SALEM AVENUE

SALEM AVENUE

AND OTHER TALES OF TERROR

JOSEPH THEIS

Raymond,
Thank you so much for all of
your support!

NEW DEGREE PRESS

COPYRIGHT © 2020 JOSEPH THEIS

All rights reserved.

SALEM AVENUE

and other tales of terror

ISBN   978-1-63676-579-2   *Paperback*
                978-1-63676-195-4   *Kindle Ebook*
                978-1-63676-196-1   *Ebook*

CONTENTS

AUTHOR'S NOTE

———

"...people have worn green glasses on their eyes so long that most of them think it really is an Emerald City."[1]

—THE WONDERFUL WIZARD OF OZ

The view was bleak beneath the pavement, buried beside the metrorail that ran the length of the city. It was there, below the concrete and the steel, along the avenues and alleyways that wound an undiscovered way among the homeless and distraught, that I encountered the vagrant citizens of the streets.

———

[1]   L. Frank Baum, *The Wonderful Wizard of Oz* (New York: George M. Hill Co., 1900), 188.

When I first moved to Washington, DC, I was overcome with expectations for the future. Visions of soaring skyscrapers and marble monuments glittering in the sun. This was a city sparking with energy, the pinnacle of progress and peak of political power. But I soon discovered that the fireworks could only be seen from the penthouse, and that far more people cowered in the dark. Instead of a tenth-floor terrace with a Capitol view, I found myself living underground.

Riding one evening at sunset between Rhode Island Avenue and Brookland Station, I witnessed the profound declarations of a man besieged. Dressed in the ragged trappings of the destitute and displaced, he staggered unsteadily onto the train.

"Sorry for the smell. I promise, them maggots ain't gnawin' at my leg no more."

He presented an oversized club foot wrapped in bandages and gauze as he leaned dependently on an adjustable aluminum cane. Falling into a seat not far from my own, he dismissed the other passengers and proclaimed himself alone.

"I must be the Last Man on Earth. Ain't no other man would let me live like this."

In that prophetic revelation, I understood there was something deeper than the metrorail roaring underneath the blacktop, a more sinister force at work in the city. A darker chapter yet to read.

In the ensuing years, I have poured these pages over, studied the stories of the city, and found them full of horror. Homeless huddled helpless on the streets, houses fallen down in disrepair. The muddled masses disregarded like garbage soaked by sewage and the stains of wasted years. Strangers in the night that never ceases, a million masks marching silently alone.

As the plight of the poorest worsens by the day, politicians preach of progress achieved for the very same. Cries for social justice fall short beside the sight of something real—an underpass encampment and the isolated inhabitants therein. Aimless in their days, dead but for their own shallow breath hanging frozen in the air. Excised from the city and left instead to their own devices, I have seen them waste away. Blinded by the glaring truth refracted through tinted windows towering overhead, those apathetic faces maintain their tunneled gaze. Hypocrisy of the highest order, a schism of the mind cleaving through conflicting depictions of Metropolis. Images of elitist airs rallying against indifference all the while forsaking those who cannot live among the clouds.

The story of the city is one of aspirations, of striving toward an ideal. But the view from the ground looks much more like an abandoned dream. It is a delicate balance by which we live, poised above the precipice of horrors old as time. Concrete is all that keeps the earth from reclaiming those most vulnerable from the streets. From atop the towering citadels downtown, the nobility has forgotten the history of the world. The natural state of man is one of poverty, homeless and hiding in the dark. Without the invaluable institutions of civility safeguarded by the stronghold of the city, we would all be swallowed up in the night. Nature is a violent, brutal force that will drag us screaming back beneath the dirt.

Disillusioned with popular pretenses of the powerful that conceal an unattractive truth, callouses growing like contusions in their hearts, I considered returning home to Hagerstown and leaving the broken city behind.

The Wonderful Wizard of Oz similarly depicts a city adorned with false color, granted by the Great Wizard's deception, disguised by the green-tinted spectacles that each citizen had been compelled to wear. Upon Dorothy Gale's arrival in the mystical land of Oz, the Good Witch of the North sends her on a journey to the Emerald City, assuring her that the Wizard can whisk her away back home to Kansas. But the Emerald City soon loses its luster as Dorothy discovers the truth. The Great and Terrible Humbug abandons the city after confessing his treachery against the people of Oz—the Emerald City is no more green than any other. After the conclusion of her adventures, triumph and tragedy alike, Dorothy chooses to leave the city behind and return home to Kansas.

Although Washington fails to attain the height of its lofty ambitions, I have chosen instead to stay. I have removed my own rose-colored glasses and seen that the city still catches the sunlight, shining in spite of its shadows. And the shadows are dark and deep, filled to the brim with terrible tales of misery and grief. As an outsider from a small town on the edge of Appalachia, I have an individual perspective that enables me to honestly examine the city and critique its often-overlooked flaws. My hope for this book is to distress and disturb the reader from a place of quiet complacency to reconsider the city as something more than the skyline and to experience the horror of those living underneath.

Perhaps the stories that unfold in the following pages are no more than works of fiction, figments of my imagination invented for your entertainment, but perhaps there is an element of truth. If you ever walk down the streets of Metropolis, look in the shadows of the skyscrapers.

The horrors contained therein are real.

THE BLACK SPOT

OR

AN ACCOUNT OF THE FINAL DAYS OF

M. CHESTER PEMBROKE

EVIDENCE

PERTAINING TO THE ALLEGED HOMICIDE OF MALLORY PEMBROKE

Note:

Neither before nor ever since in my tumultuous career have I encountered such an altogether unnerving set of peculiar circumstances. Cases of mutilation have rarely upset me, but this particular incident has disturbed my iron countenance and distressed me to the core. A black and putrid sludge has stained the countertops and torn the faded wallpaper from its place. Severed limbs lay discarded on the floor, liquid meat made to molder in the aftermath of something cruel. An apartment turned to ashes and a life reduced to rubble, smoke still rising on the air. *Disfigured faces haunt me from the scene, charred expressions broken in the crucible of flames.*

Though we have secured a suspect in custody, his conviction is far from guaranteed. An elderly lunatic swaddled in the trappings of a leper. He was apprehended in the lobby of Mr. Pembroke's apartment building, muttering to himself and stumbling over his bare feet. The evidence against him is weak and a jury would be loath to convict. He will likely be locked away in an institution, to be isolated from the dangers he may pose, or else released to aimlessly wander the streets of the city once more.

Hereafter lies an excerpt of the personal diary of Mallory Pembroke, documenting the final hours preceding his death. I cannot confirm the ravings of a dead man, nor can I discount the clues contained therein. Delirium may be an effect of an isolated mind, made to conjure up illusions in the suffocation of confinement. Quarantine can do little to cure what cannot be seen. In the wake of something more sinister than salvation, the searchlights fade away and we drown.

April 17, 3:30 p.m.

The afternoon has been accented by inconvenience. Train was delayed on account of rioting at the multiplex—fourth event this month. Rumor contends that a man had been thrown onto the tracks when we barreled across 49th Street. Will inquire further when home.

Dismissed from work early after complaining of fever and acute sensitivity. Sunlight pierced my sandpaper eyes through the open office window. Shimmering arrowheads bursting through yellowed blinds and embedding themselves into my brain. Each and every mark of pen against paper etched itself into my skin, like the constant, whirring hum of a needle driven relentlessly below the surface, injecting ink to affect a stain. The metal chattering of typewriter teeth fell like bullet casings against my skull.

The head absorbs the senses as a weary, ravaged town bombarded by the shells of war. Gone are the roaring days of my youth, the glittering nights bathed in sparkling liquor, drowning in neon lights. I am enduring the descended years, gripped by global depression and ravaged by the tyranny of decline. The dazzling parties had ended and the lights had all burned out, a rusted skyline silhouetted against a gilded sunset. My own body has succumbed to the same fatigue, the vulnerable state of an exhausted nation overwhelmed by the dust gathering in storm clouds from the past.

These concussive irritations have persisted throughout the morning and well into the afternoon. The world has assumed an oppressive face, its every outward force pinning me in place as the entomologist secures his invertebrate prey. I wonder at the cruelty of my fate. Perhaps my condition is justified, some universal restitution. Shall I attribute my pain to the cosmic will? I am unsure which is the more frightening disposition: that my suffering might be nothing more than the indiscrimination of an arbitrary existence or that it is the deliberate work of an omnipotent fiend.

Train has reached Flint Station. Must continue in the evening—respite awaits.

8:00 p.m.

Collapsed upon arrival home, awoke in a stupor evocative of drunkenness. Or an ethereal dream. Left arm is numb, punctured by pinpricks—must have lain upon it.

Flat is in a state. Papers strewn across my bedroom floor, window left wide open. Unfinished and unpublished manuscripts sit indiscriminately in boxes piled to the ceiling like the evidence locker of a station house downtown. The wallpaper curls where it is peeling and rises in enigmatic contusions where it is not. Color has faded, which is an improvement upon its original noxious yellow. An unusually humid spring has caused it almost to sweat. Surely there is mold growing underneath. In fact, I can identify a darkened stain above my bed.

Curious, I stand upon the mattress and reach out my arm to touch it. It seems to recoil at my approach, or perhaps it is my own hesitation. Concealed beneath the warped and damaged paper lies something that inspires in me disgust akin to insult or offense, that such a grotesque and meager thing should invade my home.

Hatred moves my hands closer, a fist forming in one as the other extends a finger toward the swollen spot. It seems almost to breathe, to rise and fall in time with the steady rhythm of my own respiration. But I catch my breath and hold it tight inside my chest. My heartbeat crashes against my bones as everything inside me screams, pleading with the pulses in my veins. I press my finger gently to the budding bruise protruding from the wall and let a panicked sound escape my lips. Like a heavy, bloated corpse or the stomach of a woman engorged with child whose labor is nearing its end, the wallpaper gives way to a black liquid that seeps lazily through, viscous and slow, leaving a dark, translucent stain.

A thin but definite trail of fungal puss falls in a steady, oozing stream, accompanied by the smell of inundated garbage, the foul afterbirth of a dying creature.

I am tempted to burst the swollen mass all at once, as the temptations of the boil would dictate, to splatter the blood and the juice across the room. A perversion rising from someplace in my stomach compels me to approach, to bring my face near enough to shift the focus of my eyes like a telephoto lens. The smell is unlike anything I have known before, dead meat and curdled blood burned beyond belief. Casualties of the warring fields strewn with careless disregard, poppies for Her Majesty. But the graves have been ripped open and the rotting bodies are beckoning me to crawl inside.

The tension contained beneath the surface becomes almost too great to bear. A stillness that dries the throat. My heartbeat suppresses every breath, quickening the pace of my mind, disturbing the even, faithful tempo of the world.

8:49 p.m.

With a spare bit of Muralo Spackle, I conceal the spot beneath a thick layer of putty. It hardly looks contained, but at the very least it is obscured. Anyway, it is a temporary irritation—my lease expires within the month. If all ends as it should, I shall never see this place again.

As I prepare for the ending of the day, and perhaps a moment's dedication to my work, the city comes clamoring to life. Electric lights burning like neon candles in the dark, humming over the sound of the traffic and rumbling underneath the pavement like the rolling thunder of the metrorail. With a Lucky Strike held casually between my fingers, I am pulled toward the edge. Smoldering tobacco and paper perform an exotic seduction in my mind. Through my open window, from someplace beyond the veil, I breathe it all in—the essence of the night. Every sight, every sound, every intonation of the roaring beast bellowing with dynamic vigor. It lives in clarity as fine as a needle, it exists in lucid picture sharp as wit.

I imagine some affectation of the mold has heightened my awareness, brought every minute detail screaming to the forefront of the windowsill. Each sensation drives me deeper within myself. The hysteria of the madhouse approaches bedlam. Twisted lanes of captive streetcars, frozen channels of traffic crying out from far below. Burning billboards and midtown marquees humming in their neon masquerade. The breadth of the city reaches farther than the boundaries of the earth.

A warm, inviting glow beckons me outside, pulls me toward the window—I slide one leg into the night. It grows suddenly heavier, pulled violently away from my body with an overwhelming downward force. An intensity that tries on my weary arms holding fast to the walls of my apartment. Terrifying heights, the likes of which only birds should know, compel me to avoid the ground. I crane my neck in a desperate maneuver and stare up into the clouds. Far beyond the fading glow, the horizon of stars expands forever.

Perched on the windowsill, stretching high above the concrete plane, air as I have never known floods my nostrils, expanding my lungs, threatening to burst them, and I drown.

Bound by instinct, I drop my head and see the rushing headlights streaming down every avenue below. My leg dangles carelessly as blood rushes like vertigo, filling my head too fast. The hypnotic allure of the streetlights calls me down into the brilliant, orange sea. A sudden urge to hurl myself headlong toward the pavement rises in my stomach, creeping upward along the back of my throat. I grow top-heavy and teeter toward the edge, groaning as it becomes almost too great to bear. But I resist and turn away.

Intend to phone California in the morning. Have a man in Los Huesos whom I would very much like to meet. Must secure travel and living arrangements. He promises the future.

2

2   Tania Bustamente, *The Black Spot, 2020, acrylic ink on watercolor paper.*

April 18, 10:00 a.m.

Slept well. Fever is reduced and sensitivity is lessened. The light no longer causes me to close my eyes in pain. Strength has returned to my bones, and there is no sign of swelling in my throat. Remained home from work to facilitate recovery.

No answer from California. I believe the number that I have on record is correct, though I really have no means of making sure. Will phone again in the evening.

An entire day lies stretched out before me. Tendencies toward accomplishment compel me to stand. The endless projects that I have at one time or another assigned myself convene in a conference before me, inviting me to choose one and seize this day to complete it. Poetry, novels, manuscripts of all kinds that desire of their own accord to be finished. I desire this for them, too, but have failed in regard to each. Every instance of freedom in my days promises this opportunity; and yet, in all the sundry hours, I fall short.

On this day, however, I am filled with a sudden euphoric relief unlike any sleep nor stupor I have experienced before. My head swells with the thrill of intoxication at a thousand feet, a rush of helium that lifts me off the ground. A revelation of an empty grave from which I have leapt unscathed. Not since Christ walked from His tomb has Death endured such a sting.

From among my countless documents, stuffed within overcrowded drawers and folded between verbose chapters of more celebrated works, I select something practically forbidden. A large volume, old as I can remember, gestating within me long after its appointed date of delivery. A crisp and weathered page, stained yellow in the corners, reads dramatically across the front—*Anathema*.

Although I had written the words myself, there is the suggestion of a much older tale. Perhaps these thoughts have been attached to my blood for generations, these very words inspired by the voices of a time long dead. The wisdom of ages alien to me reaching out across the expanse of time. Inflections of another era entirely, screaming out at me from the dark. I turn the tattered pages with a delicate precision, scanning the handwritten lines and identifying the familiar markings of my own pen. Elegant trails in ink, scarlet flourishes dripping with style, if not slightly fraught with signs of distress. Of course, no publisher would accept a manuscript in this state, and I have yet to purchase a Remington.

4:00 p.m.

Before I could continue to write *Anathema*, this weathered fiction before me—thousands of words scrawled in faded ink, barely legible even to the man who had composed them—I had sat down to transcribe what I had begun. I do not remember what happened next, but I have awoken disturbed. Strewn across my desk are papers bearing strange and foreign markings, evocative of my own words yet unrecognizable, exceptional to everything I know. I cannot replicate their design, though they are so plainly written as I am writing now. They must be in my own hand—the curvature of certain symbols too eerily resembles that of my cursive letter "*S*." Like a mirrored image grotesquely distorted by its refraction, as a beam of light through a single drop of water, they astound and distress me.

A familiarity undermines and betrays their exotic masquerade, which would assume the face of horror had they not inspired a more reticent feeling of unease. Like a splinter of wood burrowed just beneath the surface of the skin, a foreign shard of shrapnel entrenched and inclined to fester. Though it will find its own way, in time, to tear surely through, it will be enough to consume its host in an obsessive fit of fixation. Or some wayward bit of dirt that has wedged itself underneath the fingernail, which grows in size and irritation and, after some time, stings the rotten flesh as infection turns the finger black and spreads. Visions of my own familiar hand tempt me toward an isolated fate.

The air is thin—will clear my head outside.

4:30 p.m.

The city smog hangs low in the late-afternoon, diluting the smoke from my Lucky Strike. Wandering aimlessly among the faceless horde, I breathe it in. Thick, it fills my lungs and weighs me down.

Still, the expanse of streets like jagged spokes radiating in every direction opens my world beyond the insular apartment I've often considered home. The heights to which the city rises verge upon the sublime. Their gargantuan impositions shame the mountains of Tibet, and I live but in the valley of the shadow. I contort my neck to steal a glimpse of their peaks.

An unnerving dizziness throws me off my feet and I stumble into a man tightly bound in tattered, worn-out clothes. A drifting vagrant swaddled in the threadbare tapestries of his youth, the moniker of a man left behind in the gutters of his golden years. He smells offensively of urine and offers a subtle yet unmistakable scent of gangrene. His beard is an unkempt tangle of white tucked carelessly about that hangs as regally as Sunday vestments. But his eyes startle me the most. Vivid and blue, electric with an unpredictability that conveys some greater notion of understanding. A sudden, indescribable contempt for this man boils in my stomach. He seems to know me, in an unsettling, aberrant way. I despise him. I see myself—

But I look away. I need a drink and fall into the nearest, most disreputable dive I come across. I didn't catch the name.

Dimly lit and clouded in a thick and musty smoke, rich in flavor. The atmosphere resembled those establishments that had been engaged in bootlegging during last decade's dry spell. Secretive, concealed behind the veil of propriety, demure in all the trappings of their disguise. But I had found them smiling underneath.

I avoid the bar and seat myself in a tight, secluded corner booth padded with burgundy leather, torn and peeling on the sides. The walls are adorned with framed photographs of the city, crisp monochromatic vignettes that challenge our memory—how is the world? An incandescent glow softly hums throughout the otherwise silent and abandoned place. I take a sudden interest in the tabletop and find that it has been marked by whoever had sat here before. Enigmatic messages meant for other eyes, etched either in extraordinary carelessness or in haste, bemuse me from below. Verses of regret, notes to vagrant lovers. Expletives intended for the same. I think to add my own and wonder at what I had lost. I had never held anything worth losing for fear of it being lost, and now, having lost nothing, I have nothing left at all. Perhaps, one time, the table was bare, and there were no regrets. Nobody mourned and everything was glistening and new. But the years lie thick in dust.

A gentleman approaches from the bar and I ask him for cheap bourbon and ice. He frowns disapprovingly, as though I have offended him, but emits a compliant grunt before returning to the bar. As I wait in the darkness, unassuming, an incessant itch creeps along my left hand, gently tingling the hairs as though some many-legged insect seeks to burrow into my skin. In the instant before I bring my hand reflexively from underneath the table, my mind concocts a vision of something parasitic, with mandibles and feelers, surgically depositing its eggs into my warm and virile flesh. A spark of fever ignites and I begin to sweat.

The barman returns with a stout glass, which I hastily drain before pressing to my forehead. My throat and stomach burn, but the ice relieves the fever, if only for a moment. I ask for another, and the barman retreats to the bar.

Droplets of sweat comingle with water and whiskey as my vision doubles under a clouded film. The fever returns with a vigor as the sour, salty taste of sweat runs into my mouth. I wash it down with another glass, followed by another. A shudder chills my blood, the fanatic rhythm of my heartbeat quickens in anticipation, struggling against itself. I find it difficult to breathe. Violent tremors seize my body as the image of the old man grips me more vividly than pain. His piercing eyes that must have known me, must have been watching me—I can see them even now. Paranoia that catches in erratic bursts but builds to conflagration burns like fanaticism in my mind. The atmosphere grows oppressive, and I shrink.

April 19, -:-- a.m.

A gutter overrun with vomit and blood, teeming with refuse of all kinds. I contribute my own share of filth. Clothes are ruined, soaked through and stained by all manner of rancid waste and foul smells now sewn into the fabric, intertwined with yards of wool and silk.

The night has lost its novelty, and every hope is death.

This aft-ward tumbling toward day's end disorients and upsets my otherwise firm and famous countenance. Something gravely unsure of this drunken escapade and its effect on my constitution has gripped me by the throat. Retching on the street and struggling to breathe. The blush of intoxication has worn away its welcome and my head throbs with the ache of dehydrated wit. I have awoken newly perturbed, as though an inner voice from deep within me has been violently made aware.

9:30 a.m.

The disturbances of last night's ventures through the city have left me lethargic and spent. My bed has been the only comfort. Not even the temptations of breakfast nor the stubborn churnings of my bender-busted stomach can summon me from rest.

This black and offensive stain that had appeared several hours ago at the center of my left hand refuses to quit its place. No larger than a pinprick, though as effectual and piercing, it has since with pulsating rhythm sent beats of throbbing pain coursing through my arm. Despite its diminutive size, its incessant stinging has driven me insane. It must have been the work of an insect, a spider or otherwise invasive thing. What other explanation could there be for such a spot? Perhaps I had grazed an outward jutting needle, or a rusting metal spoke. However the cause of the marking, it does not seem to have broken the skin, though its irritations persist underneath. It appears little less than the suggestion of a freckle, or a faint but conspicuous scar.

Will monitor closely.

12:15 p.m.

Have not yet left the confines of my room. I had opened the window when I stumbled in through the darkness but shut and latched it not long ago. The smell of the city had wafted in, like the carcasses of carriage horses baking in the sun. Isolating myself against the world has become this morning's routine—it is preferable to enduring the stench of the streets. Even still, the sounds of fresh rioting beat against the windowpane, threatening to break through and flood my room with violence. Paupers in the penthouse, turning the world on its head and shaking every coffer free. Without a minute's foresight, they would tear it all down for a scrap of côte de boeuf and send the castle crashing to the ground. They would choke on the dust in their wake.

Something in the air today is different, somehow thinner, less inviting. Hostile to the peace of days. A rotted perfume inviting scavengers and parasites, as if the world had already perished and the living were anachronisms, remnants of a bygone era, feeding like maggots on the corpse. A decomposing Wonderland rotting just beneath the pavement, buried below the city streets but protruding like weeds through cracks in the concrete. Slipping across the surface and spilling over into the world, corrupting with tendrils that poison and spread. The rioters carried the stench with them, clinging to their unwashed coats and whatever cause they had adopted today. Scavengers waiting for the vultures to descend.

2:19 p.m.

The spot on my hand has grown and spread. Little larger than a quarter, and nearly just as round. Tips of my index and middle fingers are discolored and swollen, as though constricted. Purple blood pooling beneath the skin. Hint of numbness. Will soak in Epsom solution.

5:32 p.m.

Something is eating me from within. Those eyes—neither empty nor soulless, but overflowing with life. Piercing blue and frozen in time, tearing into my own. Eyes that had seen more than their share of years. The eyes of God.

And He demands a sacrifice. The streets burn like incense, offering up prayers atop columns of smoke, worthy beams to prevent the heavens from crashing down upon us. The rabble below me, a selfish crowd, make demands of their own. Like children, useless things, crying for food and warmth. But their mother has abandoned them—the weakest of the horde, each of them clamoring, pathetic runts. So their tantrums echo in the caverns of the mind, building to a dissonant chorus, which they sing until they are hoarse or else consumed. They are fortunate not to have been eaten alive.

I retreat from my view of a fragile world and fall, recumbent, into bed. The days grow longer the less I sleep, and exhaustion beats me down. Time presses onward, waves against the sand, until the shoreline has been swept away.

The black mold has crept along the wall and across the ceiling, growing with tendrils reaching outward like skeletal spokes from a central point. It has adopted a darker hue, as though some greater depth lies underneath. The patch that I had concealed seems to have consumed the Spackle, or else become so overgrown as to have itself concealed it. I am at a loss. Its stubborn occupation above me depresses the entire room and diminishes my place within it. Not only is it living, but it expresses primal thoughts—simple, carnal desires. My stomach convulses, brewing hatred, a guttural repulsion to this intelligent thing.

7:43 p.m.

Swelling has not decreased and my hand has gone entirely numb. Discoloration has progressed to a deep lilac, punctuated by black markings with no indication of order or significance. To confess that I am concerned for my safety would be a disservice to the virtue of honesty. I cannot sleep, cannot turn my back to the rotting walls for fear of what the foul mold might do in the absence of my attention. Its appendages grow in strength and size and extend its reach across the ceiling, grasping at any footholds to reinforce its garrison against the world. A black cocoon nurturing infection inside, fit to burst without hesitation. If I were to turn my eyes away, it would spread beyond its lonely station and consume me where I lay. How long until it overruns my weakening defenses?

April 20, 5:29 a.m.

I have decided to return to the office for the day. I am relying on a restoration of order and a retreat to monotony to foster my rehabilitation. The familiar sound of the typewriters' song, a metallic chime to welcome me home, will surely assuage this fever dream that has consumed my weary days. Afterward, I will visit St. Anthony Regional Hospital and speak with Dr. Reinhard, who nearly treated my father's influenza. I know him to be a good enough man, knowledgeable in his field. Perhaps he can uncover the matter with my arm.

Train is brimming with anticipation, on the verge of something sudden and anarchic. The skyscrapers above tremble at the precipice, shuddering with every new approach of the riotous horde. Each character in the narrative plays a willful harbinger of the new age, having eaten his fill of this present time. They consume its passing with soulless eyes and bottomless throats, inhaling as the maelstrom does each wandering ship. Governed by garrulous stomachs and insatiable appetites. And they are all themselves consumed, each by another, and their impossible lust for blood.

In an effort to conceal the deep discoloration, I have worn a pair of Perrin leather day gloves on my hands, dark and inscrutable, yet ordinary enough in the fashion of the day. It is a simple thing but has drawn the attention of several sneering passengers. Beady-eyed inspectors, noses in the air, sniffing out the scent of dissidence—and they have found it. Perhaps too highbrow a statement for a man on the metrorail, but I dare not remove them for fear of what they might say to the horror underneath.

9:37 a.m.

The office has assumed an air of conspicuous and deliberate surveillance. The eyes around me have all trained their sights like vultures on my hands, or at least on the pair of leather gloves that have concealed them. They are nothing so out of the ordinary as to inspire such scrutiny, and yet my coworkers have all paid them more attention than their work.

I try to ignore them and carry on with my assignment—a distracting narrative about the doubtful prospects of the annual Onion Festival in Elba. I would prefer to cover the riots, spinning a fabulous fiction about the man who had been killed on the tracks at 49th and Broadway. Some thrilling narrative worthy of the front page. A singularly mysterious man, I would write, with no family in the city, no friends to speak of, and hardly a record of existence at all. Or so my sources say.

The marvelous Mr. Pembroke, dedicated investigator that I am, would discover his connections to the Lombardi crime family of the Chicago Outfit, who had seized power and prominence in the wake of political disaster. I would detail his unforgivable betrayal of Joe Lombardi's illegitimate daughter, Alessandra Isa Borelli, and the hurricane of violence that had since torn the country apart. The tragic demise of the man on the metro tracks was just another casualty marring a twisted trail of bodies and blood.

But Mr. Mercy granted that assignment to Cecily Moreau—little wonder why. Regular morning rendezvous earn the little louse front-page coverage, and I have to fill the space around the classifieds, caught between an obituary of Howard Phillips and an advertisement for Florsheim Shoes.

My typewriter clacks with sarcastic vigor, inviting the attention of those whirring drones seated all around me, whose own ignoble efforts to conceal their curiosity betray their every pretense. I sneer at the feeble attempt. The cacophonous arrangement of their gossiping flaps obscures the consistent metallic thrum of productivity. It is simultaneously amusing and wearing on my patience.

11:24 p.m.

Monotony and routine seem to have restored my collected disposition. Apart from the cool fabric of my leather gloves and the burning sensation underneath, the day has passed as all days have—constructed but orderly, arranged but by design. Safety and contentment persist in mediocrity, which is much more dependable than excellence.

As the afternoon approaches, I prepare for an hour of lunch, a brief respite from the flavorful, cigar-laden atmosphere of *The Daily Maine*. Instead of choking on the perfumed scent of fattened men, I indulge myself in the thin and dizzying air enveloping mountains made of steel. Though I do not ascend their vertical slopes today, I seat myself comfortably in their shadows at a little sidewalk café called The Plum.

I slip a Lucky Strike between my fingers from within my suit pocket and ignite my Colibri lighter—black and tortoise-shell enamel encased in chrome. It sits heavy in my hand as I taste the toasted tobacco flowing over my tongue. Playful like a dancing sprite, it trips over itself and falls down my throat. Thick and bitter, the smoke fills my lungs. I breathe deeply, exhaling fire that flies high above the city, rising over the mountaintops. My day gloves receive considerably less attention in the publicity of the streets, intermingled with the boisterous anxieties and concerns of the rushing millions. The gentle shade of my street-side seat offers a slower pace.

Held comfortably in my hand sweats a Golden Afternoon, bourbon and iced tea glistening in a crystal glass. Here, the sound of Pembroke inspires reverence and compels respect. These people do not know me. Dressed in my finest pinstripe suit, accented by a patterned bowtie, I may as well be a reclusive magnate or tycoon, a financier discriminately venturing out to play. To watch, and to listen. Powerful moguls and successful entrepreneurs walk alongside children of refuse and creatures of despair. Homeless vagabonds without a hope for reprieve, penniless drifters indebted to the mercy of the tides. The beggars in the street.

A beggar in the street.

I see him. From across speeding lanes of distorted streaks of traffic, as though I have fallen out of time, I see him. A singular, ragged figure, bearded to the waist, girded in sheets that reveal spindle-legs cracked like neglected porcelain, disfigured by protruding veins. His mane of brilliant white encircles those same, electric eyes, like those of a blind man, but illuminated from behind with an immortal source of light—

3   Justin Rohr, *A Beggar in the Street, 2020, pencil on paper.*

9:16 p.m.

I recall that my fingers had loosened as the glass fell forever toward the sidewalk below. I could not move. Frozen in fear of that figure before me, I gazed dumbfounded and slack-jawed, as though I had suffered a stroke. My body sat paralyzed, trapped within that moment, so particularly framed with a scalpel's precision by an inexplicable and terrifying isolation.

My recollection after the fact remains perfectly preserved as I record the details of the day. Burning like a cattle brand seared into my mind, I can see the crippled man as clearly as if he had invaded my home and sat himself at the other end of my dining table. He had begun to cross the street, fixated upon me, ignorant of the traffic speeding all around. The figure that had found its way again into my afternoon defied the screaming traffic in the streets and made its way toward me.

The advancement of its slight but imposing frame jolted me to life and I ran aimlessly away. Breathless down side-streets and through alleyways, staggering blindly, limping lifeless anywhere to escape it. But it persisted, determined, marching onward as I ran. The city fell apart around us, each towering colossus turned to rubble in a hurricane of fear, roaring like an engine in my ears and crashing like the breakers of a monsoon against my head. I stumbled over legs reduced and useless, brittle and snapping in the heat, struggling against myself to keep ahead.

I don't know why I ran, which frightens me all the more. An instinctual compulsion, driving me with a terrific urgency from my seat. A hive-mind with the most basic of desires, screaming with a thousand primal voices all at once for the chance to survive. A language I didn't understand, a tongue that no one speaks, so ancient that it has been lost and returned to the earth. The breath of life, the rot of time, and the bitter, violent rattles of the end.

And this vagabond was all of it, loosely bound in bandages and sheets, practically falling to pieces. Crumbling under the oppressive weight of his age, his bones snapping and his joints popping out of place, uncertainly supported by brittle limbs that clung to him still. An insect scurrying along a predetermined path, a trap set and sprung in the early afternoon. For a moment, it seemed as though his prey might manage to slip away, but he pursued, unrelenting, unashamed, and rapidly closing the space between us.

Desperate for some avenue of escape, I fell haphazardly into a second-hand bookstore embellished by the familiar, heavy scent of damp paper. The façade was unassuming, molding storefront trim and windows frosted with dust. Stuffed unnaturally between an abandoned theater and a laundromat that I knew discreetly to house an opium den, its inconspicuous exterior did little to prepare me for what I would discover inside. The sour suggestion of mildew encouraged me to turn around and leave, but the horror just behind forced me further in.

Bookshelves stood in claustrophobic proximity, towering above, tilting slightly to the left. An unmapped labyrinth underground adorned with the skulls of the catacombs, memories that linger like engravings etched by vandals on tombstones. Monuments and mausoleums. I was in a maze of Hawthorne, Hugo, and Swift, avenues intersecting Shelley, Shakespeare, and Poe. First edition printings of Sidney, collected works of Chaucer. Translations of Erasmus.

I pressed further, falling farther down this catalog of time. The lights dimmed in the backmost corners of the store, stale fluorescents buzzing behind stacks of strange and mysterious works. Hiding among unfamiliar volumes, my fingers caressed their fragile spines. Their titles sounded foreign and ancient, their binding unraveled from years of isolation and neglect. Stories older than the city, older than civilization, spoken before the written word.

From among the primeval, grimy throng, a single volume enduring inconspicuously along the farthest wall arrested my attention. Some horrible witness to every brutal, bloody age. A sentry standing watch along the ramparts, nearly unnoticed in the tangle of shadows and cobwebs intertwined among the rest. Its spine was thin and coated in dust, carefully embossed with a title I recognized all too well. Crimson thread bleeding through black leather binding—*Anathema*. I snatched it from the shelf and tore it open with a violent disregard. My own enduring fiction, the weathered novel that I had begun to transcribe but had not yet quite completed. Only I had never seen this molding tome before. It was not written in English, nor any language that I knew. But I must have—it stirred in me something so familiar.

The paper was thick, a fibrous weaving nearer to cloth than to the pages of my own. The symbols that bled across each page held no significance for me, not in the plainest sense of the word. Winding caricatures of an unknown alphabet. Not quite Oriental—perhaps a form of Arabic script. Carved into the surface of each pulpous sheet, tattooed onto pale and supple flesh. A true transfiguration, the manipulation of the earth, like clay or slabs of marble, raw and unrefined materials sculpted with skill into works of art. The butchers and their parlor tricks, turning bloody beasts to feats of beauty, monsters into modern-day delights. Taming what once was wild and consuming the fabulous feast. The author and the alchemist alike.

It held a strange hypnotic sway over me, persuasion like a powerful trance commanded by some medium in the dark. I slid the book discreetly into a pocket in the interior of my jacket, careful not to crease the pages. I was compelled to do so, duty-bound by the forces at work in my mind. As I turned away toward the overflowing aisles I had just perused, a shriveled, tiny creature stepped out from the flickering shadows.

A woman overcome with age, the embodiment of all my fears falling from the darkness and spilling out into the world before me. The manifestation of my most sacred thoughts. She wore a tattered frock and spectacles that magnified and distorted her kaleidoscopic eyes. Her hair fell in a disheveled cluster of cobwebs over her sharp, uneven shoulders. Spindle arms and spindle legs crept slowly toward me, a smile with crooked, broken teeth. She hunched so severely that her frame doubled over on itself. The matron of whatever gateway I had accidentally discovered—she was the porter and I had stumbled into Hell. But something in the smell of the place seemed familiar to me—I must have been there before.

Something older than the books she sold spilled from between her slivered lips and hung heavy on her breath. She looked as though she had been deceased for an untold length of time, animated only by sheer will or some much more sinister force. The Fates refused to cut her string. But mine was fraying at the ends and threatened at any moment to snap. The horror of every wasted year careened toward me like a freight train jumping off its tracks, demolishing all wayward hopes for the future, crushing me from within. I stole myself away from the woman in her web, rushing for the front of the store, tearing through increasingly narrow corridors overflowing with legends of antiquity. They mocked me in my obscurity as I left them all behind and burst once more into the streets.

The blur of the cityscape hurried me home. I saw no sign of the ragged man who had pursued me just before. Although the phantom had faded from view, either tiring of the chase or else retreating to design a more vicious attack, I knew that it would haunt me still, lurking in the periphery of my mind.

Even in the quivering shadows of my darkened room, this spectral figure looms immediately out of sight. Those eyes, those lingering, watchful eyes that knew me from someplace across the expanse of years. The past has pursued me throughout the city, hunted with relentless purpose. The future has found me unprepared. I will secure my own solitude and make provisions for the watch—vigilance is the price of survival.

11:33 p.m.

This city is Knossos, and I am trapped within the maze.

April 21, 12:47 a.m.

The door is latched and locked, and every window is secure. I have permitted no point of entry, nor made provisions for escape. However long this horrible figure stalks the alleyways outside my door, crawling through the overgrown underbelly of the city, I will remain here at my station, else I take leave of my resolve and wander out into the streets. God help me if I do.

So I have assumed a strategy of isolation. Perhaps against all reason, but fear does not entertain the sanity of reason. My mind is muddled in the haze of summer sweat and petrified in a pillar of salt. I succumb to the overwhelming pressures in my head and drift away. Far from the confines of the city, collapsing inward until I cross the threshold and fall to my knees. An open field expands forever, razed for autumn's harvest, and at the center stand I. There no longer exist planes of being but only being itself. Outward, gestating thought. The essence of infinity.

The incredible space induces nausea, a dizzying imbalance of my feet beneath a body that has grown increasingly dense with weight. Rather than topple to the ground, I propel upward, tumbling in a circuitous gyre toward the night. The floor falls away as the surface of the sky must appear to a stone cast below the sea.

Shallow breath flees its fleshy place and vertices abandon sense. Echoing among the stars rings an ancient voice, more primal than spoken words, more immediate than meaningful thought—a guttural, organic scream. Pure, uninhibited. The raging cry of the greatest motivator in all of living history: pain, and the often-hollow promise of pleasure. This celestial sound surrounds me and fills my stomach with acidic dread.

A steady, thrumming vibration rattles my skull. The splinters of the universe crack across the sky as blood streams from my nose. An unintelligible wail invites a whirring, fractured noise like a drill boring into my spine. This dissonant clamor steadily increases in volume and dissidence before uniting in a single, terrifying voice:

KILL.

I double over in shock and disgust and expel a torrent of bile from the back of my throat as my body falls unconscious to the floor.

3:58 a.m.

Even the city is dark. The lamplights have dimmed, and the people have died. Not a sound confesses their midnight sins, nor betrays the secrets they keep. Hidden in the furthest corner of my living room, cowering far away from my apartment door, I remember my day gloves concealing my hands. I hold them, gently feeling the sympathetic touch of cool leather against my skin. I know I ought to remove them and reexamine the progress of my infection. A thought suggests I leave inspection until morning, but now that I have remembered, I cannot ignore it for the night. Having foregone my trip to St. Anthony, anxiety has already begun to fester within me. My left hand trembles at the end of my wrist, heavy with the black spot that has undoubtedly grown darker and deeper in my skin. I tug at the tip of my forefinger, and then at the end of my thumb, but the glove refuses to quit its place.

Concerned, suddenly itching underneath, I switch on a stout lamp veiled by a stained-glass shade. Refracted ruby sparks dance among glints of sapphire and gold that illuminate my corner of the room, throwing jagged shards of light against the wall. I hold my glove up to the lamp and struggle in vain to peel it away, catching just a glimpse of my hand underneath. The skin looks as though—but I can't bring myself to say. It must be distorted by the dark.

My pulse quickens. I rummage about in breathless, panicked hesitation for any sort of tool to tear away the glove, wary, unsure of what I might find festering underneath. Throwing open every cupboard, rummaging through every drawer, I grasp a heavy pair of fabric shears inherited from my mother. Large, thick steel blades rusted from wear and age. I return to my corner, crouch beneath the lamp, and steady my hand in the light. Once more I tug at the glove, which tugs at the skin beneath, as if the two have conjoined. Soaked in sweat like a sock when worn for too long in shoes that have not yet been worn long enough. Bonded by the blisters that form, that burst and bleed and dry, that fuse the fabric to the skin.

I slide one blade between the glove and the uneven scabs at the base of my wrist, pressing forward along the skin until cold steel rests against my middle and ring fingers. The opposite blade sits raised above, Gibbet's guillotine, purposely drawing out the tension. My brow glistens in light refracted through droplets of sweat. Slowly, carefully, I bring the two blades together. They snap string and thread like sinews, cutting more precisely than a surgeon slicing through tissue. I repeat this meticulous process, nervously running the blades along my palm and up each finger, shredding velvet and silk until it falls like snakeskin from my hand.

However, my own skin has not been reborn—it has withered like a corpse, shriveled tight around my bones as though it has been doused for years in lye. A dark, leathery husk shrouds the shriven, naked flesh. Patches of torn and tattered leather remain attached to open sores. The ends of my fingers are entirely numb. I pinch the tip of my forefinger, desperate to feel something, but the nail slips out of its place and falls, black and soft, to the floor.

7:00 a.m.

Telephoned St. Anthony and scheduled a private appointment for the 26th. They do not customarily make house calls, but Arthur Pembroke had been a wealthy man. My father owned *The Daily Maine* until the time of his death, at which point it passed like plunder to Randolph Mercy. But my father had fattened the sow before its slaughter, and he had been generous with the spoils. The Pembroke Wing of St. Anthony treats the clinically insane. A loving tribute to my mother.

I remained in the corner of my living room for the night, either too frightened or too resigned to move, and my neck refuses to turn as a man might hope it would. Stiffened from the discomfort of the night, knots and kinks frustrate me like a brace secured to the spine. I crack my neck back and forth, swinging violently to the left, then to the right, snapping loudly as my cogs and joints realign.

My hand has lost all feeling, but some intangible pulsation generates vibrations along my forearm. The veins have become visibly engorged, protruding topographically from underneath the skin. Crawling with black blood. I am fortunate not to have suffered infection in my other hand, else this record would be impossible. If St. Anthony had offered an opening earlier than Wednesday, I would have secured it. So long as my situation fares no worse than it has, I see no reason to suspend my isolation. I may even rise above my fears and transfigure these days into well-spent leisure, writing as I do. A sudden swell of hope rises as sunlight spills into the room—I anticipate creation.

9:15 a.m.

I have set fire to the bridge that bound me to *The Daily Maine*. The telephone cracked with electric static in my ear, but I had no difficulty understanding Mr. Mercy's underhanded threats. A grave promise that I will be held accountable for the ruin of his paper, dishrag and detritus that it is. His voice carried a wavering unpredictability, like a child challenging the strength of his temper, unsure of the consequences should he release untested rage.

In the smoldering ashes of our former association, Mr. Mercy must have stood stupefied and staggered like a drunk. I can picture it even now, his plump and pathetic frame collapsing exhausted into his oversized armchair, stationed like a bulldog behind his desk. The sweat that had always collected in a puddle on his brow would spill over along the bridge of his bulbous nose and onto the clutter of papers below. Pages of propaganda, fictions that filled the spaces around the only truth therein—images of artifacts and commodities contained in an assortment of advertisements. The logo of Lucky Strike emblazoned underneath an illustration of a slender woman lounging across a Victorian chaise, holding a cigarette to her lips.

I had contributed more than my own share of fictions, stories that I had conjured from my own imagination and embellished with the stark cynicism of the national theater. None so peculiar as to draw the suspicions of the discerning public, less so by our own faithful readers. Whatever the narrative, we need only lace it with the truth to capture the public. Allegations of criminal conduct reported by anonymous sources levied by the power of the press, details of scandalous improprieties committed by the same. Targeted and focused, blackmail by libelous extortion if not by violation of law. Of course, there can be nothing levied against us to retract the narrative despite all available remedies, lawsuits and losses alike. The source of their suffering subsists in the minds of the readers of *The Daily Maine*—and those sources run deep.

Strewn across the carpet before me in a calculated display lie categorical stacks of projects sorted by genre, form, subject, and length. The title of an incomplete poem catches my attention. A single sheet of paper, title scrawled across the top in bold and confident script, underlined. *Farewell, Ariadne!* Rhyme scheme planned in subsequent letters falling down the margin of the page. I retrieve a bottle of whiskey and a stout glass from the kitchen and seat myself on the floor.

Note:
The following poem was discovered inserted into the diary here. The paper was folded several times across its center and burned around the edges, but the words were written clear.

Farewell, Ariadne!

Farewell, Ariadne!
Take these mortal tears with you—
Across the sea, beyond the stars,
Till sorrow springs anew.

My child, among the elder gods,
And beasts of elder might,
Not crowned with scarce divinity,
But drifting in the night.

Beware the wrath of ages past,
Consumed by rancor rage—
For, in the flames of fast resent,
Hell casts an iron cage.

Forego the cruelty of revenge,
Heed not the warmth of Mars—
From Knossos' shores to Naxos' sands,
Surrender yourself to the stars.

11:35 a.m.

It has been a productive morning. One poem completed and another well underway. The others I have not yet finished fit neatly into whatever drawers I can find, wherever I can conceal the mess. My longest manuscript, a meandering novel that I have yet to edit, sits barely settled into the bottom drawer of my bedside bureau. The stolen volume *Anathema* rests on top, beneath the shade of my bedside lamp, tempting me to spread its binding open and crack the brittle spine.

As I turn to leave the bedroom, eager for another glass of whiskey, I smell the mold that, until now, had been little more than an errant nuisance. The little, unassuming spot that had sprouted in the corner has grown more fully engorged, emblazoned with needle-like thorns. The shriveled bud of a dying rose before its petals unfurl from within. I have very little faith in the beauty of what gestates inside. Vigorous and crawling across the ceiling, massive in its bulk and burdensome in its weight. It is a black, offensive thing. Large and hypnotic, consuming my attention with its perverse invitation to approach, commanding my submission. But revulsion catches me by the throat and steers my mind away.

12:55 p.m.

Received a call from California. My father's old associates have attracted more than a few disreputable men to the remnants of his reputation. The sort of men who tend to accrue wealth and power, who collect it during days of plenty and store it for their autumn years. Media magnates and prize-winning publishers, in search of some poor sucker to abet them in their pursuits—and they have found me wanting. The son of a kingpin, sole heir to an empire, exiled by the vicious hounds that had bitten at my father's heels. Suitable for grooming into the family business. But I had become weary of my father's work.

My man in Los Huesos has informed me of an open position in his family's motion picture studio, should I want it. Consultation and crafting narratives with purpose. A call for creative compositions—advertisements, in a way. Promotion of propaganda and the like. Some inconspicuous outfit with invisible intentions, conspiring toward an unintelligible end. They offer an agenda of another kind, entertainment and the opportunity to produce a body of work that endures the testaments of time. And generous compensation. I am tempted, to say the least.

I can imagine my life out west, author of opinions approved by the board, bathed in sunsets by the sea. A far cry from the drab, distressing office of *The Daily Maine*. They will survive well enough without me. Business blooms in an eternal spring—when there is no news to embellish, there is always news to invent. It is as much an exercise in imagination as my novels and the poems I scrawl across scratch paper in the afternoon, made with as much effort.

The prospect of legitimacy sends electric currents coursing through me quicker than a bolt of lightning outshines the stars and instills hope more briefly than the violent conjugation of the heavens and the earth. This downtown tenement has proven little more than a tomb for the living. The past here is dead, and the resurrection of the future would be a miraculous feat indeed. My life lies to the west. My man will be in touch and, before long, this wayward coursing river will take me to the Promised Land.

1:00 p.m.

Sunlight streams in golden rays through each and every window, the curtains thrown wide and the shades drawn high. An exceptionally exquisite afternoon. Not a cloud above me, looming overhead, threatening to spoil this moment's tranquil balm. In the brief remission of horror, I breathe as though I were standing at a precipice, on the edge of a knife, reservedly yet with wanton disregard. Where has the peace of days gone?

6:45 p.m.

Nothing restores the soul and exhausts the body more fully than an afternoon nap. I am lathered in sweat and can taste the dehydration in my mouth, my tongue a coarse and callous strip of Holdwell's discount sandpaper. A chill wind sweeps into the room, wrapping me in a cold embrace. Seduction sweet as honeydew, temptation pure as sin. This transgression nostalgic in its simplicity. The lusting heart of a child.

And, in that moment, I am young again. My mother holds me against a winter's storm, my father stokes the fading firelight. The world is small and fresh, crisp and untouched by years of ruin and pain. Simple things and ignorant hours parade in jovial fantasies across the breadth of time. But my eyes reflect those gilded days tainted with morose annotations and all I can remember assumes a tragic sheen.

The black spot has darkened every corner and recess of my mind. It has overtaken and corrupted the walls of my bedroom and reached its rotted tendrils out into the hallway toward the living room. The ceiling has begun to buckle under the excessive weight. My own body has been encumbered too, trembling from the poison in my veins.

Scylla waits outside to devour me with her many mouths and Charybdis approaches like a maelstrom to swallow me whole. The hour is imminent when I will be forced to choose between the two.

10:13 p.m.

I am overcome by a bludgeoning headache, no doubt encouraged by this absurd sentimentality. It means nothing, the past is dead. The future, out west—there lives all that matters. Still, I am afraid. How long until this present time is dead and this day has fallen to disregard, wilted with the past? The future, too, will fade.

This nihilistic inclination haunts me, reducing each conclusion to a vapid, happenstantial whim. History breeds contempt as my own life assumes an insincerity that mocks the record of the past. Art has no place in the bestial pleasure-binge.

But the city has no place for me, and my art must be a testament to my name. The epitaph of a life well-lived, an afterthought engraved.

Night has fallen over the city and exhaustion beckons me to bed.

April 22, 2:27 a.m.

My body has been ravaged in the terror of the night. Searing, blinding pain unlike anything I have ever known. White-hot fire burned in my veins, tearing me from my bed and throwing me to the floor. I recount this with great difficulty, lying in a pool of my own blood.

The most excruciating, crippling agony ignited my arm in unimaginable flames, ripping me from a nightmare and with a cruel indifference. My body jerked and twitched in a violent and fitful display of spasms and tremors as I beat my fists against the floor. Tears fell in boiling streams down my face as my bare feet crashed into every stabbing corner within reach, but I could not cry out. My throat had collapsed upon itself, constricted as though an insurmountable weight were crushing it from inside.

My head thrashed back and forth, eyes peeled open in absolute fear. I stole half-expectant glances at the overwhelming black spot, now a thundering storm cloud overhead. With an unnerving clarity, in moments preserved like insects in amber, the spot presented itself to me as though from on high. It was a celestial messenger from an alien world—the annunciation of a parasitic host. In an instant prolonged by the eternity of pain, the bulb that hung from its center split along its seams and burst in a volley of fluids and pulp, splattering the room in amniotic sap. Black blood fell along the walls like wax dripping from the seal of high justice. The wallpaper was soaked through and stained.

In an instant, the pain either subsided entirely or else increased to an immeasurable degree. I entered into a state of delirium, though remained fully aware, terrified that the pain would return. Instinctively, without thought, I tore headlong into the kitchen and seized from my block a butcher's knife.

The blade was thick, the handle was thicker, and it all felt heavy in my hand.

Steel flashed in electric bursts, striking in rapid succession, followed by the cracking of bone. The blade swung independently, rising and falling of its own accord. Blood stained the countertop before spilling onto the floor as everything cut to black.

I awoke to the smell of something freshly-deceased, wet with blood, the flesh torn gaping wide. My left hand lay beside me, severed below the wrist. Coagulated and thick like strawberry jam left out in the sun, or the tough and tasteless rind of stale gelatin. Semi-translucent, obscured by a cutaneous film and loose particles of tissue and meat.

Lying half-conscious on the floor, I could taste the salt in the air. My vision was obscured by a heavy haze of sweat and blood. Everything transpired like a lucid, meandering dream. My head rolled lazily about on the floor, waking from whatever nightmare had played out before, only to discover that the aftermath was real. The vulgar phantasm of war. Carnage dripping along the counter base, meat spilling onto the floor. A sensation of swarming insects overwhelmed my left arm but I saw nothing there. Jutting bone, protruding from swollen flesh. Cauterized in a crude display, crusting blood concealing a puss-filled wound. Black infection razed at the root.

I could not breathe. From my place on the floor, I lay entirely lifeless, nothing more than meat. In a sudden, assaulting barrage of memory, I witnessed horror as a bystander before an accident in the street. Gore spilling out from open stomachs onto the pavement. Contorted metal grafted in a gruesome dance with broken men. I lay locked in place, secured by an invisible fastener, compelled to spectate the grinding work of steel, shredding supple flesh, tearing through splintered bone. A ravenous beast, a desiccated mob clamoring for bloody consummation. And I endured it all.

Sitting myself up, leaning my back against the wall, I cradled my severed arm close to me, sobbing a breathless, gasping torrent of tears.

6:19 a.m.

Throughout the morning I have woken in petrified screams, reliving in gripping nightmares the horror of the night before. Sweat has streamed from my pores and sallowed my skin. I wonder at my fate, that promise of tomorrow, wherein all my favors lie. Caked in dried blood and numb from exhaustion, the doubts of all those promises taste bitter on my tongue. I pick flakes from the crust of my skin and fail to fathom where my future has gone. A rancid odor hangs like ammonia in the air as I drift off again—

9:47 a.m.

Perhaps the infection is contained. I have wrapped my arm in bandages and retreated from the kitchen. I have frozen my severed hand in the ice chest, hoping beyond reason that it can be preserved and perhaps returned to its proper place. But each passing minute makes my plans more and more a fantasy.

Reclining on my torn and tattered sofa, arm elevated, there comes a buzzing in my brain. Softly at first, then building, louder, to a steady hum. A probing noise. Aware that it has intruded where it does not belong.

I hold a glass of chilled whiskey to my forehead, ice cubes sweating into severely diluted liquor. A sudden roar of confused, chaotic voices clash in a violent, brutal contest. Has the rioting begun so early? I stand and walk to the window, glaring out across the city. There rushes no horde, no madding crowd scurrying through the streets, setting fires and looting the ashes. But I hear them as acutely as tinnitus, ringing with a wretched fervor. The floodwaters beaten back against the crumbling levee, whispers leaking through that promise to burst and kill.

Then, from out of the corner of my eye, I spot a darting, many-legged thing scurry across the floor. An insect, perhaps. Some scuttling spider or centipede that had found a crack in my defenses. I drain my glass and approach the corner of the room, standing cautiously beside my desk. Holding the glass firmly in my hand, I disturb a stack of stout boxes filled with papers and poems and who-knows-what.

The thing scurries upward along the wall, maintaining a calculated path that defies our natural laws. Countless spindle-legs, like hairs, rise and fall in undulating waves mimicking the motion of the tides. I press closer, staring spellbound at its distinctive markings, dark-colored bands wrapping around its slender body. Antennae sprout from its beady head, reaching blindly about. Without a moment's consideration more, I bring the glass crashing against the wall, trapping the thing inside. My headache suddenly increases in severity and pain, pulsating inside my skull. The thing contorts its body inside the glass, bending over backward, its legs flailing helplessly in the air. A vulgar smile breaks across my face.

But I know that I cannot hold it trapped in this position here forever. Almost as if in mockery, this thing wriggles its legs about, brandishing appendages to spare. Should I let it go, I may never see it again. My arm begins to shake. In a swift and skillful motion, I slip the glass beneath the insect, catching it inside, and bring it over to my desk. It flails helplessly, little legs useless against the glass. With a precise gesture, I overturn the glass and trap it once more. It follows the perimeter of its prison in a dreadful panic that stirs sweet satisfaction in my stomach.

In this more vulnerable state, it assumes a pathetic face. Nothing more than a worm, wriggling in the dirt. Recording as I can in my wounded state, I take greater pains to preserve each distressing detail of my plight. From my place of power, I observe it more closely. A pair of dark stripes run parallel along its back, end to end. A pair of needle-like, twin feelers extend from its face and rub against the glass. Piercing bolts of pain strike the forefront of my head as it throws itself aimlessly against its cage. A gleeful thought as I continue to observe its erratic behavior.

4

4 Tania Bustamente, *Mazuku Parricidium, 2020, acrylic ink on water-color paper.*

2:19 p.m.

The most vivid dream, vibrant and hypnotic—a frightening allure of language conveyed in color, thought manipulated through a surgeon's probe. Animals from ancient worlds, grunting out their primal groans as they crawl out of the mud. My single hand proves insufficient, details fading faster than I could possibly record. Half-remembered notions of a life unlived slipping like grains of sand from the shore, lost to an evening tide.

However, my headache remains as persistent as ever, beating with bricks against my skull. There must be cracks in the bone. Fever boils my blood and my skin catches fire. Either the infection has spread throughout my body or else some new disease has taken hold inside. Black veins run along my left arm where my wrist had been cleaved and disappear beneath the skin. I unwrap my sticky bandages to reveal a butchered limb, a mess of meat and bone. But it is not bloody—instead, the flesh has been sealed. A soft, translucent sheen glistens over a thin layer of toughened muscle, deadened nerves and congealed blood coagulated in a column of pulp penetrated by fractured bone. I touch it, but I feel nothing—only a static numbness. It transfixes me, and I cannot look away.

6:43 p.m.

Received a call from St. Anthony. Dr. Reinhard still harbors guilt regarding my father, or else he maintains a vicious loyalty to my family. He inquired of me the progress of my infection, the stability of my condition. Considering the incredible occasion of my circumstances, I had no choice but to lie. I would not risk a diagnosis of insanity. Of course, I told him that my condition was worsening by the hour, that each day invited some new degree of self-atrophy, that I was surely boiling from the inside out. But I omitted that I had severed my left hand in a feverish bout of madness. That detail would come to light in time.

He promised that he would see to me at the most immediate convenience to St. Anthony, which he guaranteed would be within the next few days. His services had recently been made appreciably more available. A particular patient who had occupied much of his own time and his colleagues' concern had finally succumbed to his condition. A man who had thrown himself onto the tracks running across 49th Street.

April 23, 4:36 a.m.

A muttering tangle of voices expressed in forceful whispers. Sinister sounds that ricochet and intermingle with the dark. The thrumming buzz of a thousand flies swarming overhead. Lying on my sofa, recumbent in my pain, I freeze at this new invasion. The surgeon's instruments begin to pick once more as they tear my skull apart. An abstract cryptographer, determined to crack the cypher of my mind. I fall imbalanced and weightless, turning on my head, which fills with a faint humming followed by a fit of nausea. The sound comes ringing through the darkness with an unnerving clarity.

KILL.

But it does not stop. Guttural, aggressive intentions. Primal and instinctive, impulsive urges not tempered by the civil soul. Whatever the source, it intends for me much harm. Paralysis grips me and I am strapped in place, unable to run, unable to breathe. Short and shallow gasps of air stave off my suffocation.

KILL.

As if the voices are learning, as if these impulses are drawn like venom from within my own thoughts. My own words assigned to sudden compulsions, a pressure that demands to burst. A boiling over of emotions that are not my own.

BREAK.

BLEED.

The insect underneath my glass snaps its spine in a helpless spasm. Its legs all twitch and its antennae stand on end, but all it knows is pain. Pain, and struggle, and the onward-slogging slaughter of the damned. Messy creatures cursed with carnivorous appetites, compelled by instinct to kill. This creature is one of them—and, perhaps, so too am I.

7:21 a.m.

Severe numbness in legs. I find it impossible to stand. Perhaps some side-effect of infection, or perhaps I have lain too long at rest. Slight constriction of the throat. As the atrophy of my body becomes more and more severe, I must make every effort to preserve this record of my life, documenting until the end—

My glass has shattered on the floor, and the insect is nowhere to be seen. There comes a low murmur like radio static, humming excitedly in the kitchen. The noise grows louder with each passing moment, a crescendo building to the beat of my pulse. Like a persistent drilling into my brain, chipping away at fragments of skull and loosing vital tissue. I fall from the sofa and drag myself across the floor. Arm outstretched in front of my useless mass, fingers digging into carpet fibers, pulling my slack body toward the kitchen. Every inch a struggle, clawing across mere feet that might as well be miles.

From my position on the floor, the kitchen seems a faraway vision, a nightmarish mirage hurtling suddenly toward me. The buzzing becomes unbearable as I touch the kitchen tiles and my fingers turn red with blood. Bits of meat and fragments of bone wind their gory way to a murderous scene. The ice chest has toppled over, and the remains of my arm lay torn to pieces on the floor. The back of my hand had burst apart and a torrent of wriggling larvae had spilled like rainfall from the clouds. There, in a sea of hungry mandibles and eyes peeled open wide, a swarm of perilous insects consumes my flesh in a Eucharistic rite, drinking their fill of my blood. A throng multiplied to a confoundable degree—innumerable bodies, innumerable legs, all moving in a terrifying rhythm. The noise grows immense and drowns all other thoughts.

My head fills with the sound, inflated to the point of bursting, membranes stretching against the skull. Some unnatural compulsion eclipses my thoughts of horror, alien commands overruling my will. A glint of steel flashes from the kitchen floor. I am not myself as my arm stretches out ahead, reaching for the knife. Fear does not drive me as it did before—someone else has entered my mind. The knife rises high above me only to come clumsily crashing down. Hacking and sawing just below my left shoulder, severing nerves and cracking bone. I cannot hear my own screams.

11:19 a.m.

I have confined myself to my room, though it has been beset on all sides. The walls are crumbling under an oppressive weight—I know they cannot hold. Clamoring shoots of mold, larval infestation dripping with the moist breath of a newborn thing. Self-interested, instinctive, indifferent to all else, in singular pursuit of survival. I dare not touch it again. Whatever its origin, or its ignorant intentions, its invasive thirst overshadows it all.

A stronger man would burn this building to the ground. Given the condition of my legs, I would not escape in time. A selfless man would sacrifice himself, but a selfless man would not hold his own life in any great esteem. His death would mean nothing to him—his suicide, a hollow spectacle for the rest.

The end of my shoulder has coagulated like my arm had done, hardened in the heat of my fever and dried like salted meat. The squirming bodies of larval worms crawling inside me, swarming throughout my body. My limbs have been seized by a numb paralysis—I cannot feel the pain. But the pressure of little bodies, little legs scurrying beneath my skin writhes between my muscle and tissue. Protruding like a boil against the surface. Mincing the meat on my bones. This record has proven nearly impossible as I fight against the spreading numbness in my bones. My fever has risen and a constant, dehydrating sweat has left me in a stinking pool of salt. I will be a putrefied, liquid stain before my days are done. There is no returning from this.

April 24, 2:47 a.m.

There is an archway above the entrance to St. Anthony that reads *Memento Mori*. I haven't forgotten. In fact, I am reminded all the more by the horrid purple hue that has blotted my skin. As though I have bathed in wine. Careless, meandering stains spill from vein to vein, tripping over capillaries and contusions. My limbs are all consumed, drunk in the relentless delirium. Whoever discovers this record, may you not judge this wayward winding narrative too harshly. Know that I am distraught.

I pray that Dr. Reinhard has abandoned his post, absconded from his duties and left me here to die. There is no sense in rushing to my aid only to succumb to the very same disease. No cure could save me now.

--:-- a.m.

The telephone rang for countless minutes, shrieking with a shrill, metallic urgency. The screeching cry invited me to answer, taunting just out of reach. Concealing a riddle in a song, an irony befitting a cynic and a bard. A chance to warn forthwith of danger, if I hadn't suffered it myself.

I reach out with my left hand, only to be reminded in a gruesome display that it is not there. A phantom loneliness that haunts me still. I had tried clumsily to crawl across the floor, throwing my weight with what power I had, only to hear the song die before I reached the door. I opened it just a crack to see the hall covered in tiny bodies and tiny legs, an army of insects brimming from the ceiling to the floor. The telephone began to ring again. I knew that I would not reach it, and I knew that I would die, alone but for a million murderous minds.

KILL.

It screamed a desperate, piercing scream. Before its congregation, from atop its pretty pedestal, from its sleek, unerring pulpit, the painted pastor preached.

FEED.

The swarming assembly listened. They grew restless, and I grew in despair. The telephone continued to ring, a tremulous, glacial vibrato. Steely and raw, incessant chiming enough for a quarrel of sparrows. And, in that moment—in that haunting, soulless refrain—I accepted that I would die.

April 25, --:--

From within my bedside bureau, it whispered—this dark, foreboding thing. *Anathema*, bound in leather, pages scrawled with deep etchings carved like claw marks into skin. Passages dripping black with blood, the life of a time long dead struggling still to survive. This alien fiction feeding dark fantasies to my battered brain. Like the hot breath of some predatory beast, patiently stalking just behind. A deep but deliberate exhalation, heavy and wet on my neck. Weighted with the violence of bloody gore, caught between the teeth. Thick with the smell of decay wrapping around my throat. These whispering intonations tear the flesh from my bones, building to an irresistible refrain. Bursting inside and splattering across the room like a blood-smeared canvas.

I cannot read the words, but I hear them. Suggestions from the illusionist.

--:--

A lesion has pressed through my abdomen, some dark hernia protruding and twisting like a child. Black vomit covers my legs and spills across the floor, already sprouting a fungal, hairy growth. This journal too is stained, splattered with bile and blood. The pages stick together, sealing my testimony inside. Distinct, offensive voices find weaknesses in my mind like a fresh assault on a fortress crumbling from a successful siege. I am my bloodline's peak.

Chittering mandibles click between the broken walls of my apartment, echoing the rhythm of these voices in my head. Responding in unison to the periodic thrumming of this alien infection—I am host to a hive of parasites. Reliant on this damaged vessel, a conduit for their procreation.

Possessed as I am, taken by the appetite of a tumultuous horde.

--:--

This dark contusion on my stomach struggles against the skin. My body has dried and withered, been consumed and leeched. The labor is ending, the feast diminished to scraps.

I am sorry for the incoherent ramblings of my mind. This record serves as a witness to my pain, some testament that I have lived. No matter the state of my recollection, I must preserve my name. The fears of all tomorrows have fallen away in the wake of my own despair.

April 26, --:--

Have not eaten in days. My throat is parched and my stomach has been constricted, as if tied in rope or bound by piano wire, cutting through my abdomen. Spilling out onto the floor.

My legs have become spotted with plum-painted bruises and succumbed to the entropy of meat. I am nothing more than rotting beef, though I more closely resemble a leper than a tender, hindquarter cut.

The strength of yesterdays has dissipated into the air, and my consuming sense of powerlessness remains my only companion. My resolve has been exhausted, and I cower against the certainty of death. But it will not come quickly, preferring instead to creep along with a tired disposition, drawing painfully out. Patient to the last.

Dr. Reinhard will not see me before I am dead. Mr. Mercy must find another man to spin his weary fictions. The studio whose open position awaits me in California will plunder on, proliferating whatever propaganda their business traffics, attracting some other ingenuous prodigy. The world outside has ceased to exist.

--:--

Let this record serve some greater purpose—a warning, a history, some simple documentation that I lived, however briefly. I fear that by the time this is discovered, it will be too late. Not for me—I will be dead within a day. These insects, these parasites, whatever they are, they will spread. Locusts to the fields. Throughout the building, throughout the streets. Infection proliferous as the plague. Whosoever finds this record, in greatest urgency, you must believe what I have written and listen to what I say—burn it to the ground. This building, this city. They will consume it all with poison and with pain—they will overcome the world.

--:--

I must consume them first, not as flesh but as flames. There is no longer any choice. The ceiling has buckled under and the floor has cracked from the weight as the mold gathers in excess, shrouding the earth in darkness. But an idea has sparked the embers of my mind—a terrible, deliberate idea. My gangrenous limbs must obey me once again.

Carrying this journal with me all the way, I begin to crawl across dry and splintered hardwood. Unfeeling bits of leg, purple pieces of skin scrape off like an apple's peel, exposing raw and naked fruit underneath. I would writhe and cry out in agony if I could feel the flaying meat, but it is little more than the latest horror. I have grown numb to it all, turning my attention instead to the far end of the hall.

Beside the front door of my apartment, my suit jacket hangs from the coatrack. My lighter sits comfortably in the right-side pocket. A pack of Lucky Strike cigarettes waits expectantly in the left. In the hallway between are sure to lie a thousand little bodies and a million little legs, all wriggling in the spasms of their hunger, instinctively drawn to the smell of a wounded beast.

The bedroom door swings painfully open as I press tentatively against it, hesitant and afraid of what I might see. Peering out into the hall, I find that it is empty. A greater fear grips me than had I seen the ravenous swarm—they could be hidden anywhere. Burrowed into the floorboards or nestled into the walls. Growing, spreading, multiplying in the dark. I push these thoughts aside and struggle forward, dragging broken bits across the floor.

My dead and useless legs catch on the splinters, hooking on an uprooted nail. Cold, purple blood pours out onto the floor as I try to crawl forward, ripping my right leg open from the thigh to the calf. Tendons untangle and spill from my leg like capellini pasta, thin and membranous strands of flesh. But I do not scream—I cannot feel it at all. My leg hangs limp, torn wide, attached at the knee only by a thin strip of sinews and nerves, already black with decay. Without thinking, I rip it apart, severing what strands of meat had held the several parts of me together. It resembles an alien piece more than my own flesh and blood. I toss it callously, dismissively aside.

A dull and sudden silence. The walls stand stoic, concealing the writhing mass within. Behind them lies a hidden hive, clawing for their queen. They will burst through soon enough.

My jacket hangs like a lynched man from the coatrack, dangling high above. Desperately now, I knock the coatrack to the floor and plunge my bloody hand deep into the pockets of my jacket, searching breathlessly for its contents. I grasp my lighter and pack of cigarettes and lean against my apartment door. It is my turn to lie in wait—I know what I must do.

--:--

Exhausted and out of breath, I have sunken into myself. These words assume their own significance, adopt an air of historical importance. Too often have I dedicated my days to languishing at my desk, devising verses and narratives of empty, hollow tales. A selfish, ignoble effort to preserve my sorry name. Now I sit surrounded by towering pillars of my own work, crisp and weathered columns of yellow paper glowing golden in the light. An undiscovered Parthenon, a sacristy sinking into uncarved stone. The epitaph will remain unwritten, my works the only witness to my name. A longer-lasting instrument than flesh and bone but only a lonely vessel stranded in a midnight moor. It is an imprint on the immortal mind but a shadow on the wall. Brittle marble monuments to unremembered men.

--:--

My stomach has burst from within and my bowels have fallen onto the floor. Pale, translucent larvae spill out across the room, wriggling and already sprouting legs. Drinking in my purple afterbirth collecting in pools of blood. Writhing responsively to their surroundings, drowning in the sensation of life.

A violent, bitter hatred rises in my throat. I hate how innocent, how pure they are. Untouched but for instinct, driving always to kill. I take my lighter in my hand, choking on bile, gagging on the taste of blood. The enamel and chrome cold against my skin. With a deliberate flick of the wheel, it ignites in the dark. I bring the flame close to the larvae, heating their little white bodies until they catch and burst. Dark juices splatter across my face—and I am satisfied. A perverse sensation of pleasure, power over these vile, despicable things.

I slip a Lucky Strike out from within its blood-stained carton. It fits comfortably in my mouth, sitting loosely between my thinning, splintered lips. My tongue touches the paper but I taste nothing. I bring the lighter close to my face and listen to the paper catch flame. A soft, crinkling sound as smoke falls effortlessly down my throat. Drinking it down like smooth whiskey. Filling my head with the most compelling, horrifying vision. An incredible, delicious dream.

Instantly, a barrage of clamoring voices erupts in my mind, beating against my skull. Desperate, unintelligible cries, the shrieking sound of a hive in panic. They understand what fiery, blistering violence I intend. The screams of a dying forest as its limbs burst and snap in the heat. I look at the trees around me, standing tall. A vicious mausoleum, a grave wood marking my most promising accomplishments, amounting to nothing more than ink assigned in arbitrary symbols, impressed upon wasted sheets of pulp. The bloodsoaked hill of Calvary, dripping with my sins. And now I condemn it to Hell.

Smoke pours from my mouth as a dragon belches fire and I throw my cigarette across the room. I watch in prolonged moments suspended in the air as it turns somersaults overhead. My pen presses faintly against the page in a desperate, final endeavor. The cigarette lands atop a tower of manuscripts and sets the city ablaze. The paper roars and the voices shriek as the *Inferno* swallows up the world.

Note:

This is the final entry of Mr. Pembroke's diary. It was recovered from the smoldering apartment unit, along with various personal items and other written works. They have all been accordingly documented and preserved as evidence. The fire was extinguished before it engulfed the building entirely, and much of the body had been preserved.

The events recounted in this diary cannot be corroborated by any witnesses, nor can our forensic sciences reveal more than the identity of the deceased. Reason and justice demand prosecution of our suspect to the fullest extent of the law. Though arson is an appalling crime committed against the estate of man, murder mars the soul with the stain of immortal sin. Madness makes a man commit all manner of offenses.

The gruesome homicide of Mallory Pembroke marks a turning point. Something evil has taken root in this city and it can no longer be ignored. It has festered for some time in the minds of its citizens and finally embedded within our very selves, deep beneath the skin. We cannot contain it and, like a pestilence or the plague, it will burst above the surface and spread. Whether through the air or by our blood, we will play host to its parasitic pupae and feed the fires of its grip, extending its reach across the earth. Our histories will fall and the future will fade as we huddle in darkness by the sea—and we will all say farewell when we do.

SALEM AVENUE

PART ONE

[1]

Sunlight spilled over the brim of the valley as Jonathan Hager crossed the purple mountain ridge and descended the rolling hills below. The land was untouched, an immaculate sea of emerald greens and a royal coronet of wildflowers dancing in the afternoon breeze. Carefree and innocent, the thoughtless charade of a child, whose mind had invited a symphony of song. In that elusive sense of wonderment and splendor, Jonathan Hager found himself longing for home.

But this was a foreign land, a new world, untested and unchallenged by the hands of civilized men. The overgrowth teemed with the lush of life, thick forests and militant woods marching unchecked into the fields. Jagged mountain peaks surrounded the valley like the jaws of an ancient beast, gaping wide to swallow the peaceful landscape whole. A playful brook skipped aimlessly through the grass, laughing to itself as it wound a meandering way across the clearing.

Jonathan Hager led his horse by the reins as he climbed unsteadily down the mountainside. He had brought little from the other side of world, and even less from Providence, packing only what his horse could carry. She was an old mare, withered in her bones but strong in her spirit. Her coat shone dark in the glare of the sun, black as pitch and smooth as Arabian coffee. He had called her Elsabeth, after his mother. Sturdy and strong, stubborn in the face of hardship.

He followed the little stream across the valley to its source—a pair of natural springs bubbling up from deep within the earth, frothing white as snow. They leapt from the dirt with the vigor of a newborn fawn, gentle and unsteady but eager and unafraid. The two collected in a small pool before flowing from the clearing, giving life to the cool hollow. He bent low to the dirt and found that the water was cold to the touch. He brought it to his mouth and tasted the sweetest, purest drink that had ever passed over his lips.

It filled him with remarkable clarity, a strength to forge ahead. He surveyed the land around him, breathing in the faultless air, crisp as an autumn breeze. Here, in this primeval place, a land hidden away from progress, he planted his weathered boots. He would stand against the creeping weeds and wailing woods in hope of fostering something that might live in spite of bramble thorns.

The old iron axe felt right and just in his hands as he swung against the forest. They were rough hands, calloused and swollen with the scars of unforgiving work. Twisted and torn by years of sweating in the sun. Bits of bark flew through the air as the axe splintered ancient wood, trees standing tall as ramparts and wide as a city square. He swung against the hardened wall, a fortress to the world. It had stood as a tower without a watcher, no alarm bell to be rung. The quiet had caused the countryside to sleep for a thousand years. But their conqueror had come, strong and determined, fearless in the face of the unknown.

Another swing and the tower fell, splitting the sky with the sound of thunder. It crashed to the ground with a shattering force and crushed the saplings underneath. The blade cracked across the valley as he shaped strong walls from the woods. Mud and leaves packed between interlocking logs would shield against the midnight chill. It was to be a sorry house, simple and stout, a provisional shelter from the wilderness that yet lay undiscovered.

Sitting at the edge of the forest, the scant hovel resembled little more than a primitive shack, a surrogate for a proper dwelling, at least until he could construct something more permanent. Something to last. Still, the outpost far exceeded any other evidence of man, wrought from raw materials ripped from the womb of the earth. This sturdy structure, skillfully razed from the dust and the dirt, struck a bruising blow to savagery.

And it was a savage land, bestial to the bone, brutal and begotten by the natural law. There was no legislature here, no court to call the accused. Justice was a foreign word that had never tripped from the tiger's tongue. Tyranny burned like wildfire through the world, catching in the most vulnerable places, dried and snapping in the heat. Once aflame, there was little hope that cruelty could ever be extinguished. These woods had turned black with char. Another mighty pine crashed to the ground as Jonathan turned toward the woods. Leaping through the forest floor, he thought he saw a little flame. Fallen leaves rustled in the undergrowth, followed by a flourish of russet fur. A small creature cried out with a pitiful shriek before the fire found its throat. Foxes followed an ethics of their own.

Darkness cloaked the mountains as evening descended on the valley below. The nighttime air crashed against the cabin walls, cutting through and piercing Jonathan's face. He lay exposed, staring up toward the stars. He hadn't yet completed the cabin's construction, but its progress promised solace from the storm.

The howling of the dark sounded either from wolves or the wind, both of them lonely and calling out for a companion. He couldn't see those hungry eyes, dark and painted over, frozen like the glass eyes of a doll. Black as midnight winter, invisible and cold. However many there might be, their numbers mattered little when the pack hunted together as one. Deep in the darkness of the woods, there opened a single cavernous throat. He envisioned rotted scraps of flesh, gangrenous decay caught half-consumed between its teeth. An unnamed beast stalking primal in the night, not yet discovered by the voyeurs haunting from the shores.

Such thoughts ran wild through his sleepless mind, afflicted by terrors he couldn't see but which had seized him in their stiffening grip. The infinite gullet that swallowed the sun would vomit its warmth at dawn. Until that more promising time, he would shiver alone through the night.

But Elsabeth lay slumbering beside him, her great nostrils flaring from the visions of a dream. She expelled hot air as she snorted aloud at some invisible fiend. Her ears twitched and her hooves unsettled the dirt as she huffed and pawed at the air. He smiled at the sight, comforted by her presence and filled with peace from her warm, mountainous frame. He would stare down a villainous pack of wolves prowling about the field with Elsabeth at his side.

She may have been an aging mare, but her hooves could still split skulls and spill the contents on the ground. Her muscles stretched taut beneath her skin, rippling strong and tensing at the chill. She had carried him across the world, seen more magnificent splendors than the kings and queens of old. The mountains and valleys had chiseled her broad shoulders and carved her strong legs like rivers that cut through limestone cliffs. She had been sculpted by the glorious hands of God, masterfully crafted in the fires of His forge. And she remained as powerful, sleeping peacefully in the night, as she had ever been in her younger days across the sea.

There, back home in Siegen, she had trotted about with careless vigor, free in the simple mountain air. They had grown together, known no one else as companions in their youth. The other children had always been cruel to the boy with a horse for a mother. His father had bought her after his mother's death, but Jonathan had named her after the woman he had never known. She brought memories back to him that he had never had, reminded him of a time before he was born. He reached out into the hole sinking in the back of his head, the dark void where another life had been lived. His fingers felt nothing but the cold, empty autumn air slipping out of his grasp. Wrapping his fur coat snug around his face, Jonathan moved closer to Elsabeth and drifted off to sleep.

5

[II]

The air had begun to change as it always had in late October, but something different was carried on the wind. Elba pulled her jacket close around her face, bracing against the chill. Blazing autumn colors had robbed the trees of their summer splendor, leaving none of their warmth behind. The cold streets of the simple city led her downtown, past the dancing fields and faded farmlands and toward crippled concrete walls. Gravel grew together until blacktop tore the ground in two. Deep in the pit of the valley, at the core of the timeless town, industry sputtered like an engine sipping on fumes. Without the fuel to feed the flames, the fires had died and the embers had been all but left behind. Elba's eyes found cracks in the foundation, snaking in jagged lines underneath an institution that could not stand. The pavement met her footfalls as she pressed unsteadily on.

But the streets of Hager's Fancy resisted. The crumbling towers that lined the concrete stretch at the center of town cast shadows from perilous heights. Down in the gutters below, in the overflowing pools of rain-soaked sewer drains, Elba stepped with cautious independence. Every alleyway beckoned from the dark, luring with uncertain promises for tomorrow. Calling with a siren's song, sweet to the untrained ear, they told of treasures in the mud.

The most malicious of these lay between Jonathan Street and Salem Avenue, sunken in between the cracks of neglected pavement. Elba lingered for just a moment, peering with some difficulty into the darkness. Disregarded refuse stretched end to end, strewn as rotten roses in a graveyard for the damned. A deep groan emanated from within the mausoleum. A woman, or the figure of one who had been, stood silhouetted against the rising sun.

An undead mirage, emerging from the grave, abandoned by all who had once held her near. Her hair fell in a matted mess across her face, obscuring her eyes and tangled in knots between her teeth. She took a single step forward before collapsing headfirst against the concrete. Another groan, louder than the first, and the gargled sound of a broken nose. Elba imagined the blood streaming from her face, the bridge of her nose jutting outward in the wrong direction. A stray swallowed up by the streets, struggling to survive. But the streets had won another round, taken another soul down below where she couldn't hope to escape. Her body soon disappeared in a shroud of smoke and early morning fog, rolling in from the forgotten fields. Elba felt a sting of pity but wandered on, admitting to herself that there was nothing she could do.

She trudged on through the early morning, down the primrose path that wound an errant way until she reached a singular colossus. There, on the other side of the city, sitting solitary at the edge of town, rose a towering edifice of education. St. Matthias Catholic Prep impressed itself upon a solitary field, surrounded on all sides by broken blades of grass that had died and snapped in the heat. The rains had come too late, and the summer had done its worst. A blanched, withering yellow had swept through the town, reaching beyond the edge of the woods—a dry season that left in its dusted wake a collection of faded, brittle bones.

Elba crushed the fragile brush underfoot and marched toward the doors. Golden sentinels standing watch at the gate, guardians of the priceless power beyond. A concrete castle casting shadows across the tired old town. Turrets towered overhead, garrisoned against the city as though preparing for a siege. She wrapped her hands around the handle and threw her weight against the door. With a slow and deliberate movement, she entered the hostile place.

The first half of the day passed with amenable inconsequence. The halls inside St. Matthias were quiet as a tomb, breathless as the morning air on the precipice of afternoon. But lunchtime was another matter. While the classrooms kept her peers in line, they roamed the cafeteria like predators prowling on an open plain. Elba did not care much for parochial tedium, but she cared even less for the commonplace drama of twelfth grade. Simple misunderstandings or trivial disputes that turned anger to bloodlust in a moment. Sitting alone in the swarming cafeteria, Elba observed from a distance something primitive and cruel.

A lioness and her mate, primped and pruned but for the blood in their teeth, lorded over the pridelands below. The Serengeti sun had bleached the grasses white and raised the fever of the fields. Overrun with fodder, teeming with indolent beasts, the blood ran hot across the grasslands. An antelope grazed with impudence. The hunt began.

Rebecca Larsen strode purposefully across the room, prowling among the buffalo and gazelle. Her shoes clicked loudly against the tile floor, shots into the air, bold forewarning of her approach. Slinking through the savannah like a cobra in the grass. Muscles tensing, tendons taut. Her prey remained oblivious, vulnerable in the open plain.

"Hello, Hanna. How's your mother?"

Suddenly, there was blood in the water. The beasts looked up from their disparate meals and stared at the pitiful scene. The lonely girl with raven hair sitting at the far side of the room looked up with worry in her eyes.

"What?"

"Sarah told me she saw her stumbling out of the woods out past the interstate. In fact, I heard she has you living with her in that old crack-house on Salem. Is that true?"

The beast was wounded from the striking blow and crumbling to the ground. Her legs had folded beneath her frame and started shaking from the weight of their burden. Her blood was letting in streams onto the grass as she struggled to stay on her feet. Limbs trembling, she raised herself off of her knees as the pride moved in for the kill.

"Fuck off, Rebecca."

Silence fell over the room like a controlled demolition. Dust gathered in rolling clouds at the approach of a thundering storm. Heads turned with caution, eyes glanced fearfully about. Nobody rebuked a viper.

"Excuse me?"

"I'm really not in the mood," the timid girl replied. She stared intently at her lunch, which had already cooled in the compartments of the plastic tray in front of her. But Rebecca wouldn't accept surrender so easily.

"The only reason you're even here is my daddy's scholarship. You're just a charity case from the other side of Salem."

"Fine."

A flourish of long, pitch-black hair as Johanna Parker rose abruptly from her seat.

"My mom doesn't own a mansion on the North End. We sleep in a shit-stained gutter with the rest of the hopheads. But I've heard much worse about your father. I'd rather she were high as Harlem than face-fucking every whore in Hager's Fancy. Oh, and—"

She smiled, paused, and caught the lion by the throat.

"Your dad's cock tastes like shit."

Johanna fell to the floor faster than the blow that struck her across the face. Nobody dared to breathe. Rebecca's bloody fist hung limp beside her, bruising a deep shade of blue as purple pigment spilled underneath her skin. The Savannah had fallen apart and its inhabitants returned to the cold fluorescent light of the lunchroom. Teachers on duty discussed the strikes in Albuquerque and hopes of snow days this winter, willfully ignorant of the Larsen girl. Mr. Larsen contributed generously to the annual fund, trusting that no mind would be paid to his daughter's improprieties, or to his own indiscretions.

Blood pooled around the body of the lonely girl too foolish to stay in her place. The hierarchy was rigid, the rules were strict—poor girls from the other side of Salem didn't belong anywhere but the underside of the city. Elba crawled out from underneath the sorry streets of Hager's Fancy every morning only to wander woefully back every night. Her own hovel hidden away on the South Side of the city stood uncertainly in the shallow grave of her years. She had received her own share of the dirt. She turned away from Johanna's broken body on the floor and took a sudden interest in the lump of mashed potatoes on her tray.

[III]

"Come, you spirits that tend on mortal thoughts—unsex me here, and fill me from the crown to the toe topful of direst cruelty!"[6]

"Jesus, Becca, no."

A thin man with thinning hair held his fallen face in his hands. His oversized clothing, wrinkled in the seat and faded from the sun, seemed several decades too old. The thrift stores downtown served all manner of customers, from vagrants and vagabonds to sage style savants. Studying the figure of Bishop Ford, it would be difficult to know which camp he called home. Students lingered confused around the stage, holding crumpled scripts and neon highlighters. A crude battlement constructed out of wood groaned painfully behind them.

"Do you even know what you're saying?"

---

6   William Shakespeare, *Macbeth, The Folger Shakespeare, Folger Shakespeare Library*, 2020, 1.5.47-50.

Rebecca stared blankly ahead, genuinely unsure. Thanes and witches held their breath in nervous silence around the theater. Macbeth stepped out from behind the curtains.

"Mr. Ford—"

"What?"

"I have to leave at four."

"Goddammit. Okay, everybody—take five."

The group of students dispersed, some to the dressing rooms, some to center stage, while others still retreated to the back rows of the Pembroke Theater's polyester-blend seats. Elba found herself sitting alone, several rows back from the stage. Her legs brushed uncomfortably against the thick, woolen fabric that had torn in too many places. Crusted stains blemished the cushion like faded motel bedsheets.

It was an old theater, built of brick, wallpapered with dust. The smell of it hung low, like something stale rotting in the sun. A large fissure in the foundation darted uncertainly along the height of the western wall. The weathered years had worn away at the ancient stone, threatening to raze the entire structure to the ground. Though it spent much of the year unused, these tenanted days brimmed with activity. Elba listened to the whirring of buzz-saws, the adamant droning of power drills against stubborn planks of wood. A hive mind bustled below, restless insects, driven tirelessly to task by an obstinate queen.

"Have you memorized your lines?"

Mr. Ford approached without warning. Elba hadn't memorized them at all, but she was hardly concerned. Her part amounted to a small paragraph in the middle of Act II—she played the part of the Porter.

"Here, run lines with Hanna."

Johanna stepped out from behind the slender frame of Mr. Ford. A dark bruise had begun to form around her eye and her bottom lip had visibly swelled. She held tightly to a torn and ragged script with her name scrawled across the front in red.

"I'm the third witch," Hanna said, her voice cracking just a little. She opened her script to the first scene and fell into a seat beside Elba.

Mr. Ford left them both and returned his attention elsewhere. The disparate groups scattered around the theater had begun to talk amongst themselves, their voices rising above the rusted radiators that rumbled and shook in a fruitless, insensible din. Hanna looked up from her tattered seat with a half-expectant look across her face as Elba flipped to the opening scene.

"Alright," Elba began, "act one, scene one. You say whatever you have memorized, and I'll read everyone else."

Hanna stared blankly someplace far away, gazing through the shuttered windows and falling fast in thought. In the silence of her vacancy, Elba turned toward a deserted moor, mist rising from the heat of battle and blood staining the grass across the field. Lightning cracked open the sky as thunder crashed into the mountainsides and spilled a storm out onto the rumbling earth below. Three witches dressed in rags hobbled unsteadily into view.

"When shall we three meet again—"[7]

"I'm glad..."

Elba looked up from her script, ripped away from the gruesome scene playing out spectacularly in her head. The

7   William Shakespeare, *Macbeth, The Folger Shakespeare, Folger Shakespeare Library,* 2020, 1.1.1.

girl seated beside her had begun to cry, tears spilling delicately down the side of her cheek. Elba didn't know Hanna very well, but she understood the darkness in her eyes. A deep, fermenting hurricane that could make landfall at any moment and wreak all manner of untold havoc—a maelstrom made flesh.

Hanna gestured to her swollen face.

"I'm glad Rebecca hit me. What I said to her—I meant it. So did she."

"You're glad she hit you?"

Those eyes like storm clouds rolling overhead at once broke free and bellowed out the truth.

"I'm glad I made her lose control."

A strident whistle sounded throughout the theater. Mr. Ford stood at the forefront of the stage, summoning the room to regroup around him. Elba closed her script, smiled faintly and with abundant caution, and turned away from Hanna toward the stage.

Mr. Ford gestured excitedly as the cast and crew filtered back into the auditorium to wait expectantly at the edge of the proscenium. Their chattering voices fell below the murmur of a few wayward whispers while a metal clanging resounded in their place. A steel ladder reaching to the rafters shook unsteadily as an elderly man adjusted industrial spotlights just above Mr. Ford's head. He hadn't noticed the perilous placement of the ladder—it had been carelessly planted atop the old trapdoor at the center of the stage.

"Everyone, I've just been speaking with Becca here about character motivation. Can anybody tell me what that is?"

Several hands shot up into the sky, shaking with the excitement of an assuredly correct answer. Mr. Ford pointed to a small boy in the front.

"It's the reasons why a character does what he does."

"Exactly," Mr. Ford replied. "Now, who is your character?"

"Fleance."

"And what does Fleance do?"

"He runs away."

The ladder trembled as its weight shifted precariously, teetering atop uneven legs as the trapdoor began to give way. Mr. Ford crouched down low from his place on the stage, leaning closely into the crowd. He allowed himself a hesitant pause as he built anticipation at the approach of his next lesson, stressing the significance of this exercise. His voice dropped just below a gentle purr.

"And why does he run away?"

The boy thought in silence, careful not to answer incorrectly. He settled on something safe.

"Because his father tells him to."

Mr. Ford clapped his hands together and sprang to his feet.

"Yes, because his father tells him to! His father, who has just been fatally wounded by assassins. But why doesn't he fight back? Why does Fleance obey?"

The boy looked up unsure. He had no answer.

"Well, I can't tell you!" Mr. Ford exclaimed. "I'm not performing Fleance—you are. Only you can determine your character's motivations."

The boy stepped back into the crowd as Elba heard a feeble groan from somewhere behind her, a weak confession of pain. She turned to see Hanna staring vacantly in the direction of the stage, lost in the sight of something unseen. Her empty, tempest-torn eyes gazed where Mr. Ford had risen once again to his feet, almost as though she were looking right through him. Looking toward some faraway place that nobody else could see.

"Assignment—each of you define two motivations for your character's actions. Be prepared to discuss on Thursday."

The groaning grew louder as saliva spilled over Hanna's parted lips. It traced a lingering trail along her chin and spattered in droplets on the floor. Her eyes widened and her body shook just enough for Elba to notice.

"Thank you, everyone. You're dismissed."

With a horrible crash and a metallic shriek, the trapdoor swung open to the crossover below and the ladder collapsed violently to the floor. Mr. Ford jumped toward the wings as the elderly man who had been balanced so unsurely came hurtling headfirst from above. He gave a feeble cry before his neck snapped and his skull spilled open across the stage. His broken legs jerked and his jaw hung slack in a ghastly, undead scream.

***

In the humming, golden light of the Hub City Laundromat, Elba studied the faded words printed in justified paragraphs across the folded pages of her script. The rhythmic sound of washing machines persisting like a steam engine rumbled in her mind as she struggled to imagine what the Porter might be thinking. He was a vulgar, offensive character, a clown for the audience to ridicule. The part was little more than a page, a comedy routine to relieve the audience of the murders that Macbeth has just committed. Elba couldn't conjure up motivations for a fool.

And in the quiet abandon of her imagination, the face of the elderly man who had fallen from the rafters gazed lifeless and still from the void. His eyes like saucers were peeled open in a terrified and silent stare. The back of his skull was split open like an egg, fragments of bone floating in a glistening pool of blood. His neck had snapped and his spine was twisted from the fall. As Elba watched the life drain from his eyes, his fingers convulsed and grasped at nothing as it drifted away. A grave opened for him in the center of the stage as he sank without a sound into the earth.

"Need another quarter?"

Elba looked up from the misty moors of Scotland and the bloodstains in her head to see her father standing before her, holding a roll of coins in his hand. His eyes were kind and his smile was calm, but she had known him long enough not to let her gaze linger there for long. Burrowed beneath that glistening visage lay a grimace like a snake, coiled and caged, prepared at any moment to strike.

She smiled faintly at her father's gesture, but gently shook her head. He slipped the roll of coins back into his pocket and placed a crumpled paper bag and a pair of strawberry milkshakes on the counter beside her.

"Suit yourself."

The two devoured their dinner in peace, pausing only to share a knowing glance and a smile. Their lives had never been filled with riches but their hearts were full every Tuesday evening in that laundromat. In the absence of more worldly treasures, they clung to what luxuries they had.

"Your mother would be happy to see this."

Elba's stomach caught in her throat. Her mother was rarely mentioned out loud, and never in a pleasant tone. Her ghost lingered on her father's lips, haunting from somewhere beyond the grave. The sound of creaking metal kept the room from falling silent, but Elba understood that something had been said her father could not take back.

"You can tell me if you miss her."

The truth, of course, was more complicated than that. Elba often felt an absence, some gnawing pit that had sunk into the back of her mind, but she could never truly miss what she had never really known. She had no memories of her mother to keep her holding on to phantom whims.

Without holding tight to that missing piece, her father remained a mystery. His temper, short like a fuse, would forever burn for reasons ineffable, undiscovered oceans of history and loss.

Night had fallen fast over Hager's Fancy and cloaked the valley in darkness. Mourning doves made their sorrows known for the death of the day. Under cover of encroaching nightfall, Elba and her father spent the remainder of the evening eating Krumpe's burgers and shakes as they waited for their wash to dry. Before their last few loads could finish, the front doors to the laundromat swung open and a disheveled man stumbled inside.

"Got any change," he said, his voice a clumsy blunder that slurred those stolen words like a lazy painter blotting a canvas without regard for tact or taste. He looked like her father, only aged by untold years of living on the streets. He smelled like vinegar and stale beer, and the stubborn odor of cigarette smoke clinging tightly to the unraveling fabric of his coat. His shoes were weathered clubs caked in crusted mud, oversized but somehow still sewn together.

Her father turned to face the stranger, clearly cautious of this slight but shadowy figure. A tension rose between them as Elba sat perched on the ledge of the counter, craning her neck to get a better look. With a swift and mindless motion, her father tossed the crumpled Krumpe's paper bag behind him to the floor. The steady thrumming of the laundromat like an anxious heartbeat throbbed in Elba's throat. The man approached with persistent vigor, either unaware of or unaffected by the distressing limp of his uneven legs.

"Just need a little," he muttered as he nearly fell over his own unbalanced feet. His voice clawed its way out of his graveled throat, spilling freely into the laundromat and filling the air with what amounted to a desperate groan. The smell of gangrene and gout stifled his senses and clouded the evening sky. Elba looked deep into his bloodshot eyes and pitied what she saw.

But her father had been calloused against the compassion of younger years. Wearied by his own inescapable past, his sympathies had dissipated into thin air. He stood from his seat with aggressive speed before planting himself firmly between his daughter and the figure of a man who had fallen too far. The coil of the snake had begun to unfurl as he raised his head above the dirt. Elba was unsure what he might do.

"That's far enough." Her father's words were blunt, brief but stern. "We don't have anything for you."

But the man pressed forward as though he couldn't hear or else refused to listen. He slipped a slender arm into the folds of his overcoat and raised the other in Elba's direction, pointing a gnarled finger at her face.

"I see them lips is lined with grease."

Her father's fist collided in an instant with the man, snapping his nose like something brittle underfoot, splintering out of place with a violent crack. Blood poured deep and dark as hidden histories down the front of his shirt, soaking through to his skin. The brutal consequence of overstepping her father's bounds, of challenging the authority of his parental instinct, stained him on the surface.

As the echoes of this sudden savagery rang out in her head, Elba was powerless in the face of conflict. To sit helplessly sidelined at the mercy of her father's fists frightened her more than the threat of bloodshed at the hands of the city's sorry few, those lost and wayward souls left abandoned by the faceless figureheads above, forced to fend for themselves.

Holding his face firmly in his hand, the man faltered backward into the front doors of the laundromat as blood flowed freely from his nose and slipped between his fingers. Elba shared a troubled look with her father, who turned around with worry in his eyes, as the man tripped out the door and disappeared into the night.

[IV]

Morning fog rolled down into the valley as dewdrops collected on the grass. Jonathan Hager woke from a dream that he couldn't quite recall. The fading memory of an alternate life, some inexplicable adventure in an inverted world. He had fallen below the crust of the earth and sunk like a perilous stone. Through dirt and through mud, swallowed alive by an insatiable beast. Into a grave of his own making, buried beneath ages of bones. His own singular impression would be added to the rest, consumed by the onslaught of time. And suddenly he soared through the stars, shooting like an arrow arching high across the night. But he collided with the clouds and came crashing back to life with a force more powerful than fear.

He leapt from the dream as he jumped to his feet and saw that Elsabeth was gone. The imprint of her body lay still in the dirt, undisturbed but for hoofprints leading to the door. Gathering his heavy coat about his shoulders, Jonathan stepped out into the field.

Across the valley, where the twin springs bubbled

gleefully in the mud, Elsabeth drank freely from the stream. Drifting along with joyful abandon, the babbling brook laughed loudly like a child, a sound Jon hadn't heard in an age. In truth, he hadn't heard the sound of another human's voice in—well, it must have been over a month. Not since he left the little settlement up north, Providence by the sea. He had lived on the coast within its wooden walls in a small house made of stone. He had built it with the help of others, like the sturdy houses built back home. Thick walls and broad doors, a pointed roof of heavy timber that shielded against the snow.

They were quiet towns, simple in design, safeguarded in their ignorance against the wild woods beyond. That sorry sentiment of safety defended their inhabitants from the brutish bloodshed of every era that had passed. In the complacency of comfort, they had grown weak. Jonathan resisted his own attrition, actively ensuring that he endured the hardships of his ancestors. He had often tasted blood. Few people lived in Providence who didn't know his name— rumors traveled quickly in quiet, simple towns.

But here he would build a house of his own, establish a homestead unique in its freedom, singular in the extent of its liberties. Here, he would do what he wished. Governor of his fancies, executor of his will. In exercise of his authority, he pulled his cock out of his trousers and let a steady stream of warm piss fall onto the grass. It spattered in the dirt, a wellspring of its own, as wisps of steam rose on the morning air. He shook out the last drops and tucked it back inside.

His stomach rumbled and he thought of food, wondering what rations remained. From a small sack, he removed oats and salted squirrel, apples and dried beef. Buried at the bottom, he found scraps of turkey and chicken. Morsels enough for a few more meals, sustenance sufficient for the week. But he would need to hunt if he were to survive the coming winter, let alone through his paltry stores. He grabbed his flintlock rifle from beside his short stack of belongings, wiped off what dewdrops had collected, and slung the faded leather strap over his shoulder. He tightened the laces of his weathered boots and marched into the woods.

The brisk morning chill gave way to a blustering afternoon storm. Winds gathered from the south and pushed billowing clouds across the sky, stretched taut until they snapped and showered the earth below. Jon pulled the hood of his coat up over his head but the rain soaked through the fur. He had made the old coat of black fox and beaver skins during his time in Providence. He had learned the fur trade from an Englishman and carried the knowledge with him, prepared to stake out a claim in the wilderness unknown.

He had never before considered himself a man of business, an entrepreneur of the feral woods. Lying still in the thickets and the heavy brush, he felt the thrill of the future stalking toward him. Snapping twigs underfoot, sniffing for the scent of his approach. But the rains had washed all trace of him away, swept him with the stream toward someplace he had never been.

Jonathan held his rifle close to his chest, his finger tracing the brass trigger guard. Something pressed slowly through the dense forest walls, brushing against pine branches and upsetting fallen leaves. He dared not breathe and disturb whatever creature came carelessly his way. The damp had slipped into his throat, sliding along like black mucus, infected from the rot that hung in the air. He pressed his lips together to stifle any sound as his stomach rumbled against the dirt. His legs were numb from the cold and the uncomfortable position in which he lay. The handle of his hunting knife had been shoved deep into his side, digging into his ribs. His arms began to tremble as he tried to support his weight, gripping his rifle with hands he could no longer feel.

Slowly, the animal stepped into sight, a graceful silhouette of light brown fur and slender legs treading purposely between shadow and raindrops falling between the canopy. Hot breath gathered in a cloud of vapors rising on the wind, wisps like smoke from a fragile fire burning in the faded daylight. He rested his rifle in the crook of his arm, lifting the hood of his coat above his brow.

Dark eyes like marbles peered through the underbrush, large round baubles glinting like glass. A small, black nose of coal rooted through the sticks and the leaves. A white-tailed doe, innocent and unsuspecting, untouched by the artifice of man. There were imperfections in her skin, traceable patterns like ripples in her fur, dirt that clung in matted clumps to her underside.

Jonathan brought his rifle level with his eyes and smelled its polished wood. Steady, with a firm grip between his frozen fingers, painfully uncertain of the barrel. He exhaled slowly after holding a shallow breath, careful to do so quietly, lying as still as he could. The doe stood no more than an arm's length away, nearly within his reach. With another breath held tightly in his chest, he squeezed the trigger and a burst of fire blew a bloody hole through the beast.

The bullet brought it down but had not yet stopped its heart. Jon felt a foreign twinge of pity for the pathetic beast, wounded and broken, writhing and screaming in the muck. The sound of its cries echoed through the forest— desperate, bleating whimpers unbearable to his ears. He drew his hunting knife, a large blade gleaming in the rain, clean and thick and sharp. Careful of the flailing hooves that lashed and kicked in his direction, he pressed his knee onto the stomach and dragged the blade across its throat. Blood spilled bright and red from its thrashing neck onto the ground, staining the woods like wine. It soaked into the dirt, diluted by the rain, never to be drunk again. In a moment muted by thunder overhead, the creature stopped wriggling, stopped screaming to the clouds.

Dragging the creature along by the legs, Jon struggled through the woods and the mud back toward the peaceful hollow of the valley. A deep trail carved itself into the grass as he carried the doe behind him by a rope, tied securely around the hooves. Its head slumped lazily to the side, its face skipping undignified in the dirt. Blood mixed in the mud as it dried black and purple, crusting in its fur.

Elsabeth stood dutifully by the unfinished house, sniffing at the air and flicking her tail to the side. Her unease showed as Jon brought the doe, mangled and bloody, beside the house. It had been a messy kill, more violent than he intended. She huffed in his direction, stamping the ground with her hoof. The advance of the gruesome sight like a lingering phantom toward her haunted visions in her mind. A bloody premonition of her natural lot, the gory, ghastly atrophy of rotting, liquid flesh. The specter broke unspoken rules regarding the unknown, unveiling to the innocent her finite, mortal fate.

Panic gripped her by the throat, crushing her windpipe and constricting her breath until the veins in her eyes engorged. Sensing the worry in her bones, Jon dropped the carcass behind the house and gently patted her coat. He spoke softly to her, reassuring with an even tone, a chorus of comforts together like a song. She seemed to calm, eased by his touch, consoled at the sound of his voice. Taking his knife again from its sheath, he stalked toward the rear of the house and prepared to gut the beast.

[v]

Elba slept in resounding peace. She dreamed of silence and seasons and unbroken things. The ellipses of time tearing through the universe with a callous disregard. A runaway wheel of fortune that never turned in her favor. A dream without ending, infinite spaces stretching outward in all directions.

And in her dream she fell, farther down the rabbit hole than she had ever been before. Vanishing vertices and vexating vertigo, a cosmic complication of our fragile physical plane. Far below, or through, or after, she—but she didn't fall. She flew. Not through space, not through time. Transcendent of it all.

"Elba—"

She woke with a start, taking a sharp breath that stung in her throat. Her eyes were torn open by a panic that subsided in an instant. Her father stood at the door, leaning inward with care.

"Time to wake up."

He entered the room slowly, approaching with a cautious disregard. The smell of years hung lingering in the air. He surveyed the wistful walls, the colorful photographs and drawings that adorned every lonely corner, and smiled at the records of a life. Evidence of happiness, irrefutable proof of his parenting prowess. Still, there lingered a cold emptiness in the air. Something unacknowledged haunting the silence. He moved beside Elba's bed, placing his hand on top of her sheets, and sat at the end of her mattress. His hand moved softly along the outline of her body as he kissed the side of her face.

The shower ran cold as Elba let it fall over her, running in frozen droplets down the quivering contours of her body. A shallow pool had begun to gather around her feet as the water refused to drain. Numbness crept up her legs as she wrapped her arms across her chest in a futile, icy embrace. The shampoo had dried up and the soap was worn down and her skin had grown rough with goosebumps.

She took a final breath and shut off the shower with a decisive twist of the handle. Her hair hung thin and flat against her scalp, heavy with water that dripped onto her skin. She wrapped her towel close about her and stood shivering for what felt like an eternity. The tile floor below promised the sensation of a thousand knives. After a moment's hesitation, she lifted her leg and stepped down.

Slipping out of her towel, she laid out her mass uniform—today was a holy day. At least, it was the funeral service for the elderly stage worker, the man who had fallen from the rafters. The man whose head had spilled open like an egg onto the proscenium. The entire school was expected to attend. She fell into the same clothes she had worn for every Feast Day, Holy Day, and First Friday of the month. Black knee-highs, a pleated, green-plaid skirt, and a matching tie wrapped around the neck of her button-down blouse, distinguished by a silver coat of arms. Ornately sewn beneath, the motto of St. Matthias Catholic Prep—*Virtus Vocat Fideles*. And she was called. An inward beckoning to some higher place, to some power she didn't understand. Her father could do little to foster her potential, not without neglecting what passions he had. Virtue did not call him. Elba slipped on her shoes, slung her book bag over her shoulder, and headed out the door.

The basement of St. Matthias Catholic Prep housed a small chapel framed by simple panes of stained glass. St. Matthias was not an ornate structure, but it was austere. A byproduct of unfortunate renovations undertaken in accordance with 1970s brutalism. An unencumbered cathedral to the pitiless, new-age gods where a simple schoolhouse once stood. The chapel offered a tenuous respite from the towering concrete and steel. Elba descended the spiraling staircase to an underworld buried beneath the surface. The smell of perfume filled the room as incense burned above, rolling in purple clouds against the ceiling. Candlelight offered a soft glow that flickered like a host of timid angels. Elba took her seat in a pew toward the front.

Father Brian read the rites with a delicate musicality that echoed softly through the chapel. The body of the elderly man lay displayed in a simple casket before the altar. The morticians had done the best they could but there was no disguising the scars that stretched like cracks in porcelain across his face. A morbid memento of her mortal fate. Fragile frames of splintered bones, constrained within a clockwork cage, held together by a tangled thread. His had come unwound, the broken visage of a murdered man. But Time and Death and the cruelty of Fate did not bend their will to the whims of Justice. Her scales were unbalanced, and they shifted in the wind.

Mass moved quickly as Elba stood to receive communion. She processed with a steady rhythm toward the altar. The body of the elderly man shone dull like plastic underneath the flickering candlelight. Elba thought he might melt from the heat, a mannequin figure made of wax. There was something artificial in his brow, an expression not of sleep but of absence, less than unconsciousness. There was no promise of recovery, no hope in waking from a dream. Empty eyelids and hollow head, stomach pumped and spirit dead.

She saw the imperfections in the mortician's handiwork, the cavities where the stuffing had collapsed, the blotting of cheap makeup in patches across the face. The blush had been applied too liberally, painting the unhappy canvas rouge with embarrassment at his state. A drunkard perhaps, rosy in the cheeks, a tired, old man who had passed away to the sound of a whiskey lullaby. She wondered at where he was, where he had gone having left this vessel behind. She tried to imagine nonexistence, contemplated oblivion, and came up empty-handed. Still, it was difficult for her to envision the transposition of a soul. Like musical notes soaring on sound waves from the yellowed pages of a hymnal, Elba could not read the arrangement of his mind.

Father Brian's outstretched arm trembled gently as he placed each host into the hands of her classmates with an understated significance. Elba bowed her head in reverence before she approached. She received her own, ate of the Body, and stepped aside to receive the Blood. The wine tasted like sorrow on her tongue. She returned to her pew and fell to her knees as she watched the rest of the school come forward. Hanna was among the last in line. Her face was contorted, fixed in a frown that caused Elba concern.

In either devotion or despair, Hanna pressed on toward the altar, stumbling over herself as though she were wearing someone else's shoes. Father Brian failed to notice as he offered her the host, which he placed into her outstretched palm. Elba watched a tear fall slowly down Hanna's cheek as she shook, almost as in pain. Though Hanna brought the host close to her lips, Elba caught her sleight of hand and saw her slip it inside her pocket.

Mass concluded without consequence and they all filed back to class.

***

Rehearsal came with the familiar, tedious drudgery that it always had, the school day passing with brief but precious moments in which Elba drifted off to sleep. Her dreams had left her disturbed for countless nights, unable to find the peace of days she had known as a younger girl. She rested in the front row of Pembroke Theater's crusted, fabric seats, waiting for rehearsal to begin.

"Hello, again."

Hanna dropped into the seat beside her. Elba shifted herself uncomfortably, unsure of what to think of this girl who had taken such a sudden interest, though she was happy to have the company.

"Have you memorized your part yet?" Hanna asked, unaware that Elba hadn't opened her copy of the script in weeks. She was only participating for the extra credit—and even then, she wasn't sure that she really needed it.

"Alright, everyone! To the front, please." Mr. Ford had jumped onto the stage and stood beckoning the room toward him. The stage itself had been stained a deep, unsettling red where the elderly man had fallen. Where his brains had leaked out through his ears and soaked into the old, untreated wood.

"You all remember our last rehearsal. All things considered, it was an unmitigated disaster."

This was largely the truth, although Elba was unsure if Mr. Ford was more upset at the death of an employee or the indolent youth of high school students.

"I'm going to trust you all considered your assignment. Rebecca, why don't you come forward and show us what you've prepared."

Rebecca strode down the aisle and onto the stage beside Mr. Ford. She performed an awkward curtsy before assuming an unconvincing air.

"Lady Macbeth considers her sex obstructive to her desires. She calls upon supernatural forces to strip her of feminine weakness, which she understands as incompatible with power and success. She cannot reconcile her womanhood with her ambitions, so she chooses one over the other."

"And how does that work out for her?"

Rebecca took a moment to consider, hesitating at her conclusion. "It drives her mad."

Mr. Ford clapped his hands together. "Exactly."

Elba rolled her eyes. Lady Macbeth was not a complicated character. *Not many of us are*, she thought. A woman who wanted more than what she had but who was unprepared to pay the cost.

"You disagree, Miss Reed?"

The theater turned its eyes toward Elba, who sank just a little into her seat. Mr. Ford reached out his arm, motioning for Elba to join him and Rebecca on the stage. Reluctantly, she stood, climbed the proscenium steps, and gazed out into the audience.

"Why don't you tell us about your character's motivations?"

She hadn't prepared anything. Her character was a drunk—that was it.

"I'm not really sure," she said, her voice breaking in the sour theater air.

"Who are you?"

Elba understood this in the most literal sense, but she also knew what Mr. Ford was asking. Her character was simple, her part was brief, and her lines were not in the strictest sense complex. All of this was more than welcome.

"The Porter," she mumbled.

"Yes! And what is the Porter?"

"A gatekeeper."

The intensity increased as Mr. Ford burrowed deeper into her mind. "Now, *who* is the Porter?"

She did all she could to keep from running backstage and hiding in the dressing room. Every blazing stare burned into her skin, glaring beneath the surface into her sinking stomach. The bile crept along the back of her throat.

"I don't know."

Mr. Ford didn't believe her but understood what she meant. He sensed her discomfort and pressed further.

"He's a clown," he said, saving her from further embarrassment. A soft laughter floated across the room on a sigh of relief.

"A façade. He's a smiling face painted over a moment of despair. You have to look deeper than the mask."

The laughter ceased.

"What has just happened in the play? The Porter pretends he is the gatekeeper to Hell just after King Duncan has been murdered by Macbeth. He laughs at the fate of sinners, all the while Duncan's body bleeds and Macbeth scrambles to wash his hands. He is, in one sense, speaking about them. The ironic levity is meant to disturb the audience. He makes them afraid of what's to come."

Applause sounded throughout the empty theater as Elba's face burned a deep shade of pink. The color of discarded bubblegum decaying on the underside of a rusting, metal desk.

Mr. Ford gestured for Elba to return to her seat. As she descended from the stage, she found Hanna's face in the crowd. It had contorted into a troubling grimace, twisted unnaturally with an unmistakable expression of pain. Elba felt something unsettle in her stomach, something more sickening than embarrassment. An ache that grew with a swelling disproportion—soon it would have to burst.

"Clearly, some of you have not taken this assignment as seriously as others. To those of you who did, I'm grateful for your cooperation. To those of you who did not—I expect better. Now, let's take places for Act Four, Scene One."

A flurry of movement as students rushed into place, glad to have survived the lecture unscathed.

"Oh, Rebecca—does your father remember he's meeting with me after rehearsal? I need to discuss next year's budget with a member of the school board who is remotely invested in our drama program."

"Yes, Mr. Ford."

8   Justin Rohr, *Elba Reed, 2020, pencil on paper.*

[VI]

An unforgiving wind swept like violence across the empty plains hidden below the frozen mountains. Never had the earth looked so desolate as under siege of winter. Swelling thunderclouds overhead trumpeted the fatal approach. Nights passed slowly and the stars faded in time as Jonathan Hager struggled against the cold.

His half-assembled hovel shivered through the dark but withstood the wilding winds as they battered for days on end. The promise of progress burned within him and kept his spirits warm in spite of the murderous chill. Standing resolute in the face of brutal forces, the simple structure shrank into the shadows of the surrounding mountainsides.

Jon dreamt of a stone house, sturdy and strong, resilient like the houses of his childhood. They had stood for hundreds of years, monuments to men of progress, testaments to the cruelty of time. In all the merciless minutes that passed him by, that passed the world by without a second thought or a glance behind, those houses would endure in the dust. He hoped that he, too, might build something that would last.

A legacy silent to his name, speaking only to the strength of his hands.

When day broke, the sky split open and rain fell like hailstones to the ground. Deep, violent cuts into the earth, bullets piercing through and ripping dark mud from below. It was not a day for great accomplishments, but Jonathan felt compelled to try.

The mountains surrounding the valley were weighed down with stone, heavy and rich as the elder mines on the other side of the world. Instead of glittering gemstones and cities built of gold, ocean blues and brilliant whitecaps rose atop the ancient mountain peaks. Limestone like jagged teeth in the maws of a mythic beast, more useful to Jon's purpose than all the valuable jewels in the halls and hordes of mighty kings.

There across the valley, rooted in the rolling hills, hidden away from the envious eyes of meddlesome men, Jon harvested the fruits of the earth. Stone fruits, hardened in the crushing crucible below, sculpted through ages of fire. Once ripened, they burst forth from the core and shattered the crust to hang high above the clouds. Unattainable, forbidden by the jealous gods, purposely placed out of reach.

But Jon had awoken determined to pluck them from their jagged branches, to haul his house piece by piece down from the mountainsides. Elsabeth was too old, too burdened with the afflictions of her age to be of much use making her troubled way up the wooded slopes carrying cargo from the clouds. He would gather the harvest himself and plant its seeds in far more fertile ground, where he would watch it grow more powerful than all the mountains in the world.

In his own silent, secluded citadel he would cultivate the seat of progress, an encampment from which he would wage unholy war against the savage lands beyond. The state of nature was a tyrannical plot, beset by oppressive forces without mercy or consideration for justice or liberty. A nation unknown, its borders boundless and its people primitive, subject to the dictates of a despot. Mother Nature reigned supreme, unconquerable and unassailed by the insignificant insects crawling on their hands and knees across the forest floor.

Progress was made swiftly and with ardent expectations for the future. The foundation was laid around the twin springs bubbling from someplace undiscovered under the mud. A deep cellar set below the dirt, buried beneath the stone walls that would rise high into the air above. He had dug a grave into the earth, pierced through the soft exterior and made short work of supple flesh.

In the consequence of hours racing by, a sizeable cellar had been carved into the ground, large enough to allow the springs to pool and collect before flowing from the foundation and forming a stream through the center of the valley. This would secure his source of drinking water, keep the lower level of the house cool during the sweltering summer months, and provide for safe and fortified food storage. A thin column had been sculpted for the chimney of a stone hearth, one to serve as a small stove.

At the far end of the room, he made an alcove for storing what provisions might spoil and rot before he could consume them. The falling temperature would preserve them for the future and deliver him from starvation. There, in that cold and hollow void, an empty promise of tomorrow's sure success, the future of his empire would stand firm and tall. The beating heart of the valley would pump living blood through the very veins that wound their way into his own swelling muscles, tense and stretched taut underneath his calloused, weather-worn skin.

He had been conditioned by the work of days, sweating underneath stifling beams of sunlight. The charge to establish something civil in a ruthless, brutal world would be fulfilled from this wellspring of hope in something greater than he would know. Already the walls were taking shape, rising faster than the dawning of a new day as stone after wary stone settled comfortably into place. From the mud and the dust and the earth of the valley, Jon created a mortar to hold it fast together.

The gears like clockwork meshed together in symphonic harmony as the machine chimed the hour of his triumph. Day by abundant day passed with righteous consequence as the great stone structure rose higher and higher into the air, the monument taking glorious shape. First the ground floor, formed by sturdy hands, then another built above, separate rooms centered around a rugged hearth to civilize a savage land. Strong walls supported by a stronger will, wooden floors and wooden beams framing the future Jonathan envisioned. Several stories tall, intruding into the eagle's domain. There, where he didn't belong, venturing beyond the safety of the fertile fields below, he ascended to the dizzying heights of the clouds.

9

9   Tania Bustamente, *The Work of Days, 2020, acrylic ink on watercolor paper.*

With his glinting axe and his sharpened pick, he gathered his bricks from the mountainsides and placed them in a worthy sack. Not far from where he worked, leaning against a protruding boulder, rested his slender, flintlock rifle. In abundant caution of the careless woods, Jon carried it with him whenever he stepped foot across their darkened threshold.

Along the razor-blade ridge of the summit, the sun pierced through the storm clouds and shattered over the valley in shards of stained glass. The rain had cleared in the afternoon and the air turned thin and dry. A slight breeze carried a new scent over the mountain peaks. Something sweet and fresh, the smell of cool moss clinging to the cracking bark of an ancient oak tree. Jon placed another stone in his bag, gathered his tools and his rifle, and started his climb down the mountain.

Through the impenetrable woods, passing between towering trunks and scattering underbrush, Jon pressed toward the valley below. The rising walls of his resolute house stood dutifully waiting, and Elsabeth no doubt stood beside them. His entire world lay quietly nestled in a comforting cradle of verdant fields, a peaceful façade fallen over the feral frontier.

But it told a terrible lie, a fable devoid of conflict, no lesson to be had. A false front to the terrors lurking underneath the surface. There, below the tranquil sea, unimagined monsters tore with violent fervor at the mounting wake. Ancient oceans hiding the horrors of the abyss, undiscovered demons dancing in the depths of Hell. The mountain peaks imprisoned the past in a tomb, buried beneath ages of the earth. Shadows of primeval people caught between the teeth of an eldritch beast, one that hungered not for blood but for their bones. The forests surrounding Jon's pitiful plot of land teemed with incongruent life, monsters of another kind. In the darkness and the thick of the woods, he thought he heard a noise.

He paused briefly in his tracks, crouching low to the ground and carefully setting his tools and his bag of stone down in the dirt. His rifle hung at the ready around his shoulder. From behind the cover of a moss-coated tree he caught a glimpse of some lumbering creature moving steadily toward him. He couldn't quite discern what it was, only that its sturdy frame upset the otherwise impenetrable woods. A mass of dark fur moving at an alarming pace, deliberate and toward his place of cover as though it had already discovered his hiding spot. He figured it was most likely a deer or even perhaps an adolescent bear. Nothing so vicious as to vitally endanger him but large enough still to feed him for several weeks. He would need to be cautious—mountain lions also prowled the forests beyond the western territories.

He took his rifle in his hands, loaded it slowly and with deliberate care to be quiet, and pointed it in the direction of the creature. He hardly dared to breathe as its heavy footsteps crushed the underbrush with callous indifference, thoughtless to the disruption of its path. A broad mass of black fur marched a lonely way through the brambles and the branches, pushing past the dense forestry and toward the clearing of the valley. It lumbered in no particular hurry, nor was it wary of disturbing the silent hills. Whatever it was, Jon was not eager to collide with a blood-lusting predator in the woods. Easing his rifle against his shoulder, sliding his finger against the trigger, he took aim at the faceless figure and fired a bullet toward its heart.

A terrible scream pierced through the daylight and broke the silence in the air. It hung low and thick like mud from the branches as it cracked and splintered, falling heavy to the dirt. An inhuman shriek, the sound of a screech owl falling from the sky. The creature collapsed with a sickening thud onto the frozen forest floor, scattering the leaves and snapping twigs underneath. A heap of fur, a mass of meat lying lifeless and still on the ground.

Jon removed himself from behind his hiding place and cautiously approached his prey, keeping his rifle pointed squarely at its chest. Careful not to lose his footing in the mud and the slick carpeting of leaves that had fallen across the forest floor, he stepped purposefully and with a painfully deliberate pace. Pausing at the foot of the beast, he noticed something disconcerting showing through underneath its thick coat. A pair of bare feet coated thick with dark mud, bright pale toes shining like iridescent pearls. Human feet, human toes protruding from beneath a billowing fur cloak. A hole was torn where his bullet had struck—blood was flowing through.

Suddenly panicked, his breath short and quick, Jon knelt down and reached out his trembling hands, turning the body over onto its back. A heavy hood lay over the head and hid whatever face lay underneath. The cloak was clasped around the neck and wrapped tightly about the body, obscured for warmth or disguise. Its black fur was coarse and thick, the hide of a bear fashioned into the shape of a man. Jon thought to leave the body bleeding in the dirt, to collect his things and run down the mountainside to the safety of the valley below. A deep, undying fear grew stronger and more fervent in the pit of his stomach, pleading from someplace at the forefront of his mind to take to his feet and fly from this place. But an ache like guilt, a dull pain wearing away at the back of his throat, trapped him where he stood.

Compelled to remain and uncover what he had done, he removed the hood to reveal the slender face of a woman. Her deep-set eyes had fallen shut and her dark hair had become a tangle of black spiders all wriggling and caught in their own webs, falling down behind her ears and spilling onto the ground. He traced their twisted way across the dirt. Pulling back the oversized fur cloak, Jon found that the woman was naked underneath, save for a leather satchel slung loosely around her shoulder. Her fair skin gleamed in the sunlight streaking through the treetops as blood streamed from her side.

He touched his finger to the wound as her blood smeared thick across his hand, the gore sticking to his fingers and staining his skin. Her body stiffened and her breath slipped away as her chest weighed heavy with lead. Her mangled breasts rose and fell with a faint but steady rhythm that beat the uncertain promise of life. And she was alive, barely breathing but stubbornly refusing to die. She continued her silent, subtle song with a painful rasp at the bottom of her throat. A dissonant chorus, a horrible dirge in a minor key. There was unfinished work for her to accomplish before surrendering her spirit to the unknown.

With an undignified effort, Jon wrapped his hands around the woman's body and lifted her into his arms, cradling her broken frame against his own as he made his careful way down the mountain. Stone after unturned stone shifted precariously with each hurried footstep, dirt and dust disturbed in the descent. He abandoned his tools and his sack of limestone in the woods and struggled with a new burden toward the valley, back toward the twin springs bubbling joyously from deep within the earth.

There, where life burst forth fresh from the ground, where the frame of a new colossus already blossomed in the dirt, he would care for the woman in his arms. Jon could still smell the gunpowder in the air, the sparks and the smoke lingering like afterbirth on her skin. Blood pooled in the cradle of her stomach, spilling over and falling in a viscous stream down Jonathan's leg. Seeping through the heavy wool of his trousers, it felt warm and thick as it stuck to the hairs of his thigh. He tried to ignore each droplet that joined the others in what had quickly become a river flowing from the woman's open side. A beautiful bottle of the vintner's own beloved wine, broken and burst as the fruit of countless years fell wasted to the floor.

Moving faster, running into the open field at the base of the mountain, Jon felt the weight in his arms increase tenfold. Delicate and fragile, the woman's face had fallen a distressing shade of pale green, pallid as a corpse and slender like a snake. Maybe it was the glinting of the afternoon sun against her sallow skin, but she seemed somehow to shed her own visage. He thought for a moment to take her to the sorry wooden shack by the edge of the woods, to lay her broken body down and tend to her in the dirt where Elsabeth slept, but his tormenting sense of guilt forced him to carry her into the safety of his stone house.

Through the wooden frame of the doorway and up the single flight of stairs that climbed to the second floor above, he brought her to a simple room overlooking the length of the valley. Bare but for the shadows on the wall, sunlight streamed in through the window to bathe the floor in gold. There, beside the open window and beneath the slanted bit of roof he had constructed, Jon eased the woman onto the floor.

The billowing cloak that clasped tightly around her neck cradled her broken body, softening the hardwood against her spine and supporting her brittle bones. Blood spilled unceasingly from an open gash ripped through her side, a gruesome scene of gore where his bullet had blown her breast apart. Careful not to press against her bruising ribs, Jon removed the satchel from around her shoulder. He tossed it thoughtlessly aside as an assortment of herbs and black moss scattered across the floor. Unsure of what sort they were, he turned back to the woman he had brought into his house and tended desperately to her wound.

[VII]

Ted Larsen met Bishop Ford in his office promptly at six, whereupon the two men began to undress. They had first seen one another several years ago, sitting at opposite ends of a long, mahogany conference table. Mr. Larsen had been a member of the school board for many years, ever since his eldest daughter had begun school at St. Matthias. But Mr. Ford had only just been hired as drama instructor when he noticed the rugged man in a suit, the one with a hint of grey in his beard.

Without a word, Mr. Larsen stripped out of his clothes and pulled off Mr. Ford's, careful not to tear the buttons from his shirt. His swollen hands fumbled as he felt blindly in the dark, brushing against smooth, unblemished skin. A shiver, half in anticipation and half in boyish fear of brutish strength. Breath against breath, blood pumping freely, almost afraid of letting go. Afraid of what he might do. He ran his fingers along the other man's torso, across his chest, and around his neck. He touched his lips, soft and pink, and tasted them with his own. He felt the other man gasp, breathing faster now.

Identity disappeared as skin melted into skin, thoughtless wants and hollow hearts, daring to be free.

He grabbed the other man by the neck, forced him around, and pressed his naked body down. His hands traced the length of the spine as he shaped it like clay, sculpting marble into a triumphal arch. He pressed his lips to the small of his back and held him tightly by the hips.

But he slipped out of his mind as something else entered in his place. It swelled like a bruise beneath the surface, a tumor that had found its place and ruptured in the brain. An emptiness akin to slumber, an absence that consumed him from within—and he was gone. It reached out with arms it didn't know, with hands larger than it had wielded before. The power filled it with a feeling of lust, of wanting more without knowing where it would end. It couldn't think beyond its fingertips, beyond the man bent over before it.

"What's wrong?"

It slipped its hand around the man's neck as he let its fingers slip into his mouth. His tongue tasted salt on its skin, his teeth coming together ever so gently. Its fingers slid further toward his throat. He closed his lips around them.

It seized the man's jaw and tore it from his skull.

"The f—!"

The man stumbled to the floor, clawing at his throat, gasping like a gutted trout. A stupid creature, broken and brainless. He rasped in panic and pain, tears spilling from his eyes. Each breath drawn grew sharper and more shallow than the last. It watched as the shattered man slowly died.

***

Johanna Parker stood secluded in the dark, watching as they wheeled Mr. Ford away under flashing lights.

THE DAILY MAINE

LOCAL DRAMA TEACHER FOUND DEAD IN APPARENT HOMICIDE, "VIOLENT" SCENE SUGGESTS MURDER... AND MORE

Hager's Fancy—The small town of Hager's Fancy, Maryland, is mourning the loss of Bishop Ford, a drama instructor at St. Matthias Catholic Preparatory School. Ford, who had just begun teaching at St. Matthias last year, was found naked and unresponsive in his office on the school premises late Thursday night. An anonymous source familiar with the matter detailed the scene at the time of the discovery, describing the sight as "vulgar, violent, and beyond human imagination." The investigation is ongoing, though early reports have strongly considered Mr. Ford's alleged sexual relationship with a member of the schoolboard to be a motivating factor.

Ford was just thirty-one years old.

[VIII]

St. Matthias closed the following day as the community prepared to mourn. The city would struggle against apathy, conjuring in spite of itself a pretense of pain—at the very least, they would pretend. Though a handful of staff undoubtedly felt Mr. Ford's absence, most were disinterested or indifferent, and the students rejoiced in an early weekend. Reportedly, the body had been found in a compromising position on school grounds, which the local press largely ignored in favor of announcing a vigil that would be held later that evening. Elba didn't think she could make it.

"I'm going out!" she cried to her father, hoping that he wouldn't hear her or else would let her go with just a warning. But she knew his overbearing heart and anticipated his response.

"What do you mean you're going out?"

She planned to spend the day perusing the palling shops withering away at the Valley Mall. Most would be gone by the end of the year, and she wanted to take advantage of their beleaguered summer sales, extended long past summer's end. Industry in Hager's Fancy was doomed to go the way of the railroad—sunken into city streets overtaken by rot and weeds.

"You aren't going anywhere on your own."

Elba's father rushed into the living room as she prepared to step out the door. His face was full of fear and there was worry in his eyes. The lines around his lips were drawn thin and stretched tightly across his forehead. The death of her mother had driven him to hold her entirely in his arms, to push the world away and secure her in his house. Elba thought to press her luck and taunt her father's possessive instinct.

"You're welcome to come with me," she teased, half in jest and half in daring provocation.

He was reluctant to take the bait.

"Don't get smart with me. I have to be at work in half an hour."

He would lock her in a cage if he could. Elba had heard as much before, been told to beware of the horrors on the streets. But her father saw horror in every alleyway and down every avenue, conjured up in his mind and ascribed to the many faces of Hager's Fancy. Tying her to the radiator was the only way to save her from the city.

"I don't care that they cancelled class 'cause of your dead fuckin' teacher. You're staying put right in this goddamn house."

As much as his anger seethed at the edge of his teeth, rolling like thunder off the tip of his tongue, his concern for her safety shone through the tears in his eyes. The powerless desperation in his voice sparked sympathy in her adolescent soul. But Elba didn't care about easing her father's pain as much as she despised being told to stay put.

"I'll be back before dark."

With an effort like skipping over the railway tracks that ran the length of town, Elba leapt toward the door as her father impulsively reached out his arm. His fist closed around empty air, and she escaped like a wisp of smoke. Her feet carried her freely from the fallen house and the sounds of her father's screams as she raced down the streets of Hager's Fancy, smiling brightly in the breeze.

***

The Valley Mall was a remnant from another time, the ruins of an industrial past that echoed the hopes of the little town across the years. Faded colors and forgotten dreams, the neon lights burned out in a flickering display of declining Americana. Where the glittering storefronts had before tempted hordes of swarming scores, the bare boutiques sat boarded up and abandoned by the same.

After breaking open the quarter gumball machines and collecting $3.75 in change, Elba fell into a familiar thrift store called Second Chances that she had visited several times before. Racks of old, discarded clothing hung anonymously on racks, soaked in untold history that blotted the fabric like bloodstains. The aisles were populated like the city, dressed in the worn and tired trappings of decades that had slipped away. The rest had been devoured in darkened closets by dusty moths in years lost to the wastes of time. Where most saw filthy flotsam floating in the aftermath of a wreck at sea, Elba found the fruits of a life well-lived, or at least some proof that a life had been lived at all.

The city was old and the future was bleak, but she understood that it had all been done before. The distress of the streets and the panic in her heart had been lived a million times over by a million different faces in the dark. Her happenstantial lot drew no ire from her lips further than the occasional condemnation of the cold as she shivered through the night. But she knew that she wanted something more, and that she was powerless to attain it. For now, the tapestries she discovered abandoned in bargain bins would have to keep her warm.

"Elba?"

She whirled around to see Johanna Parker standing incredulous, her face an unconvincing combination of bewildered and amused. Elba Reed was a ragged girl from the other side of Salem standing like a reflection, staring with a lopsided grin at the girl in front of her. And yet, Elba had always thought that she was different, that she had to be somehow exceptional. Looking at Johanna Parker like a mirrored image in her mind, she wasn't so sure.

"Imagine meeting you here," Hanna said. There was something deceptively honest in her voice, an affected happiness that had been practiced to a fault. But Elba understood what it was to be earnest, and so she played along.

"I guess you heard about Mr. Ford," Elba said. She considered the other girl's face, testing the gleam in her eyes. There burned for just a moment something a little too eager, a flash of unspoken words. Twin rings of distant blue that encircled spiderwebs of green.

"I did," Hanna responded, purposefully vacant. "It's awful. Did you read what they're saying in the *Maine*?"

"I try not to," Elba replied.

A silence wherein Elba questioned the other girl's intentions, wondering whether she had misunderstood Johanna Parker. Perhaps her sincerity was real.

"Well, are you going to the vigil tonight?" Hanna asked. Elba smiled as the other girl poked and prodded, investigating with iridescent eyes. They shone like stained glass at dawn, backlit by a crystalline display. Hypnotic hues of ocean blues and deceptively deep emerald greens.

Hanna took Elba by the arm. "Why don't we? The entire cast will be there."

If this was an act, it was a good one. Convincingly played, pitch-perfectly performed.

"I think it would mean a lot," Hanna insisted.

Elba gave in just enough for Hanna to drag her from the store, headlong from the mall and down the streets of Hager's Fancy. Downtown, further from the remote peripheries of sprawling suburbia and deeper into the beating heart of the city. Blacktop crept like a thousand tendrils through its veins, outward-stretching spokes on a rusted Cavalier.

The two found themselves falling into a simple sidewalk café, sharing the afternoon underneath a yellow, canvas awning. Elba couldn't quite remember the name—something fanciful but painfully dull. She had wandered past the blinding storefront countless times without taking note of the hideous writing scrawled in faded paint across the front. Chrysanthemum? No, that wasn't it. She turned her head to see the window beside her and the blazing letters that spelled out "Buttercup Café."

"I'll have two blueberry scones and an iced caramel mocha frappé, with foam."

Elba scoffed at Hanna's order, not only because it reeked of pretense but also because Elba wondered at how Hanna could afford it. The ragged sweater she wore around her shoulders betrayed any assumptions otherwise. Perhaps she had raided the pinball machines at the Midway Action

Arcade. Elba felt the impatient eyes of the waitress on her as she returned her attention to the table.

"Nothing for me."

With an indignant huff and a turn of her heel, the waitress marched back toward the kitchen. Elba smiled to herself as Hanna unfolded her napkin onto her lap. She was still unsure of the girl's intentions, whether she meant her help or harm, or whether she meant anything at all.

"Caramel mocha frappe?" Elba asked, her voice cracking with just a hint of sarcastic disbelief. This was a girl from the other side of Salem who couldn't distinguish Versace from Vitali. Extravagance was not a word that fit neatly into her vocabulary. Not that Elba knew any better, but she also didn't order blueberry scones from the Buttercup Café.

The two sat in enveloping silence, one curious of her part in the show to come and the other cautious to give anything away. Hanna smiled softly as she guarded the expression on her face. As Elba thought for a moment that she might break and let some disloyal sound escape from between her lips, a chill wind snapped through the afternoon and disrupted the calm in the air. Elba sensed a familiar sting against her neck, a creeping instinct like distress—a voice quietly crying against the dark.

"I bet that's what death feels like," Hanna remarked, a quiet laughter coloring her words. "A rush of cold flowing through your body, like freezing water into your lungs. Only you aren't drowning—you're being emptied of everything."

The waitress watched their table from inside, marking on her notepad what she saw. The girl with auburn hair who struggled uncomfortably in her seat and the girl who sat upright and poised to strike, muttering something she would never hear.

"I bet that's what he felt," Hanna continued. "Mr. Ford. Cold and alone. Standing in a spotlight on stage. Only you can't feel the heat from above because your blood has been drained from your face and your feet have been nailed to the floor."

She gave a meaningful nod in Elba's direction.

"I felt terrible when he made you stand there, obviously afraid. Frozen in place. I would've done the same thing—gawked wide-eyed and dumb."

Whether the air had thinned or the trees had died, Elba found it difficult to breathe. She couldn't speak, couldn't respond to Hanna's account of yesterday's rehearsal. But something in her wanted to agree.

"This town is sick, you know. Men of meager means who tell us what to do."

Hanna spoke with a troubling conviction. Those eyes that beamed with incandescent fire from within burned a hole through Elba's heart. Her own blood ran cold.

"Bishop Ford was a rube and a tyrant. And he got what he deserved."

A sickening fear weighed down Elba's stomach, a fear not unfounded in the gleeful expression on Hanna's face. It said more with a half-hearted smile than she ever could with her twisted words. It declared some uncertain degree of pleasure at the thought of Mr. Ford dead. Elba worried how potent that pleasure might be, how satisfying it must feel for ill wishes to come true.

"I never wanted that."

"Maybe not like this," Hanna argued. "Maybe not so soon, but a very small, very powerful part of you wanted this to happen. And that part, as small and as powerful as it was, got just what it wanted. You hardly had to ask for it at all."

Elba wasn't sure if there was some truth to what Hanna said or whether she might be searching for something that wasn't there. When she learned of Mr. Ford's death, Elba had felt nothing at all. Perhaps that was enough.

Before Elba could confess something to expose her own misgivings, the waitress returned with Hanna's coffee and scones and retreated back inside.

"The universe is so much bigger than you know," Hanna said. "But it listens—parts of it even respond."

The streets of Hager's Fancy felt suddenly very strange. Familiar features turned putrid with a distant, untold age, torn from their skeletal façades by an alien encumbrance. The unhallowed ground on which it stood gave way with the passage of time, ravaged like a dream in an instant. It was fragile, held together by improbable powers come to be in the blink of an eye. Whatever was watching need only fall asleep for it all to come hurtling down.

Paranoia crept into Elba's mind with a purposeful disturbance, seeking each of her insecurities and exploiting every doubt. She thought against thought in a debate of wills, her own oppressive weaknesses against all fears of losing faith. Hanna's eulogy for the same sounded distressingly like the words of an older woman, jaded by the weary world. Used by the city as cinderblocks on which to mount an emerald cathedral—but cracks had already begun to show.

Although she was not, on principal, opposed to seizing power for herself, Elba recognized a darker intention behind Hanna's words. A desire deeper than joy, more menacing than pain—Hanna enjoyed the taste of fear. Elba felt it flowing from her skin, bursting through her veins and bruising underneath. She was suddenly aware of her own scent, how sweet she must smell to a hungry beast. The eyes of the one before her practically gleamed. A tortured, self-satisfied grin spread across Hanna's face. Elba was unamused.

"If Mr. Ford got what he deserved," Elba asked, "why go to the vigil?"

Hanna finished her coffee and the rest of her scones and beamed at the approach of the night.

"I guess you'll have to wait and see."

Elba did not trust the young woman glaring gleefully across the table underneath the horrible yellow glow of the Buttercup Café. Foam laced with caramel lay trapped in the corners of Hanna's otherwise immaculate smile. The inquisitive mind of Johanna Parker protruded forcefully into Elba's brain, prodding through the muscle and the meat until she found something worth the effort. Something to draw Elba like venom from the quiet confines of her shell. Despite her unequivocal unease, Elba felt compelled by a force far greater than fear to maintain her position in the dark.

[IX]

Daybreak fell in a shimmering cascade over the crest of the mountains, shattering against their peaks and crashing over the stone house that stood at the far end of the field. The bright morning star deceived the inhabitants of the valley, casting a golden net over the rolling hills that sealed in the bitter chill. Jonathan Hager had watched the night fade away from beside the lonely window of his bedroom, whittling with his hunting knife—from a supple piece of idle pine, he produced a wooden horse.

Not far from his stone colossus stood the sorry shack he had first constructed from the immaculate woods, which now served as Elsabeth's own shelter. When the weather turned for the worse, he would bring her inside the cellar and keep her safe from the winter storms. Through the cracks in the crude shutters he had devised, he saw Elsabeth and her sturdy frame standing as if on watch, guarding the renegade garrison against the world. She was the last living vestige of a time that had died, the only witness to an unremembered age wherein Jon had belonged. Whether in the parish of Providence or Siegen across the sea, his place had been appointed and he had always been at home. But his exile had been swiftly decided and he was forced to set out alone. At the approach of every isolated fear, he reached out to Elsabeth from the dark and found comfort in her constancy, steadied himself in her calm.

Sated in the absence of unrest, he set his knife down by the window and returned to the other side of the room where his newly constructed bed lay dutifully unused. He hadn't been able to sleep, not since bringing that broken woman into his house. She had fallen in and out of consciousness from her place on the floor above, though she had yet to utter a single word. Her wound was worsening by the hour, festering a putrid yellow and smelling of rotten meat. He had done what he could to stop the bleeding, to stopper the hole in her side, but he did not have much experience in medical treatment. Providence had preserved the profession in a solitary man and his apprentice, neither one of whom had any interest in sharing their sutured secrets with their poor, pathetic brethren.

Instead, Jon relied on his experience with the flesh of animals and the sewing of textile furs—his knowledge of the trade leant itself toward an understanding of the complicated clockwork that comprised a living thing. Twisted sinews and muscles stretched taut as he flayed the skin from the meat. Fresh pulp and cracking bone pulled apart with careless ease. In the natural atrophy of all rotting beasts, Jonathan followed their innate retreat beneath the dirt. An inclination toward decay that cannot be ignored, a despotic mandate on its face that could not be refused.

No earthly clockmaker could unwind the hands of time and reverse its cruel accomplishments. He could only measure them all under the auspices of the undeniable watchman in his tower. The unassailable trajectory of his iron arms turned in bloody circles, a dizzying ballet steeped in gore and triumphant chimes upon the hour. Their tumbling somersaults rising and falling with the ease of an avalanche, rushing downward as if it were an inevitable force, compelled by the power of gravity.

Still, repairing what had been damaged was a more complicated matter than tearing apart what was whole. He had done what he could with limited supplies, but the result was hardly sufficient for a successful recovery. She would not survive the end of the week, not with a gangrenous hole gaping in her side. The putrid stink of a festering wound would stain the house and sink into the cellar below, where it would turn sour and rot. Thinking of the paltry reserves he had secured only for himself, his stomach turned inside his throat and cried out to be fed. His stores of food needed to last him through the coming winter, and he couldn't waste them on a dying girl.

He decided in that moment to relinquish his weakness and compassion, to sever that human part of himself that held him secure to the ship on tempest-tossed seas, that held him back from taking the helmsman's wheel and guiding the wreck to balmier tides. He understood what would be required of him to safeguard his future. This time, his resolve would be steady—this time, he would not hesitate to strike.

Rising from the futile comfort of his bed and climbing the creaking stairs to the room above, his heart strained against his chest to beat sense into his blood, to tempt him back to bed and the yielding relief of sleep. But the effort was in vain, useless to prevent his determined advance toward the woman he meant to kill.

Step by groaning step, he thought of how best to accomplish the task. A quick shot to the head, a blade across the throat. But these methods would be messy, bloody deeds that would stain his hands. He did not want to leave such a gruesome mark on the history of his house. Another step higher, another step closer to the task. Smothering would be painless, stainless, and intimate in the undertaking. He felt a rush of excitement at the thought, of feeling something slip away between his fingers. He tried to suppress the sensation, the thrilling, static buzz of lightning in his brain, but his hands had been commandeered and his thoughts were no longer his own.

And he was there on the second level, at the room where the woman lay unconscious on the floor. She had rested wrapped still in her cloak and reclined uncertainly on an old pillow from across the sea. Jon had done what he could to bring her comfort—he had given her water from the springs and covered her shivering body with a heavy blanket of wool. But the fear of this fading corpse threatened his own survival and eroded his final sympathies.

He had meant to snuff her out quickly, to bring the douter crashing down upon the flame, but something stopped him where he stood. The woman's eyes were peeled open in a horrified look of fear, or perhaps some more inscrutable expression of pain. Great, distant orbs staring blankly ahead, clouded over with a milk-white film that hung like foam in the crest of a wave. She could not see Jon make his patient way across the room, but she could hear the sound of his fatal approach.

"Where am I?"

The words caught him by the throat and pinned him in his place. In the terrible commotion of his bloody mess, he hadn't considered this crippled woman as the first visitor to his new homestead. The name of this frontier had been a secret all his own, kept close to his chest and held hidden away from the world. He had spoken it to himself many times before, privately in the confidence of his head. A fitting name, one to stand the test of time.

Jon had envisioned his own society, a shining city on a hill—but he sought not to establish some colony subservient to the laws of ancient men residing on the other side of the world. Here he would be free. He had surveyed the valley and the woods beyond, finding them pleasing to behold and pleasant to command.

He assumed the role of ruler over an estate that had, only a short time ago, existed as nothing more than a brutal battlefield subject to the false clemency of Nature. In bold defiance of her will, he maintained a fortified position against the world. This would be his country, and it would serve his interests well. The woman had trespassed onto conquered land, wrenched from the iron grasp of the mountains. Perhaps she was an outcast too.

"Hager's Fancy," Jon answered. "This is my home."

Her satchel lay on its side where Jon had thrown it, its contents spilled out across the floor. Various herbs and bits of black moss, strange stones and peculiar fungi strewn like flowers from a wicker basket before a grave. But this woman had come back to life, clawed her way from underneath the earth and stumbled haphazardly into the world. To Jon's own amazement, the color had returned to her face and her strength had found its place again in her bones.

She rose to her feet with an uncertain waver in her legs, the heavy blanket falling in flowing folds to the floor as her billowing fur cloak framed her slender body. Her eyes were filled with a darkness like the sky, rolling clouds that held back a hurricane of tears, or something far more fatal. She stood naked before him, trembling from the cold or the fear of an unknown place. She shivered as though panic had gripped her in her bones, cornered as a bristle hare caught dead in a trap.

Jon sympathized, though he could not help wondering at the feat of her recovery. Not a day before, her skin had been a pale shade of green and her wound was filled with pus. In the low morning luster of the upper room, her smooth body glistened as if she were standing in the soft glow of faded moonlight. The wound in her side had all but disappeared, a small scar overshadowed by something silver growing out from underneath her skin.

He thought at first glance that it was a spider, some monstrous insect with wandering limbs creeping its way across her skin. But as he continued to stare, he saw that it was some sort of fungus or moss, stiffened and sparkling in the light of the upper room. It reached out from within her stomach, nimble boughs like the gnarled fingers of the eschenfrau. Perhaps she was a spirit of the woods, a dangerous faerie guarding the forests from ill-intentioned intruders—perhaps she was something more sinister. A vagrant woman deranged, exiled from her own people for some unspeakable crime and forced to wander the wilderness on her own. He didn't believe in the fairytales of his homeland, but he was uneager to embrace the more honest truth that stood starkly before him.

In the absence of identity, the woman adopted an enigmatic air, one that suggested she might be desperate enough to do anything. She had been injured to the point of death and had made a miraculous recovery. But miracles derived their power from above, not from digging up rotted things in the dirt. Jon stared for a moment longer and saw that the spider on her side was a black spot of mold, a fresh patch of moss that had closed her wound like a professional suture. It stretched across her skin with tendrils dark as ink, a living colony breathing life into her veins. He would have sworn that he saw it move.

"What is your name?" he asked.

She gazed into his eyes from someplace far away. Her own eyes shone opaque, unreadable orbs swirling like opals set in silver. Whether she was disarmed by his apparent innocence or the genuine curiosity expressed in his quivering voice, there came an answer soft and low.

"I am my Mother's Mouth."

In the quiet chamber of the upper room, Jon was unsure if she had spoken aloud or whether he had heard her response in his head. The words floated like a feather on the air, light and fluttering with every waver of the wind. Free-flowing strands of dark hair rose and fell on the same, wisps like spiderwebs clinging to the thorns of a rose. The woman walked with her head held toward the sky, her arms hanging loosely at her side. Effortlessly, as though she could see everything before her, she shrugged her cloak from her shoulders and strode across the room.

Jon held his breath as she drew nearer to him, hoping that she might pass him over like the angel of death. But she crossed over his threshold all the same, reaching her hands out toward his face. He stood helpless against his instincts as she brushed her fingers across his cheek, stealing the breath from his lungs. Her lips came within inches of his own before she whispered delicately into his ear.

The words were of a different kind, a language that he didn't understand. Her body, cold as stone, pressed briefly against his own unsteady frame as she swept hastily from the room. Her shameless disregard for decorum in his house angered and amused him. This creature, who had been in the maws of death not a morning ago, sauntered naked from her deathbed to the door. Insulted to say the least, Jon grabbed her by the arm and demanded she answer him directly.

She considered the contours of his face, as though she could see right through him with those dead, unseeing eyes. Jon felt the scrutiny of her judgement on his skin, crawling underneath his clothes and embedding in his veins. She turned his blood sour and burrowed into his brain. There, beneath the surface of his scalp, she worked upon his weaker senses, eroding his steadfast resolve. Without the promise of an answer, the woman laughed at the force of his protest, the effort to hold her in place. Something in her broken laughter told him that she could not be held for long.

Whether her bravado was a bluff or genuine amusement, Jon let his hands drop to his side as she descended the stairs below. He hesitated for a moment, uncertain of the specter in his house, a haunting shadow risen up from the depths of a grave predestined for her molding corpse. But the rot had receded and the gangrene had gone, the venom evacuated from her body by a magical source or else some natural cause that he had yet to understand.

He sensed that his designs for dominion over the valley and the broken world beyond had been irreparably disturbed. What had before been uninhabited mountainsides and immaculately preserved country plains were suddenly settlements teeming with activity, brimming at a boil from the work of a mysterious woman who had emerged wordless from the woods. His mind spun in circles at a breakneck speed, humming with thoughts loudly repeating like a desperate chant in his head. He wondered almost aloud at her place in his world, whether she would merely disrupt or altogether destroy the foundation of Hager's Fancy. Following her distorted shadow hurriedly down the stairs, he vowed to discover her intentions.

Before Jon could catch her as he raced for the floor below, the woman flew from the front door of the house and disappeared into the valley. He sought frantically for his hunting knife in the place where he had last laid it but could not find it in his haste. Grabbing his rifle from beside his bed, barefoot and barely clothed, he burst with a panic through the door and out into the field.

The grey sunlight like an arrow's head hit his eyes with the trauma of an assassination, blinding his pursuit and shielding his prey from his rifle's aim. Naked and glinting in the light, she pranced like a fawn freely through the field, faster than her legs could carry her, aided by the fury of the wind. Storm clouds billowed over the mountain peaks above as Jon tore across the sea of grass and through the breaking waves.

As Jon gained steadily on her swiftly fleeting frame, she sank beneath the pale green breakers and vanished entirely from view. The ripples flowed through the field faster than he could fire off a shot, but he aimed where she had been and pulled the trigger. His bullet sailed like a cannonball from a galleon, soaring through the thinning air and cracking like thunder against the mountainsides.

The frozen dirt underneath his feet propelled him to the edge of the forest, where he paused for the briefest moment in fear of the dark. In the frightful specter of the woods, Jon saw faces in the trees. Where he had been before was suddenly overgrown with foreign fears, an encumbered labyrinth of daggers waiting like vipers to strike. Under every leaf and behind every limb lingered the faint suggestion of something perilous wanting to do him harm. His heartbeat clamored to escape his throat, threatening to leap from his tongue and let the world know that he was alone.

But he ventured forward, crossing over the threshold and stepping into an unnamed realm that he was dreadfully aware was not his own. His rifle provided little comfort against his chest, inept in the hunt for his otherworldly game. He could see no footprints in the mud, no sign that she had come this way. Still, his instincts drove him on.

The rolling clouds overhead heralded the approach of night as he stumbled over the underbrush, losing his footing and all sense of the day. His body twisted in the air as his head hit the mountainside and he slipped away. Hours passed him by in a flash of lightning, leaving him discarded on the forest floor. Worms crept through the dirt where his body lay, impatient parasites eagerly expecting to reclaim him from the earth. Lying on his back, listing toward the sky, disorientation turned him on his head. As he fell above the barren trees and the frozen valley below, he tasted snowflakes on his tongue.

He opened his eyes and found himself face-down in the dirt, breathing in the smell of the woods. Damp and full of life, old but perpetually renewed. A cycle of rot that recovered all that was lost, the Coroner Royal who exhumed what carcasses remained. And Jonathan was counted among the dead.

But his grave was shallow and his death was short-lived. In the dawning of his rebirth, Jonathan Hager rose from his crypt in the mud, brushed the dirt from his hands, and started to make for his home. Hager's Fancy in the valley, that elusive settlement of safety and right that he had worked so hard to build. Abandoning the hopeless pursuit of some woodland faerie, he stepped free from the forest and the interment of the trees and made his homely way across the field.

As the sun sank below the striking mountain ridge, concealed by swollen velvet clouds, a light flurry of snowfall dotted the valley in white. Blossoms like daisies blooming in the storm, bursting through the frozen ground and budding in spite of the chill. The butt of his rifle dragged in the dirt as Jonathan trudged across the field. He could no longer feel his bare feet and his skin had broken out in goose pimples. He ignored every indication that his body had been beaten by nature's blows and forged ahead toward his home. Even from a distance and through the bluster of the snow, he saw his great stone house standing tall and the sorry shack beside where Elsabeth would be waiting.

But something was wrong—the nearer Jon drew to his dwelling, the more the marrow soured like curds in his bones. He quickened his pace, flying full of fear as a hopeless dread seized his heart and screamed at him to run. His breath was stolen away from his lungs and his chest collapsed inward on itself as he came upon the shack at the edge of the woods. There, twisted and torn to pieces, lay Elsabeth in ruins on the ground.

Every gruesome detail of the gory scene tore into Jonathan's head and embedded with sadistic permanence in his mind. Her powerful neck spilled out into the dirt from a deep and deadly gash ripped ruthlessly across her throat. A river of blood still flowed thick through the grass. Her bright eyes had gone dark and grown cold, empty ornaments of glass that sat useless in their sockets. Her knowing smile had receded and a pair of withered, leather lips revealed a grotesque sneer in its place.

From within the very pit of his stomach, a breathless, gasping sob escaped him as he collapsed in a wretched fit to his knees. He crumpled onto his side and stared with unseeing eyes at nothing at all. His vision blurred and his voice fell flat in a rough and rasping cry as his body contorted and he vanished like vapor into thin air. In the dissipated apparition of the world around him, weeping for the rotted spoils of the past and the broken promise of the future, he understood that he was entirely alone.

[X]

Ted Larsen stood in the shadows, watching from the dark as the town of Hager's Fancy gathered under cover of night. The steps of St. Matthias Catholic Prep were prepared for a vigil, adorned with tasteful ornaments of grief. Numerous candles lined the stairs and a large, black cloth was draped across the front doors of the school. A simple podium with a small microphone attached stood at the top of the stairs. Beside it, an enlarged photograph of Bishop Ford sat propped on an easel, bordered by bright flowers.

Those gathered on the lawn breathed gently in the glow of flickering candlelight. Not many had shown—only a handful of students from Mr. Ford's theater troupe encircled by far fewer adults. They milled about the grass at the edge of the lawn and muttered amongst themselves. Ted Larsen wondered whether they truly mourned the death of Bishop Ford—he knew that he did. As his memories of the man came flooding to the forefront of his mind, an unassuming girl approached the podium, prepared to give a speech. In the unsteady candlelight of the vigil, he saw that she was his daughter.

Rebecca Larsen adjusted the microphone and cleared her throat before delivering a few stilted words. Her voice echoed in a hollow refrain as though she were performing a soliloquy on the stage. Ted Larsen could barely understand what his daughter was saying between cracks of feedback and mumbling static. He assumed whatever woeful words she strung together weren't worth venturing nearer.

He couldn't see who all stood grieving in the crowd, hidden by their jackets and the dark. Ted Larsen feared whoever they might be, whether they might have seen him and his indiscretions before. He was a prominent man gone missing, sure to be noticed should he show his face. He was the last man to see Bishop Ford, the man most likely to have killed him. Guilt, the winning weapon of his steadfast resolve, ate away at the fidelity of his conscience. But fear was a far more piercing spur, more painful to endure in the face of uncertain consequence. Ted Larsen feared what this town might do.

So he ran. He had run from Bishop's body when he saw it splayed and broken on the floor before him, bleeding unstoppably from his gawking throat. The sight had sent him tearing through the halls, crashing into every unremembered moment and trying like hell to tell himself that it wasn't his fault. But no explanation conjured up in the confines of his brain could quell the terror and remorse racing through his blood.

He had spent the day running from sirens searching for rats in the gutters. The pavement had been his dwelling place for the duration of the night, an icy, callous lover who would kill him in his sleep. But the coursing flow of the streets tended toward ruin at the center of the city, and Ted Larsen fought against the current.

Taking once again to the river, he ran from the vigil through the shadows toward someplace unfamiliar, some forsaken place he hoped might give him shelter. He had been there only once before, a burrow sunken deep into the ground where the promises of tomorrow could only endure the night. A hollow house where he would hide from prying suspicions and investigative minds. At the outskirts of the city stood a secret sanctuary whose inhabitants had been overpowered by lusts of all kinds, wayward tenants of a distant world, detached from Hager's Fancy and abandoned by the same. Under cover of encroaching nightfall, Ted Larsen ran toward Salem Avenue. The officer seated in his unmarked cruiser across the street didn't see him disappear into the dark.

Far from the damning downtown streets and through the forests at the edge of the valley, Ted Larsen tore across the city until he came to the corner of Jonathan Street and Salem Avenue. Crumbling in disrepair at the center of the abandoned lot, consumed by overgrown weeds and impenetrable underbrush, stood an ancient stone house shuttered against the world. Ted Larsen climbed the rotted steps to the front door, twisted the handle after a moment's hesitation, and fell haphazardly inside.

10 Tania Bustamente, *The Broken House on Salem, 2020, acrylic ink on watercolor paper.*

Elba stood anonymous in the crowd beside Hanna as Rebecca Larsen finished her speech. Rebecca gripped the podium firmly in her hands as her voice carried out across the grounds of St. Matthias. The few students who had gathered together in the grass began to lose interest in the wasted words of a tiresome girl. She had droned on too long and Hanna was suddenly restless, tugging at the ragged sweater thrown loosely around her shoulders.

"And I won't ever forget the last words he spoke to me: 'Becca, you're going to make it. Not many people have what it takes to succeed in this world but, dammit, kiddo, you do.' I'll always remember. Thank you, Mr. Ford. I love you."

Applause echoed faintly in the night against the trees in a hollow, clanging din. Hanna stared with unseeing eyes toward Rebecca as her jaw hung slack from her skull, her lips parting ever so slightly. Saliva spilled down onto her chin as she pulled at her sweater, chipped and broken fingernails snagging on the threads. Elba thought at first that she must be nervous, but the longer she observed, the more determined she appeared. As Rebecca stepped aside from the podium, standing alone in front of the large, black cloth waving like a standard in the wind, Hanna's focus turned to the portrait of Mr. Ford, illuminated by flames from below.

His features protruded in the contrast of shadows, cast as the garish specter of a dead man. He seemed to have already decayed, his skin stretched taut to the breaking point across brittle, cracking bones. The eyes were sunken into his skull and his nose had already collapsed. It was the image of a more ancient man, half-preserved in time by the dirt. But it was only a trick of the light—it had to be.

Hanna continued to pull at her sweater, digging her fingernails into her skin. It seemed out of habit, as though she had done this before. The threads began to come loose and unravel, tearing holes where her fingers found blood. She was transfixed, fallen into a fit of muttering under her breath. Her forearms were a patchwork of scratches and cuts, her fingernails cutting ragged gashes in her skin. Blood fell in oozing droplets onto the grass as Elba took her hand.

In that sudden, fleeting instant, the portrait of Mr. Ford burst into flames. Fire leapt from the candles to the funerary to the black cloth draped behind the podium. Hanna fell abruptly to the ground as the entire façade of St. Matthias erupted in a burning blaze. The night sky was torn away and a blinding surge of light brought tears to Elba's eyes, stinging with the force of the sun. Hannah lay stunned on her back, motionless, her mouth hung open in a lifeless scream as her limbs convulsed and her skin turned pale and cold. A soft groan like a death rattle came curdling from the back of her throat, air from inside escaping her body.

Elba fell to the ground beside her, wondering whether she was alive. Flames devoured the flowers and chaos consumed the crowd as students and teachers alike shouted frantically for help. Elba stared transfixed at the terrible sight, unable to tear herself away as though she had been turned to stone. Shadows danced in the light of the inferno like devils freed from Hell. Shrieking cries rose high above the trees, carried on swelling clouds of smoke, as the school blistered and snapped in the angry blaze. It roared louder than thunder, the bellowing chorus of a runaway train that had jumped violently from its tracks.

Unstoppable, conflagration like a murderous mob that devoured as a swarm of locusts, engulfing everything in its way. Windows burst and beams splintered in the overwhelming, insufferable heat. Then, as quickly as it had started, the fire vanished without a trace, a simmering spark extinguished in an instant. The smoldering remains of the ruined atrium collapsed inward in a pile of ash and smoke. Slowly, life returned to Hanna's body and she sat upright on her own. Elba reached out a hand to comfort her, but Hannah recoiled at the approach.

"Don't touch me—I'm fine."

Elba knew this was a lie, and Hanna understood. What neither girl knew nor understood was whether the other could guess at the truth—whether the other could know what had really just happened. As her sweater slipped from around her shoulders and fell onto the grass, Hanna rose unsteadily to her feet. Elba led her urgently by the arm as the two stumbled to the back of the crowd.

From someplace in the distance, running at breakneck speed out of the darkness, appeared a man in uniform. A man of action, appropriately festooned for the occasion, ready to help where he could. A broad man with shoulders that carried the weight of the city and seldom shrugged at the prospect. Elba saw his rugged face in the fading light of the embers, bearded but bespoke to play the leading role in any one of her favorite detective films. He stopped for just a moment, sweeping up Hanna's sweater from the ground and handing it hastily to Elba, sharing a gentle smile before taking off again.

He leapt with bounding strides to the steps where Rebecca stood stunned, staring at the flower petals lying burned and blackened on the ground. Elba watched in simple amazement as he moved fearlessly among the throng, lithe like an alpha wolf to the head of the pack. He planted himself beside

Rebecca before holding his hands high in the air, commanding the crowd's attention.

"Everyone, listen up! My name is Barry Boscoe, I'm with HFPD. I know you're understandably alarmed, but the fire department is on their way. If you could all move to safety, I'd like to ask you a couple of questions."

A few students nervously hid their hands in their pockets. Others walked cautiously away, disappearing without a word into the night. Elba stood attentive, her arm hovering around Hanna's shoulders as she wrapped her shivering frame in the comfort of her ragged sweater. She wondered whether Hanna trembled from the cold or else from the excitement of the mayhem and disarray. Before she could make up her splintered mind, the man let loose his booming voice and called out to the scattering crowd.

"Do any of you know Ted Larsen?"

The anonymous faces concealed by the dark paused in recognition of the name, returning their interest to the center of the makeshift stage. Rebecca looked to the man standing beside her, hanging her head low and hiding her blushing face from the people below.

She spoke just above a whisper, her voice a solemn apology—"He's my father."

After surveying the scorched and smoldering wreckage of the school's foyer vestibule, Officer Boscoe dismissed the remainder of the crowd and pulled Rebecca aside. In the welcome distraction of his work, Elba took Hanna firmly by the arm and pulled her forcefully away.

"What the fuck was that?" Elba demanded. The two lingered at the edge of the lawn, careful not to draw the attention of the officer, who was preoccupied for now. He stood statuesque like a monument against the night, his sturdy frame silhouetted in the buzzing lamplight. He held a radio in one hand and a voice recorder in the other as he interrogated Rebecca on the steps of St. Matthias. Elba was intent on conducting an interrogation of her own.

"Was that what you wanted to show me?"

Hanna struggled to lift her head and meet Elba's gaze, her expression heavy with exhaustion and her face full of failure. The circles underneath her eyes were deep and bruising purple, as though the blood had pooled below her skin.

"Wasn't it beautiful?" Hanna whispered.

Elba suppressed the panic in her heart and tried to contain the waver in her voice.

"I was terrified."

But Hanna had seen something else in the flames, a vision of the future that she wanted more than anything to come true.

"I wanted to burn the whole thing to the ground."

Smoke had risen over the roof of St. Matthias and spilled into the treetops, spreading like a sickness across the sky. The city was colored with the char of the embers and weakened underneath the foundation. Though the fire had died, the smell of it hung still in the air—a stale smell, the dried splintering of wood forced under impossible heat. It sank into the earth and stung Elba's skin as tears fell down her cheeks.

"What did you do?"

A thin smile spread between Hanna's lips and contorted the appearance of her face. It twisted a knot in Elba's stomach, turned the acid in her stomach to bile in her throat.

"Come home with me tonight, and I'll tell you everything."

[XI]

Alone and shivering against the cold, Jonathan Hager sat huddled in the dark and empty corner of his room. His great fur coat was draped about his shoulders as his eyes darted rapidly around the spaces inside his head. Memories of murder colliding in a terrible clash of fears and frantic hopes for the future dashed away in an instant. Elsabeth and others lying face-down in the dirt as their blood spilled from their throats and comingled with the mud.

In the shadow of the mountains, he was entirely alone. There were no more remnants of his past, nothing left to remind him of the time before. The world across the waves had sunk beneath the horizon and disappeared from view. His own frontier had already begun to fade away, invaded by a faerie in the dark. That woman he had brought into his home, that evil spirit who had emerged from the trees and retreated once more into the woods. She was a viper under the leaves, slithering across the grass and striking at his heel. But he would crush her underfoot and kill the remainder of her brood—he wondered whether she was alone.

The endless sea of shadows reaching down from the hidden peak of the mountains told him there were more, maybe a nest of these woodland nymphs burrowed deep into the earth. A den of rats readying for hibernation. The air was thin and dry, and Jon thought to burn the forests down and butcher them where they lay.

He had tried to track her across the valley and through the tangled weeds, but her footsteps had vanished in the dark and run away into the night. Returning under cover of the midnight clouds, Jon had discovered the body of his only friend—Elsabeth had been slain at the hands of this witch whom he had failed to kill. Jon had no doubts that she would have slaughtered him too, had he not been elsewhere indisposed. His own pressing sense of paranoia heightened his defenses and urged him to remain garrisoned in the safety of his house. But he swore on the earth and the mountains above that he would see her dead.

And there across the valley, from within the shadows of the forest and the deep, unending darkness of the trees, a sinister figure emerged and stalked toward the house. Jonathan strained his weary eyes to make out its face, but in his heavy heart, he already knew who she was. Her body gleamed in the light of the stars as something in her hand glinted like a blood moon in the sky. His hunting knife, the same instrument she had stolen away from him. She was determined to see it returned, sheathed deep in Jonathan's heart. But he had other intentions.

Tearing himself away from his bedroom window, Jon snatched up his flintlock rifle and loaded its muzzle full. This would be the final moment of his triumph over the wilderness, the defeat of a primitive horde. He envisioned her body falling to the floor, breaking on the ground and shattering in a million diamond pieces. His conquest of the mountains would be complete.

He rose from his place in the dark and stood squarely beside the front door of his house, aiming his rifle level with his chest. His breath was even and his arms were sure, strong, and steady as he waited. The world slowed its onward pace and the seconds passed like snowflakes drifting on a lazy wind. Jon tempered the anger in his head as his heart beat loudly in his throat. Cracking his ribs and crushing his lungs.

But the cresting wave had yet to crash, the tension rising and his anxious blood pumping faster in his veins. Perhaps she had hidden on the other side of the house, preying on his weathered senses and fatigue, waiting for his guard to drop. Or perhaps she had returned to Elsabeth's body for some secret purpose, to harvest the flesh from her bones. He resisted the insistent screaming in his head for as long as he could, but the thought of Elsabeth lying discarded in the dirt disturbed his steady hand.

With a singular motion like drawing an arrow from its quiver, he swung the front door open. But the woman was there, and her movements were swift. She knocked his rifle from his hands and plunged the knife deep into his gut. Jonathan could not cry out, too overcome with pain and the shock of her sudden appearance. He staggered backward and collapsed onto the floor. Before he could comprehend what had just happened, she fled from his side and descended down the stairs toward the cellar. His stomach bleeding out and his head spinning where he lay, Jon struggled to his feet and pursued her through the dark.

Below the mountains and the valley floor, beneath the mealworms and the mud, she led him like a stone sinking below the surface of the ocean, falling faster than the weight

Jon felt in his stomach. He descended the stairs with a gravity unlike any he had known before, more severe than he had felt in the construction of his house, more significant than his discovery of the valley.

This woman, clad in porcelain skin, commanded his approach. Her violence was a siren's scream. Under the layers of limestone and lumber, her body glistened like a pearl, vanishing beneath the waves as she succumbed to the shadows beyond the cellar door. The entrance stood shrouded in darkness like a cave in the dim light of the stairwell, the gateway to someplace just out of reach. The doorway was low, thin and oppressive, bordered by cold stone dripping with moisture from the damp. The woman's smooth body seemed not to shiver, unbothered by the frozen, shallow air beneath the ground. The sort of air that was difficult to breathe, the stale, unmoving air that hung low in graves—not that the dead needed to breathe underground.

The gases and the grime clung like desperation to the walls of the crypt, carpeting the tomb with moss. There, in the sacristy beyond the veil, in the sepulcher where the twin springs bubbled joyously to life, the woman stepped into the shallow pool where the water gathered and held out an open palm. Jon hesitated at the edge of the room, breathless at the sight. The steady sound of water flowing like music mimicked the life spilling from his bowels before splattering onto the stone floor below.

His blood raced from his heart as though he were on fire, burning and boiling in his veins, bursting beneath his skin. She held his knife at her side as she muttered something unintelligible, rapidly whispering under her breath. Her lips wavered and her sightless eyes rolled about freely in her head. He was compelled by fear to turn from the room and run far away from the house, but his legs were trembling, his heart was weak, and his feet were frozen to the floor.

The muttering words grew louder, a venomous curse filling the air with the sound of a serpent, hissing echoes that turned and twisted around him. Jon's twisted stomach crept along the back of his throat as the woman brought the knife into the air. With a crude motion like carving her name into stone, she dragged the blade purposefully across her wrist. Jon couldn't gasp, couldn't scream as blood poured deep and dark into the pool, falling faster than the flowing rains that streamed down the mountainsides and gathered together in the mud.

The woman collapsed in a vivid surge of water and blood that overwhelmed the pool, flooding the room and soaking Jon where he stood. Her body lay floating face-down in the water, motionless as Jon watched the blood drain slowly from her wrist. He stood unmoved, unwilling to make any effort to save her as her skin turned green and stiff. With the chilling shudder of her final breath, the blood comingled with the fresh water of the springs and spilled out into the world.

***

Jonathan Hager stumbled up the stairs of his house to the upper room where he found the woman's satchel filled with mosses and herbs. A small clump of silver sat innocently inside—the same silver thing that had crawled along the woman's body, sealing her silent wound and bringing her back to life. Desperate for his own salvation, Jonathan thrust his hand into the bag and seized the silver moss. Unsure of what exactly he should do but hopeless in the face of his injury, he stuffed it deep into the hole in his stomach, fingering his flesh, and gasped loudly from the pain.

In an instant, the stinging subsided and all he felt was an odd, numbing chill throbbing in his veins. His vision blurred and his stomach sank as his mind split open his skull. He abandoned his body to the gravesite of the earth and let his spirit ascend to the stars.

Days passed and nights stood still while he waited for his wound to heal. In the all-consuming darkness of his descent into Hell, Jonathan was entirely alone. A singular survivor drifting on a desolate sea, clinging to the pitiful detritus of his home. As the engulfing expanse of the ocean around him lay indifferent to his pain, he suddenly shrank into the shadows. The darkness of the mountains held him tightly and filled the valley with his fears. A terrible dread that weighed him to the ground and buried his hopes in the dirt. In all the spacious splendor that the mountains could provide, he was lost in the delirium of fever that had forced him inside his head. As exhaustion and trauma beat at his brain, Jonathan Hager passed away to dream of another life.

[XII]

The broken house on Salem Avenue was held together by rusted nails and the curses of cursed people. Its splintered door frame played maître d' to the dirtiest of downtrodden, jugheads and junkies alike. An opium den of thieves, starved of their own lives and feeding on the salt stains of others. A hive mind, commingled in blood, thoughtless in the exquisite ecstasy of pain. It was, in all ways, condemned.

Elba entered the house at Hanna's command, otherwise unwilling to approach the rotted place. The smell of it gagged her, urine and sweat dried in a crusted shell around bodies long dead or otherwise paralyzed by an oppressive weight. These were mangled corpses rotting alive, the molted skins of serpents in the grass. Only the grass had died and the soil had turned and there was no shelter from the sun. A mass grave of the poorest of souls, not in wealth but in fortitude, fallen victims of the Cheshire grin. *Come away*, it said. *Come away to Wonderland.*

Further in the labyrinth, the moaning children quaked and, as in Hell and furnaces, the skin of children baked. An inverse candle thieving light, a clock that severs time—the house on Salem Avenue proved fatal in design. The aftward tumbling toward day's end, the rush of ketamine, the feeling of forget-me-not—an effervescent dream.

Deeper in, down stairwells that led underneath the earth, Elba felt as though she were falling. Dante led her through the circles of Hell, each doorway the passage to a fresh horror, until they reached the final room. Darker than the others, and colder. Elba watched her breath escape her, frozen in the air. Hanna stepped inward to a small chamber, dimly lit in red. A tall woman in white stood at the center, her hair spilling down like black ink. Elba remained outside.

"Mother, I've brought a guest."

The woman said nothing, instead staring with intent in Hanna's direction. Hanna smiled and nodded before running from the room, closing the door behind her.

"It's alright. Mother says she's brought one too."

Elba felt far from alright. Her head was pounding from the smell and the sick and the relentless feeling of unease. In the shadows slept unwary men, and women just the same. The darkness hid their faces and, underneath, their blind intent. In the corners of the hollow house, they fell out of themselves and assumed something less. Not granted rationality but enslaved with thoughtless instinct. Insects caught in a clever web that seemed to them their home.

Hanna led her to an upper room, an attic with a door of its own. Falling inward, Elba discovered a more familiar space. An abandoned mattress for a bed, framed on either side by salvaged bits of wood that served pragmatically as end tables. A broken vase stood unsteadily atop, holding a single white rose. Moonlight streamed from the other end of the room, through shards of glass that jutted in seemingly random intervals around a perfect circle. An empty, shattered window, now a spotlight full of moonbeams.

"I've never had a sleepover."

Unsure whether to laugh in discomfort at the miserable thought or run from the impending explanation, Elba offered a confession of her own.

"Neither have I."

The two settled in, positioned intimately on the mattress as old confidants from an innocent age, prepared to whisper secrets in the other's ear. Hanna plucked the white rose from its vase, careful not to touch the thorns. Delicately, she held it out for Elba to see. Beautiful, unblemished, and just beginning to wilt. Elba took it in her hand and waited expectantly. From within a makeshift drawer fashioned in her bedside table, Hanna produced a small mouse, no larger than her palm, sniffing curiously at the air. As though Hanna were going kiss its face, she brought it close to her lips.

In the passing of an instant, Hanna opened her jaw wide before she snapped it violently shut around the mouse's neck. Blood spilled from its open throat as Hanna squeezed its stomach, letting its entrails drip down into the vase. She took the rose and set it back in its place, sitting delicately in the blood and the guts. Elba felt too sick to scream, too paralyzed by shock to run. She watched in helpless horror as Hanna doubled over, muttering incoherently, moving her hands to an erratic, ancient rhythm. Within moments, what little signs of wilt had shown were vanished, and the rose stood tall with the strength of new life. Hanna placed the fragile vase back onto the table as it shone with silver moonlight.

Elba's stomach turned in somersaults as she sat horrified by what she had just seen. She felt the impulse creeping up her throat and she wondered what good it would do to vomit.

To burn her tongue with acid rain and stain her teeth with bile. But in all her wondering, she couldn't stop it, and it spilled from her mouth in chunks of half-digested rot. It fell like wet sand over her tongue and onto the mattress, an embarrassing display of convulsions like a feral cat, retching as clumps of it caught in her teeth. When it stopped, Elba fled to the bathroom.

She rinsed her mouth with water that tasted like rust and looked at herself reflected in cracking, mold-stained glass. Her eyes were splintered like a spider's web, her head engorged like a fly. The wooden walls heavy with mold collapsed inward as she struggled against herself to breathe. The mildew stench that hung in the air whispered that she should run.

"Elba?"

A knocking on the bathroom door, gentle and familiar, enough to pull her from hypnosis.

"Elba, are you okay?"

But not enough to bring her to obey. Through the softer sound of a voice begging to be trusted, something colder threatened to surface. Despite the promise of a friend at the door, she was afraid of the girl on the other side. She was suddenly someone unfamiliar, hiding dark desires and invisible intentions. A stranger's face behind a mask, buried beneath a twisted grin, dancing in the distorted light of the occult. Elba didn't know this person, didn't wish to understand. She had touched things beyond the natural veil, forbidden things that lay purposely out of reach.

"I'm sorry," Hanna said softly through the bathroom door. "I shouldn't have done that, not before—"

Hanna stopped herself from speaking further. Elba wondered whether any explanation would satisfy her unwilling curiosities, but she wondered nonetheless. Shock began to subside in the wake of jealousy, or maybe it was some more potent desire for power that made her unlock the bathroom door. She swung it slowly inward to see Hanna resting her head on the doorframe, her eyes sympathetic in the pale blue light.

"It isn't your fault. Here—"

She took Elba by the hand. Fighting her instincts to recoil, Elba followed her back into the bedroom. The mess had been cleaned and the two sat back down on the mattress. Whether it was a trick of the mind or the fumes from below, Elba felt a sudden eagerness building inside. She stood at the precipice of something that, one way or another, would change her life.

"Show me," Elba whispered. Her voice wavered with a hesitation that betrayed her outward confidence.

Hanna had caught it just enough to let a smile crack her otherwise solemn face.

"Mother taught me how."

She held Elba's hands in her own and told her to close her eyes. Hanna began to mutter again, faster than before, her grip tightening around Elba's palms. She began to sweat, her body a lightning rod of energy, burning with an intense heat that radiated throughout the room. Elba's hands trembled as her wrists bent painfully back, locked in Hanna's grip. Her eyes were held shut by fear and focus and the thought of losing her mind. In the darkness underneath, Elba was hurtling through a subway tunnel, lights flashing by in an instant, the deafening roar of impossible speed cut through by the piercing scream of grinding metal.

Her hands slipped free, and she felt herself falling as a deafening sound tore through her ears. Backward into a bottomless pit, the void of her despair. Her eyes split open as she collided with the floor and saw Hanna standing over her, laughing and clapping her hands together like a child.

"Jesus fucking Christ."

The glee in Hanna's eyes was that of a girl who had first discovered a secret, something she was not supposed to know. It was power over another, manipulative and cruel. In the hands of Johanna Parker, secrets could kill.

"What the fuck was that?"

Hanna fell back onto the mattress and wrapped her arms around Elba's neck. "I can't tell you. Only Mother knows. Mother taught me."

"Taught you what?"

Hanna beamed with blushing pride. Elba sensed the precipice of an answer, the edge of something real. The bubbling brew began to boil over.

"Witchcraft."

PART TWO

[I]

Barry Boscoe sat squinting underneath the harsh fluorescent lights above his desk, reflecting on recollected things. He thought about the murdered man Bishop Ford, bleeding and broken at St. Matthias, his body torn apart. He thought about Ted Larsen and his sudden disappearance, and the mounting suspicions that were becoming impossible to overcome. He thought about the Larsen girl, how brave she had to be in the face of all this. But most of all, he thought about Hager's Fancy and the town it had become. What had once been a historic city glittering with optimism and chrome was now a battered hovel, beaten down by years of worry and neglect, bruising in the wake of blows.

The ruins of the city had begun to show through the rusted veneer and the open cracks in the pavement threatened to unleash something monstrous from underneath the foundation. Officer Boscoe wondered at what lay below, what ancient evils must be lurking in the undiscovered fissures of the mountains. Those sharpened crags that shielded the valley from the world, or else that held the city's population prisoner without regard for ransom or reward. But the cage was collapsing under the burden of its design and could no longer hold against the unruly throng beyond the gates, nor could it sustain the pressures from within. Lost in fatiguing concern for the future of his city, there was nothing that Officer Boscoe could do to stop it all from crumbling down.

His bulletin board had become overcrowded with faceless names and wasted pictures of missing persons, all of whom were lost to the malignant forces at work in Hager's Fancy. One in particular had caught his attention and remained within the margins of his mind—a young woman with matted hair and deep, impenetrable eyes. Her name was Riley Mason, a senior at South High who reminded him of his younger sister. In her photograph she stood forever framed beside the shallow lake at the City Park, dressed in vibrant colors to match the rhododendrons. Her fragile smile hung suspended in time, scorning the despair that creeped into Barry Boscoe's heart.

There was something sad and hopeless in those eyes, a silent misery that told him she would never be found. She had been missing for several weeks and the department had all but abandoned their search. They had overturned the city with nothing but overtime to show, and Lieutenant Davis was displeased by the added paperwork. There likely wasn't anything left to find, not so far out from the date of disappearance. Officer Boscoe pushed those morbid thoughts aside in favor of more encouraging work. Whatever Riley Mason's fate, there were more promising cases to cover for now. The death of Bishop Ford was fresh, and Officer Boscoe was determined not to let him linger like a ghost on his wall.

He reviewed his notes and statements from several St. Matthias staff members and searched for anything he might have missed. A pattern, a mistake, an unintended slip of the tongue. Something that Mr. Larsen may have left behind—or else someone he may have left behind. And a sudden notion struck him like a bullet in the side of his head, a fractured piece of his memory that surfaced in the muddled matter of his brain. A sweater on the ground, a torn and tattered thing that he had handed off to someone in the crowd. He shuffled through the papers on his desk, trying to remember what he had seen, and returned to the statement he had taken from Rebecca Larsen.

Friday evening. Vigil for deceased.

Approached Rebecca Larsen, daughter of suspect. Pulled aside to speak. Transcript of recording follows:

Off. Boscoe: You said you're the daughter of Ted Larsen?

R. Larsen: Yes. I'm Rebecca Larsen.

Off. Boscoe: Can I ask you a few questions, Rebecca?

--indistinct--

Off. Boscoe: Please speak into the recorder.

R. Larsen: Yes.

Off. Boscoe: Thank you. This won't take long.

R. Larsen: Is everything alright?

Off. Boscoe: That's what I'm going to figure out. When did you last see your father?

R. Larsen: Last night, just after rehearsal. He came to pick me up, like always. He had to speak with Mr. Ford about something. Budgets or schedules. I'm not sure.

Off. Boscoe: And did he speak with Mr. Ford?

R. Larsen: He went into the administrative building, where Mr. Ford's office is. But I don't know if they actually spoke.

Off. Boscoe: Did you see your father come back out of the building?

R. Larsen: No.

Off. Boscoe: Were you worried about that?

R. Larsen: Not really. He's had meetings with Mr. Ford before. Sometimes they take an hour, sometimes they take longer.

Off. Boscoe: Has he ever met with Mr. Ford all night?

R. Larsen: Sure, plenty of times. They'll go out for drinks after their meeting and crash at Mr. Ford's place.

Off. Boscoe: So, you assumed he wouldn't be coming back?

R. Larsen: Well, I wasn't surprised when he didn't.

Off. Boscoe: What did you do?

R. Larsen: I waited in the car. I don't remember when, but I got tired of waiting and drove home.

Off. Boscoe: Did you see anything while you were waiting in the car?

R. Larsen: Like what?

Off. Boscoe: Anything unusual. Anything at all.

R. Larsen: I'm not sure.

Off. Boscoe: Did you see anybody else leave the school?

R. Larsen: No.

Off. Boscoe: Did you see anybody else at all?

R. Larsen: There was somebody. I remember someone standing next to a tree, toward the back of the school. In the dark, at the edge of the parking lot. I thought at first it was a groundskeeper, but she ran into the building and wasn't wearing a uniform—

Off. Boscoe: Wait, you said she?

R. Larsen: Yeah, she—

Off. Boscoe: How do you know?

R. Larsen: I saw her. In the lights by the foyer. She had dark hair. Black.

Off. Boscoe: What else?

R. Larsen: It was dark,

Off. Boscoe: Anything at all would be helpful.

--pause--

R. Larsen: She was wearing this ugly sweater.

Off. Boscoe: A sweater?

R. Larsen: Yeah, this horrible, ragged thing. Tattered like an old dishrag. Sleeves torn and falling apart in strips.

Off. Boscoe: That's great, Rebecca. You did good. Can you remember anything else about her?

R. Larsen: No.

Off. Boscoe: That's okay. You've been very helpful. Did you see anything else?

R. Larsen: No. That was everything.

He turned his papers over and read through the transcript again. He had been surveilling the vigil in expectation of Ted Larsen's return, anticipating that the killer, whoever he might be, would show his face. He tried to recall everyone in the crowd, their faces hidden by the dark. Most of them were students, many of whom might fit the Larsen girl's description. Although Officer Boscoe was convinced of Ted Larsen's guilt, he was also certain that there was more to Mr. Ford's death than he understood. He had held that sweater in his hands, he was sure of it. He had seen a girl there with black hair and tattered clothes. A girl in rags, fallen to the ground.

And he saw her again, vividly in his mind, collapsed to the ground in a fit. A burst of flames as the school caught fire and burned viciously in the night. The frightened faces of anonymous fears, eyes widening in the sudden glare from the wild blaze. He saw the girl with the ragged sweater, her forearms crosshatched with scars. He watched her fall powerless to the ground, the sweater slipping from around her shoulders and disappearing into the grass. Another girl dropped to her side, concerned for the safety of her friend. As Officer Boscoe remembered running from his cruiser to the fiery steps of the vigil, he had snatched up the fallen sweater from the ground and returned it to the other girl, catching the kindness in her eyes.

Had he suspected anything further, received any indication of guilt from either girl, he would have detained them then and there. But their faces had been filled with nothing but horror, unreadable expressions of fear as St. Matthias burned out of control before them. Rebecca Larsen's statement would have to stand alone until he could identify the girl with the ragged sweater, until he could find her again and interrogate her as he had the others. And he would find her, he swore. On the beating heart of Hager's Fancy, he swore it. Barry Boscoe was prepared to tear the city apart, to overturn the moldering town until he could uncover the truth. He would search for it in the strangling weeds where the blight and the black mold spread, where the festering sores on the underbelly were ripped open and infected by parasites from the past. Underneath the cracking pavement and the rotted soil upon which Hager's Fancy stood, where the maggots and the mealworms fed.

[II]

Hanna woke in a chilling sweat, stale droplets spilling down the curves of her back and pooling in the valleys of her skin. Her nightshirt clung wet and cold to her body as she rose from the mattress and sauntered over to the attic window. Morning had just begun to climb over the treetops and shine through the shattered glass. In refractions that magnified the glare of the sun, Hanna caught a glimpse of the dawn.

She left the other girl to sleep in peace as she made plans for the day on her own. Hanna swept silently from the attic and descended the stairs to Mother's room far below. The cellar was cold and cracking with an energy that excited something terrible but thrilling within her. A hidden hoard of knowledge, a secret store of spells forbidden but to Mother and to anyone she deemed worthy enough to teach. Though Hanna had begun to unravel the mysteries of pyrokinesis and possession, she knew that today would be something exceptional.

As she descended the stairs to the cellar below, passing each heap of half-conscious vagabonds collapsed like refugees on the floor, she thought of the heat in their heads. Fires blazing brighter than neon in their brains, burning visions like nightmares into their hollow skulls. Mother had not taught them, nor would she, but she welcomed their melancholy squalor in her home. The empty doldrums of deadened thoughts masked the more riotous droning of a mind at work. Mother's mind never ceased.

Arriving at last to the icy steps outside the cellar, Hanna paused for just a moment as she observed the details of the door. A great, black thing painted unevenly in broad, indifferent strokes. It was never locked—all were welcome in this place. A rusted, metal handle curved outward like a snake, secured at the head to the heavy planks of wood that stood between her and Mother's temple to the profane. There, in the shrouded shadow of the occult, Hanna pulled the great door open and stepped hesitantly inside.

Once she was within the chamber, she found the familiar glow of blood-red candlelight, flickering as each flame danced unsteadily under the influence of a draft. The cold stone was slick from the damp moisture hanging in the air. In the corner of the room, beside the small door of a forgotten pantry, a dull glow emanated from inside a black, iron stove. Thick clouds escaped from cracks in its stout chimney that funneled smoke from the cellar. Crackling wood burned in its fat belly, heating a small pot that had begun to boil. A harsh smell rolled throughout the room, carried on the leathery wings of the fumes—the wet stink of mold. Sour and strong, Hanna tasted the mucus slipping down her throat.

At the center of the room, Mother swayed in motions like the tide, rippling waves along the shore. Her body was draped in a sheer, cascading robe that followed her movements like frothing sea foam. The breakers beat against the coast and crashed with violent rage to drown the ancient mariner caught in her trap. Mother was on top of a man, her legs straddling either side of his naked body as he lay in bondage on the floor. Her body bent and her back arched in a strange and unnatural way as both of them let loud, unthinking noises escape from their parted lips.

Pressing further in, Hanna recognized the man—Mr. Larsen was bound by shackles around his limbs and chained to stakes driven into the floor. Mother's hair fell onto his face as she danced to a steady rhythm like a snake, poised at any moment to strike. Her hips moved of their own accord and her hands reached high above her head, grasping at the air and closing in fists around nothing at all. They were both in the bed of a shallow, empty pool where an ancient spring had dried.

Reason urged Hanna to turn away from the cellar and return to her room upstairs, but this ritual awakened something more primitive within her. She wondered if Mother would teach this dance to her as she felt the answer prodding at the base of her neck. A familiar sensation, the backward slipping away of her consciousness as she gave in to the intrusion. In a soft but steady voice, gentle like a whisper, Mother spoke freely in her mind.

"*Stay.*"

Hanna moved to the other side of the room, watching Mr. Larsen struggle feebly against his binds. He was not a weak man, which Hanna knew. She had entered his mind, had taken possession of his powerful arms as she tore Mr. Ford to pieces. His mind was split open and muscles were pulled taut, capable of incredible harm. But his eyes told Hanna that he was afraid, that Mother's savagery soured the humors in his blood.

Hanna also understood that he indulged in that fear, that the loss of all control thrilled his thirsting heart. Mother held his body like a plaything in her hands—delicate, dancing with her claws displayed like switchblades at his throat. The look on Mother's face frightened Hanna more than the ritual itself. Her movements were dispassionate, her pleasure was purposeful. The man beneath her lost all identity as she dug her talons into his skin. To Mother, Mr. Larsen was a meal.

On the other side of the cellar, where the big-bellied stove bellowed from the heat of the flames, the little pot simmering above began to boil over. The lid shook and the pot rattled as if whatever was inside were clamoring to escape.

"Bring it to me."

Hanna understood what Mother meant and knew at once what was seething inside—a draught derived from black moss gathered deep within the woods. She had tasted this sacrament before. Hanna approached the stove and removed the pot from the blistering heat and peered with caution at the concoction inside. A frothy, black brew bubbled at the brim. Floating in the center bobbed a dense patch of hair, several small clumps of silver like steel wool.

At the head of the empty, shallow pool where Mother bestrode Mr. Larsen, a simple drain ran to the edge of the cellar and out through the foundation. Where a pair of frothing springs once leapt from deep within the earth, Hanna poured thick, black bile that spattered against the stone floor and flowed like mud from the house. What remained at the bottom of the pot glittered in the fragile candlelight. Hanna snatched a small piece out from the dregs and held it delicately in her hand.

It was uncomfortably warm to the touch, not only from the heat of the boiling broth but from the beating blood of a living thing. As Mother performed her serpentine dance, drawing violent groans like poison from Mr. Larsen's lips, Hanna placed the silver moss in Mother's outstretched hand. It seemed almost to move, a glittering insect like a centipede crawling across her palm with useless, broken limbs.

Mother brought it close to Mr. Larsen's mouth, touched it to his lips, and pulled his jaws apart. She forced the thing inside his mouth and pushed it deep down the hollow of his throat. He gagged on her fingers, but Mother held his jaw shut until he had no choice but to swallow. His eyes went calm, a vacant stare, and his breath fell shallow, just below the shudder of a whisper. A man in shock, or frozen in fear—a paralytic on the rack.

Then, without warning, he began to seize, shaking violently as his outstretched limbs jerked spastically at the chains. His joints threatened to snap against the shackles, to tear the muscles and break the bones. Blood welled in his eyes like tears before spilling over the sides of his face. Mother closed her fingers tightly around his neck as she continued still to dance, her legs wrapped closely around his waist. He gasped, then screamed in silent pain, his mouth held open by a pair of invisible hands. Hanna retreated from the horrible sight, helplessly afraid of what Mother might do, shrinking into the shadows until she felt the harsh stone wall press against her back. She stood in captivated horror as Mother made the man cry blood.

From the other side of the room, or from within her own excited mind, a low and steady sobbing sounded from the pantry, a pitiful cry reaching out from the other side of the small, wooden door. There was often the wailing noise of a wounded animal coming from within that cupboard. She had never seen what lay inside, nor had she ventured any efforts to discover for herself. A cage for something suffering all alone, an oppressive place, cold and claustrophobic. A damp closet that held some dying beast, moaning and rattling in the dark.

With a final gasp for air and a whimper like a dog, the ritual ended in a flourish of raven hair and Mother left Mr. Larsen on the floor. Although Hanna did not entirely understand the purpose of what Mother had done, she desired to learn for herself. To see Mr. Larsen held so powerless in Mother's powerful grip sent an envious shiver spilling down her spine. She had possessed men before, held Mr. Larsen's strength in her hands, but never had she seen such a display of unconquerable control. Hanna wondered if she would ever hold a man so exclusively transfixed, so utterly helpless.

"*You will.*"

Mother's voice came crawling again, low like a whisper that tickled in her ear, gently plucking at her mind. Reassuring, but of something she didn't expect to hear.

"*Our mind is a powerful weapon. I will teach you how to wield it with more strength than ever before.*"

She kissed Hanna softly on her forehead before she gathered the remaining pieces of silver moss together and placed them in a jar. Mr. Larsen lay silent on the floor, his limbs slack but still bound, his chest steadily rising and falling as though he had fallen asleep. His entire body glistened with sweat from exhaustion and the fire raging in his head. Hanna pitied him for the briefest of moments, but she remembered the strength of his hands. The raw, unbridled vigor that whet his veins. Hanna had possessed him for a time, but Mother had more in mind.

She had taught Hanna the curses of witchcraft, the poisonous recipes of potion-making. She had performed the rites of Maledictus and invoked the stolen souls of the damned. But this was beyond conjuring—this was an ancient power, buried in the marrow of the earth. Planted deep like a seed, sprouting roots that choke and bind. The hive mind of a higher order, the thoughtless subservience to a formidable queen. In the cellar of the abandoned house on Salem Avenue, beneath the broken people lingering like shadows up above, Hanna understood her Mother's strength. They were all of them obedient to her will, submissive to the last. This was truly power—not the exhausting command of an expedient drone, but the amenable enslavement of a happy horde. Mother held Hanna close to her chest and spoke softly in her ear.

"Our strength is like fire. Beautiful to admire, unstoppable in our hands. But let it consume you, and all you have worked for will be lost."

Hanna took these words into her heart and brought them like an offering to her mind. Mother's coven of obedient disciples would bend and do her bidding, unthinking but of the loyalty they owed their matron. The overturning of the world would be swift, and Hanna was prepared to bring it down. Mother nurtured the spark in her daughter's eyes and used it to ignite her own devices. She stoked the furtive flame and fed it brittle kindling as she gestured to the rooms above.

"Bring your friend to me."

[III]

Elba woke in a stunning calm, kissed by the sighing breeze of a seaside town. Though Hager's Fancy was far from the shore, she felt the salt in the air. Light and pleasant, it embraced her as she rose to her feet. Golden droplets like steady rain fell through the shattered window. The day was young and the dawn was new, not yet spoiled by stale apologies and promises to be. But yesterday spilled over like a hemorrhage in her mind. A dam had burst against her will and it all came flooding back.

For the most fleeting moment, she had found the peace of days, that elusive mark of childhood when all was tawdry bliss. She had been to Eden in her youth, she had drunk from the wellspring of joy. She had tasted of forbidden fruit—and in that luscious taste of sin, she lost her pomegranate smile. Hades had ripped her from the world and kept her for his own. Now all the joy that she could taste lay lost in her summer days.

As Elba reflected on the death of innocence, the attic door swung open and Hanna burst headlong into the room. Her eyes were darkened circles sunken into her skull, recessed in the strain of a sleepless night. Her skin was pale and glistening with sweat like dew in the morning light. Elba wondered what she had done as Hanna took her by the hand.

"Mother is waiting for you."

Elba had never so much as seen Hanna's mother, but she had heard rumors enough to make her worry. The things that people said were neither kind nor innocent. A derelict in her duties of motherhood, a heathen inhabiting the fumes. A practiced pagan wasting her days away in a cloud of smoke. Elba feared whether any of these accusations had honesty at their heart, but the reputation that had branded the streets of Hager's Fancy assured her they were true.

Hand in trembling hand, she followed Hanna down the attic stairwell and through corridors like crawlspaces covered in cobwebs and dust. The oppressive rooms of the ancient house collapsed inward upon her in the dizzying descent toward the cellar far below. As they passed each heap of half-conscious bodies sprawled out across the floor, dazed or else entirely incoherent, the rumors came crying loudly in her head. Soon they were a chaotic choir, dissonant voices clamoring to be the loudest, each one screeching higher than the last until they shrieked their warning cries in a single fever pitch, the sounding of a silent alarm that implored her to turn away.

Against her own volition, or perhaps in spite of her primal fear, she plummeted down below the surface. Past the empty hallway doors, the creaking of the wooden floors, beneath the smell of sour earth—and she was there, the threshold of her grave. The curdling of her blood proclaimed that she was at the precipice of something evil. Led by Hanna's hasty stride, Elba came upon the great wooden door to the cellar. It was the deepest black Elba had ever seen, as though it were painted with shadows. What morning light had found its way into the stairwell seemed to have fallen away into the void. She, too, was pulled inward as Hanna opened the door.

It was a gateway to another world, where the hour was always night. Darkness cloaked the daylight and daytime lost its sense. Constellations of candlelight flickered around the room, burning brightly in the sky. But their fire gave off no heat—only a jealous, angry glow.

As Elba stepped into the shadows cast across the cellar, she saw that other figures stood rapt around the room, gazing fixed in her direction. It was too dark to see their faces, only the milky orbs of their eyes shining white in the flames. Elba couldn't count how many there were or surmise from where they had been summoned. She could only marvel terrified at the sight of their bloody robes like gory droplets falling from above. At the center of it all stood a towering woman in white, draped in the purest sheer lace like a wedding gown. But the bride beneath it was married to the dark.

"Speak your name."

The woman's voice was coarse and low, grating against the air as she beckoned Elba inward. A sudden sense of unease sank into her stomach as Elba thought she must have already known her name, that she only asked in some deceptive effort to conceal her winning hand. There was no choice but to play along—Elba didn't want to give up the game.

"Elba Reed."

Hanna left her side and stood behind the woman, vanishing into the faceless crowd, her eyes joining the others as they shone like embers in the ash of a fire that longed to be reborn. The eyes of the woman burned brightest of them all, filled to the hearth with flames.

"Welcome, Elba Reed. I am Mother's Mouth."

Standing cold and alone, Elba began to shudder in her skin. Like a quaking tremor erupting in her veins, she shattered into pieces on the floor. The walls gave way above her and the earth collapsed under her feet, falling in an avalanche to reveal an alternate realm. Elba overlooked the world, only she controlled her fate. The woman standing in white before her offered a solemn invitation.

"Our Mother wishes that you join us."

Reluctant to remain, Elba feared that she had ventured too far, descended too deep into the madhouse to escape asylum unscathed. But the promises of power buried deep within herself were waiting to be fulfilled. She stepped forward, fixing her eyes on the woman's face. Dropping to her knees on the cellar floor, Elba submitted herself to the will of her Mother.

"Will you join my daughters in a sisterhood of service to our Mother?"

Despite the terror beating in her heart and the voices screaming inside her head to run, Elba bowed low and answered with a whisper.

"Yes."

Hanna stepped forward from the dark, holding a pair of golden chalices in her hands. Mother plucked a small, silver clump of something from the first, a tuft of hair that shimmered like starlight in the night sky. It shone impossibly bright in the darkness of the cellar, alluring like a diamond ring to an ingénue. But Elba was less innocent than she looked.

"Eat of our Mother."

She could not refuse, nor did a growing part of her want to. She was seated at the edge of power, purposely placed just out of reach. If she only stretched out her hand, she might grasp it long enough to hold on. At the insistence of her Mother's hand, she opened her mouth and let the silver thing fall down the back of her throat. It was soft, surprisingly supple on her tongue. The texture of candy floss with the flavor of stale bread.

"Drink of Her blood."

Mother offered the other chalice and Elba drank freely. The taste was intoxicating, sweeter than nectar but rich in sadness. Thicker than wine, deeper than blood. She savored the story that it spoke, the record of an order steeped in history, the hidden traditions of a secret sect.

And she was suddenly falling, broken through the floor and descending into the dark. Faster than she knew, further down the rabbit hole. Only she wasn't falling into the earth— she was flying in between space, slipping into the fabric of the universe. Moving against time as her body lost all meaning and her mind floated freely in the air. This was a sensation she had never known, tearing through the ether with the terrifying force of a freight train. Like an unstoppable engine roaring through a tunnel, screaming louder than the panic in her bones. Across the lucid apparitions of her delirious mind and the bellowing blasts of the thunder inside, a voice came calling, crystal clear.

"*Now, you are mine.*"

[IV]

In the afternoon light of her attic bedroom high above the cellar, Hanna watched over Elba Reed as she recovered from the ritual below. She recalled when she had undergone the rite herself, years ago in the springtime of her youth. The sour taste of the fruits of the earth, the coagulate juice that ran thick like mud in the veins underneath the house. She had lain in bed for an entire day, spellbound by the dizzying effects of something from another world.

Elba, on the other hand, resisted her insistence to rest. Though Hannah had managed to persuade her to lie for a moment on her mattress, she protested and implored to go home.

"My father must be wondering where I am."

But Hanna understood the desperate worry in her voice and knew that it would be difficult to keep her there for long. In precipitous anticipation of Elba's imminent departure, she relayed the invaluable lessons she had learned. The expectations of sisterhood, the effects of Mother's mold. The enlightenment of the mind beyond the limits of the earth. It was there, in that elusive place between worlds, where Hanna had been to in the dark.

"Don't you have questions for me?" she asked eagerly as Elba closed her eyes. Her anxious breath had receded and her chest refused to rise as Hanna watched her withdraw from the room and retreat to someplace else. An involuntary calm washed over Elba's mind like the concussive aftershock of a collision.

"I feel dizzy," Elba admitted, giving in just enough for Hanna to seize upon her weakness. Without a moment's hesitation, Hanna launched into her explanation. The ceremony, the sacrament, every detail of the initiation that Hanna had endured and wondered about herself.

She began with the most significant element of the rite—the silver fungus that glittered and shone even in the dark. The process by which that shimmering consecration was derived from a poisonous black moss that grew in the woods at the edge of the city, out beyond the interstate. Hidden away from the plundering minds of Hager's Fancy and the impudent eyes that would love nothing more than to tear the hallowed ground apart.

It was in those woods, Hanna explained, deep inside the forests, where the weeds grew thick and the mud ran slow, that the Mother of all the earth lived most freely. In the very veins of the old oak trees and the ancient power of their roots, breathing in the underbrush and the unencumbered clay. She slumbered peacefully in the order of her days and she raged at the interruption of her work. Lurking just below the surface of a tranquil sea surged a thrashing storm seething at the brink.

The black moss growing over rotted logs and consuming the corpses of Her fallen creatures was the living embodiment of Mother's steadfast devotion to life—that even in the wasting decay of death, the flourish of life endured. In spite of the molder of the earth, Mother made certain to survive. Through the holy communion of Mother's meal, Hanna's sisters committed themselves above all else to life's unending climb, the pursuit of a summit somewhere in between the earth and beyond. The scarlet robes worn by her sisters invoked the goddess inside their veins. In every aspect of their coven's decorum, from the poverty of their circumstance to the chastity of their blood, they obediently served the interests of their Mother.

Hanna espoused the history of the ancient order to which they all belonged as Elba grew increasingly concerned with her absence from home. Her fingers found themselves occupied with every inch of her skin as Hanna saw the worry mounting in her eyes. Swelling like a storm about to break over the town and bring a hurricane down from above. The rains were already spilling down the contours of her cheeks.

She couldn't be sure why Elba was so anxious to return to her home, but Hanna didn't want to be around when the levies break and the thunder splits open the sky.

"Alright," Hanna said, "I'll walk you back home."

Taking Elba carefully by the hand, Hanna led them both down from the attic and through the corridors of the house. Past the scattered hopheads and the homeless sprawled out across the floor. Stepping over their soft and swollen heads, the two pushed their way through the front door of the house and out into the daylight down Salem Avenue.

[V]

The heat of the day hung low like the haze of summer sunset as Barry Boscoe made his way downtown. His cruiser felt sharp and right in his hands, and the wind felt like freedom on his face. The vagabonds fled and conspiracies failed when his cruiser came around. Order above all, civility before chaos—there would be no rest for the wicked.

Which is why Officer Boscoe came abruptly to a stop at the corner of Locust Street and Salem Avenue. A pair of young women, together on the wrong side of Salem, were walking side by side down the troubled street. Their clothes were ragged from years of use and their faces were heavy with the sweat of an unexpected afternoon. The concrete had cracked underneath their feet and run slowly like creeping weeds toward wanton depravity downtown. Officer Boscoe pulled his cruiser to the curb beside them and rolled his window down.

"Afternoon, ladies."

They paused and stared wide-eyed, unsure of his intentions. If he were to be honest, neither was he. But their faces were familiar, those same faces he recalled for just a moment the other night. His memory supplanted a sudden thought, a hope against coincidence, another game of chance. But if this were to be his only hand, he would play it close to his chest.

"Could I offer you both a lift?"

The girl with raven hair seemed almost offended, as though the offer were an insult. Her response said just as much.

"No. We're just fine."

Officer Boscoe bet against the house and wagered that two young girls walking the streets of Hager's Fancy alone on a Saturday afternoon were not doing just fine. He placed his bet.

"Can I ask where you two are headed?" he said, his voice treading lightly to convey some quality of compassion. "I might be going that way myself."

The other girl spoke up, softer than the first. Not in such a hurry to refuse.

"Just walking home," she muttered.

"Walking home? I hope that isn't far."

"Actually," she replied, "it's on the other end of town. South end."

Her confession upset the other girl, who wore a scowl on her face. Officer Boscoe sensed the tension between them, some unspoken oath to remain silent that had just been broken.

"Well, I couldn't let you walk all the way across town. Do both of you live there?"

"Just me," the other girl said.

"And you?" he asked.

The girl with raven hair glared at him with an unmistakable look of offense, as though he had just spoiled the entire day. She responded with incense and rage.

"I'm not far."

With a fire in her eyes and a turn of her heel, she whipped her head around and walked the length of the street, back toward the rotted house at the end of Salem Avenue that Officer Boscoe knew all too well.

He had further questions but didn't want to officially hold her for questioning. The optics would not play well in a town already suspicious of men who held the line. An angry town, a forgotten town, whose roots had turned sour and spread. Plagued by a virus that had swept through other cities, already contaminated the swarming millions, rising like a fever and spilling over the edge. He saw it sprouting in Hager's Fancy, the weeds that grew untamed beneath the pavement, sending up shoots like wildflowers that strangled the life from them all. For as long as he could, with every breath that he held in his lungs, he would fight infection back. He would burn the broken cities to the ground to save the sorry town he loved.

Happy to help a lost citizen wandering the labyrinth of the streets, he opened his passenger side door and smiled at the quiet girl standing alone.

"Hop in."

She did, after a distrusting pause. He didn't blame her—he only wondered what her parents might say to see her sitting beside an officer of the Hager's Fancy Police Department. He wouldn't want to cause her any trouble.

"So, what's your name?" he asked.

Her eyes were sad but the tears had run dry. A weary sadness, heavy with unhappiness she must have felt many times before. They were bloodshot and dark, burdened by some exhausting matter weighing on her mind.

"My father told me not to talk to the police," she replied. Almost absentminded, her focus drifting elsewhere. Officer Boscoe wondered whether she was high—what else would a young girl be doing down Salem Avenue on a Saturday afternoon?

"Is your father an attorney?"

"No."

He didn't press the subject further, sensing the unease in her voice. She was a girl from the other side of Salem, born to cursed ancestry withering away on the wrong side of town. Hager's Fancy was divided down the center by the long stretch of road that wound its way downtown, a singular capillary coursing through the beating heart. The old railway tracks ran alongside it, tearing the town in two—the northern half held the seat of wealth while the southern half struggled to survive. In the disparities apparent in the pair of incongruent reflections, the citizens of Hager's Fancy suffered on. What had once been a booming Hub City now lay laboring in the dust.

"My name is Elba. Elba Reed."

Officer Boscoe looked to the small girl beside him, suddenly interested in engaging with him in conversation. He knew he would need to seize his opportunity with ready hands.

"Elba?" he replied. "Isn't that something. How'd your parents come up with a name like that?"

"My father named me after where my mother died."

Shit. He would have to tread lightly.

"I'm sorry about your mama. My mama died too. A long time ago, when I was just a boy. I still think about her every day."

His mother was happily retired, living a quiet life with his father by the sea. In fact, he had just visited them in the spring. Still, he needed the girl on his side.

"Elba," he continued, "is it alright if I ask you some questions about Mr. Ford?"

The girl looked down at her feet, stuffed uncomfortably into shoes several sizes too small, then out the window at the world rushing by. She remained quiet, unresponsive as a sinner on the stand. He would be careful not to press too hard.

"He was your teacher, wasn't he? I think I remember you from the other night."

A tired look, willing to respond—less willing entirely to give in. She returned her attention to the cruiser just enough to scoff at the thought.

"He didn't teach me a thing."

"But you knew him?" he asked, eager to have the answer.

"I was doing his stupid play for extra credit."

And he was getting somewhere. Slowly, stubbornly, but the dots were beginning to connect. Rebecca Larsen had seen someone in a tattered sweater on the night of Bishop Ford's death, a ragged thing like the other girl walking with Elba had worn on the night of the vigil. But the Larsen girl's account alone was not enough. If he could identify some direct link between Bishop Ford and this girl, he just might have his killer.

"What play was that?"

"Macbeth."

"Appropriate for the season," he said. "Always was one of my favorites. Witches and murder, struggles for power, and women gone mad."

He smiled at the girl beside him, who returned a half-hearted smirk in his direction. Maybe she thought the play was stupid, but she entertained his enjoyment of it. A drama worthy of the most ancient, mythic tragedies. And who was she to perform the words of the greatest playwright, practically in a foreign language? Officer Boscoe didn't know that he'd ever seen a worthy high school adaptation, and Elba doubted whether anyone ever would.

"Still," he continued, "it would've been nice to see."

A purposeful pause, pregnant with the anticipation of his next line of questioning. He waited long enough, building the silence as though he were thinking of something to say.

"Was your friend in it too?" he ventured, flippant and cavalier. He was careful not to give away the game.

"Hanna? She was the third witch."

"The girl you were walking with?"

"Johanna Parker," she replied before stopping herself, catching her next thought on her tongue and recusing herself from speaking any further. She seemed almost to catch on. Perhaps he had moved too quickly, assumed too much. She was a smart girl, cleverer than most. Perceptive of a liar—but he had gotten this far. She was a lonely girl, hungry for attention, the kind she had never gotten at home. There was something lacking in her social life, that much was clear. Maybe he could provide her with some understanding. Nothing so complicated as a substitute for her father—just someone to talk to.

"I never had many friends," he confessed. "When I was your age, I spent most of my time alone. Reading and running from the monsters I pretended were chasing me through the streets. I was pretty fast too. Sometimes the monsters were real, other boys who thought they owned this town. Some of them didn't grow up to own a thing. Some of them didn't grow up at all."

Elba understood this, the truth of it between the lies. Officer Boscoe could see her giving in, thinking maybe he was somebody to trust. She reminded him of the missing girl, Riley Mason. Innocent but vulnerable to the sound and the fury of the streets. He would ensure that she was safely returned to her home, far from the other girl walking in the opposite direction down Salem Avenue.

"I had a friend like Hanna once. At the time, she was the only one I had. Somebody I could rely on, somebody I thought I could trust. I thought we might always be friends, that we would know each other forever. But it wasn't true. She lied to me, told me things I wanted to believe. When she left, she took everything I had."

Elba said nothing, but that told him enough.

"Don't expect everyone you care about to care for you in return. Some people just want to use you for a little while until they find somebody else. And they always do."

The seed of doubt was planted, and it would grow faster and more viciously than a weed. He would only have to wait for the roots to take hold before she ripped the girl from her head.

Best to help it along.

"I do hope Hanna isn't like that. That she tells you the truth. I hope she had nothing to do with Mr. Ford's death."

Elba's eyes widened as the full truth of the inquest washed over her. Hanna was a suspect and, by proxy, Elba was suspicious. Officer Boscoe read the fear in her eyes, fear for herself and for her friend. Fear of consequence and fear of what she might have done. The girl beside him knew something more than she let on. She had seen something at the vigil, she must have—Officer Boscoe could practically see the memories replaying in her mind, faster than before, less steady as the panic of a guilty conscience made her shake.

And he joined her there, in the distance, a figure running from the dark as chaos burst into flames. He had watched St. Matthias catch fire just after the girl in the tattered sweater had collapsed onto the ground. No arsonist's hand had caused the blaze, nor had any natural phenomenon carried fire on the wind. Perhaps it was a simple flickering of candlelight that consumed the memorial in mere moments—perhaps it was something more.

"Mr. Ford's death wasn't an accident," Officer Boscoe said. "I think you know that. And I think you know that Hanna might have had something to do with it."

He was so close. He had her in the palm of his hand, eating up his sympathies like a lost mutt finding a home. But he knew what it was to be alone, to have just one friend in all the world. He knew that he wouldn't give Hanna up so easily if he were in Elba's position. He knew that Elba wouldn't either—she was eager to have him on her side, but not for the price of the only friend that she had, no matter the looming consequences.

"I don't know anything about that," she answered.

And that was it, the end of this round. Hard fought and sorely lost, but he hadn't given up everything. He had even gained a little too. The Larsen girl wasn't lying, and she hadn't entirely invented accusations against her peer. Officer Boscoe had briefly met the girl in the ragged sweater and established more than a spider's thread strung between her and Bishop Ford. She had known him, at least in a pedagogical capacity. She must have spoken to him, been directed by him on the stage. This was a lead—an admittedly meandering one until he could establish more, but it was the only real lead he had. It would have to be enough for now. He would return to Salem Avenue in the evening, to the ruins of the rotted house crumbling on the outskirts of town—he would find his answers there.

[VI]

The cruiser pulled up beside the little house on the other side of town. Elba thanked the officer for the ride and left him all alone. Her guilty heart racing, she approached her own front door. A faded plank of untreated wood cracked down the center, the paint peeling off in chips. It stood alone between the walls of a squat and unimpressive house, shrinking into the surrounding landscape of the valley, sinking into the earth. She hoped for a moment the man in the cruiser might stay, to make sure she was at the right house. To make sure that she was safe. She didn't look back to see if he had left, to dash what hopes in the comforting thought she had, and chose instead to believe that he had stayed.

With a single reckless motion, she plunged her key into the lock and swung open the door. A small step forward into the house and there sat her father, staring from the couch, switchblade in hand. He was carving a small block of wood, looking at her as though she had intruded upon something very personal. Wood chips fell like fingernail clippings to the floor.

"Where have you been?" he asked, his voice distinct and clear. The blood froze in Elba's veins and her skin crawled from her bones. There was an unmistakable underpinning of anger in what her father said. A quiet rage that lurked beneath the surface, furious at her failure to come home.

He wasn't always an angry man. Soft spoken, articulate. He retained these qualities at all times—but they were most pronounced in anger. He sounded drunk—his speech wasn't slurred, nor did he smell of stale wheat. But it was louder, just a touch, and too forward in the throat.

"I spent the night with a friend," Elba said.

"Did you tell me you were spending the night with a friend?"

"No."

"No, you didn't," her father replied. "I spent the night right here, waiting for you. Worried out of my mind."

Elba thought to leave, to turn her back and walk out the door, to run from the house and never look back. But her legs had grown roots in the ground where she stood and secured her by her feet. Her father continued carving the block of wood, chipping away at the corners and the edges. His work was focused and methodical, not much artistry to it at all. He saw a figure concealed within the pulp and picked away at the parts that didn't belong.

"I waited for you," he continued, "because you were supposed to be home in time for dinner. Because that was the plan. That has always been the plan. You stay with me at night."

He carved with quiet vigor, purposeful like a butcher. Flaying meat after the slaughter. Elba felt a sting at the base of her neck as her limbs began to shake.

"My plan keeps you safe. Without a plan, what would we do? Run wild like rats under the city? You'd like that. Running around without a care or concern for your own wellbeing. But we all need order and structure in our days."

The vibrations trembling throughout her body came even stronger now, a needle in her spine, a wasp driving its barb repeatedly into her skin. The venom flowed freely from someplace beyond the veil, filling her veins with burning acid. It erupted in her mind, her brain ballooning from the pressure. Tissue stretched and vessels burst as her blood boiled and her muscles swelled underneath. She was sure in that moment that she would die.

"You see this block of wood?" her father continued. "I have a plan for it. I have a vision. I'm carving it according to that vision. According to that plan. Each and every time I bring my knife to it, I'm following my plan. But if I get distracted or I stray away from my plan—"

He let his hand slip and sliced a deep gash across his little finger, cutting the tip to the bone. In a flash of glinting silver, Elba's mind was painted red, splattering under her eyelids and dripping beneath her skull. Her father's fingertip hung loosely by the skin, evenly cut through the knuckle. She could see the veins and the tissue exposed and spilling out where it didn't belong. Blood spilled from her father's hand onto the block of wood, staining whatever he had intended it to be.

"This is what happens when you don't follow the plan."

She felt the electricity cracking in her bones, splitting open the sky like lightning. It burned the marrow underneath and left her hollow inside. Her fingers burned white hot and her hair bristled on end, shocking every system in her body from her toenails to her teeth.

"How can I make you remember?"

Her father stood abruptly, bloody knife in hand, and stalked toward her. Elba couldn't scream, couldn't run—she was fixed, frozen in place. But she felt a sudden store of energy brimming in her brain, the deafening roar of a runaway train that rattled in her chest and crushed the breath from her lungs. Her father outstretched his mangled hand and gripped her like a vise by the throat. Blood ran warm from his finger down her neck, soaking through her shirt and staining her skin. He raised his knife level with her eyes, opening his mouth to speak—

Thunder cracked and bones split as her father fell broken to the floor. A crumpled heap sat smoldering in his place, a bloody mess of flesh and pulp. A man reduced to meat. An inexplicable mass of singed sinews and congealed fat soaking into the carpet. The spine spilled freely from the base of the neck and the brain was torn away from the head. The back had snapped and folded in half and collapsed between the legs. The room smelled of scorched earth and burnt skin.

In the ensuing silence of the aftershock, Elba's voice at last escaped her in a heartbroken, howling cry. It was a guttural sob, grieving groans forced out against her will, demanding like a dam bursting forth from the flood. An unstoppable torrent of tears and black bile crawling up along the back of her throat and falling in streams from her nose. She tasted the salt on her tongue and let in run down the front of her face as she surrendered to the pain. And afterward, she felt relieved, an ocean cascading over mountain peaks as she crumbled to the floor and wept.

[VII]

Morning arrived in Hager's Fancy and overstayed its welcome. The day was overcast by the night before, consumed by contemplation of unthinkable things. Dark deeds and the stench of death clinging to the haze in the air.

Elba sat upright in discomfort on the floor, her head throbbing and her shoulders sore. Her throat had closed and her mouth had dried in the absence of all control. The sensation of power that filled her before had left her drained and alone. She had felt it so strongly, been entirely consumed by an overwhelming wave of light that had washed her over. It had filled her lungs so fully and forced the breath from her chest and, in that moment, she had drowned. In the gasping reprieve of the morning air, she craved to feel it again. Its effects had been intoxicating, crippling to her body and numbing to her brain, but she had never felt power so pure. Though it was dangerous and deadly and so utterly unpredictable, suddenly she was free. Unrestrained by worldly shackles and the fetters of her father's steely grip. Reborn in the steaming mud that sat putrefied and stinking on the living room floor.

She reached out to the earth from someplace within, longing to feel the crackling energy that had found her before, that had bored its way inside her brain and burst forth like bullets from her fingertips. It was raw, untethered to the ground and untested by her trigger-happy hands. Invisible to her own unseeing eyes, unparalleled by any source of power. But it was dangerous, covetous, and she would need to be careful not to let it slip free from her grasp. This town was small, suspicious of greater things. That's what her father had always told her. But she had been told many things that she was suddenly starting to doubt.

"*Elba?*"

The voice came calling like a distant memory. The house was still, save for the lonely breeze that had wandered in through the walls. Carefree and thoughtless of the obstacles in its path. An envious absence that Elba longed to enjoy. Suddenly, she felt a familiar stinging at the base of her neck. Her skin erupted in goosebumps and she knew she couldn't stay. Grief was of little use to a girl in the clouds. What did she care for the sorrows of yesterday when she had killed a man with her mind?

She rose from her place on the floor, her face a vague expression, and walked slowly from the room. No one tried to stop her—no one could. The voice that spoke her name pulled her from the house, barefoot across the city, spilling headlong toward the deep and darkened woods that surrounded the valley. The streets were all but abandoned in the light of the midday sun but were doubtless teeming with clandestine activity in the shadows underneath. Elba wondered at those invisible faces, those haunting ghosts whose wasted days were depleted in the dark. She had thought one time that she might join them, descend against her will to the depths of the city streets and the underworld below. Perhaps she already had.

She ignored those trespassing thoughts that threatened to overtake her mind and passed the sunken alleyways by. The afternoon heat filled her lungs and she breathed in the open air. Hager's Fancy had adopted a different impression, somehow larger than before, less oppressive in the face of her newfound sovereignty. Though the terror of it still hung overhead like the tyranny of her past, she possessed an army inside that could wage war against an empire of fear. Her dread had diminished and her hopes for the future bounded like lightning across the sky. But the uncertainty of the path ahead gave her a moment's pause. The inward beckoning from someplace afar tempted her further in, summoning a restless spirit to command her every step. And she obeyed, breaking into a breathless dash down city streets, over railway tracks and out beyond the interstate. Faster now, a steady sprint toward the edge of the world. She had always wanted to run wild.

But she wasn't the only one. Passing through a densely brambled wall of trees and underbrush, she came upon a dark clearing crowned above by a canopy of thorns. Gathered in a ring below stood a number of women dressed in robes, congregated around an enormous patch of black moss. It stretched like a thundercloud fallen to the earth, rolling across the ground and reaching up the length of the trees. It had already strangled several in its path, devouring the life of them and leaving a trail of rotted corpses in its wake.

"Welcome, sister."

Hanna reached out her bare arms as if to embrace, but Elba pulled herself away. The undersides of Hanna's forearms were a patchwork of bruises and thin cuts struggling to heal. A slender smile pulled her lips tight across her pale, uneven face. There was something ghastly in that grimace, an unearthly gleam that pierced her skin as Mother approached from the circle behind, draped in sheer white lace that cascaded down the contours of her body.

"Mother has called you here today."

The sound of Mother's voice inside her head crept along the nerves in Elba's spine, breaking through her bones and sinking into her brain. It shocked her like a current, cracking the tips of her teeth and tearing into her veins. But she endured for the sake of the show. Whatever task could be asked of her, Elba wanted to impress. She had never known what it was to have a mother and would hate to disappoint the closest thing she might ever get.

And she sought to please the Mother of them all, the spirit that lived like running water flowing deep inside their souls. Powerful, impossible, and entirely inside her head. Yet Her presence was undeniable—Elba felt Her as strongly as she felt the dying grass beneath her feet. She did not speak, but Elba sensed Her presence through the women encircled around her in the clearing. Through their living Mother, they attained the power to conjure up whatever their darkened hearts desired. Dark, unimpeded wants that caused their mouths to hang limp and wet with saliva. But empowerment came at a cost—Elba was terrified of what it might be.

11

11 Tania Bustamente, *Häxan*, 2020, acrylic ink on watercolor paper.

"*Häxan* is one of our most ancient rituals," Mother remarked, inspiring a symphony of unintelligible songs. Elba heard the other women chittering in her mind, an excited cluster growing in volume like a swarm of locusts devouring a field of fertile crops. Mandibles dripping and wings buzzing as their thousand eyes twitched around in their heads, prepared to raze their prey to the ground.

With gentle arms guiding her forward, Mother brought Elba to the center of the clearing, right in the middle of the black moss. The smell was damp but sweet, less sour than the basement of Hanna's house on Salem. Elba could sense a change in the air, something she hadn't been able to before. It was so pleasant, so fragrant like a flower's perfume, that she almost didn't see the man resting naked on the ground.

There, lying at the center of the great black shadow, was Mr. Larsen. His body was exposed, limbs stretched outward like a star, vulnerable to the secret intentions of the women circled about. He had already been marked with purple bruises that had swollen through his skin. His eyes were torn open in a blank, unseeing stare. Peeled back like iridescent pearls sunken into the back of his skull. He began suddenly to shake, violently, seizing from a nightmare, frozen in paralysis as though he were gripped by some uncertain fear. Whatever the task ahead, Elba knew that Mr. Larsen would be fixed to the core.

She stepped forward, placing her foot gently onto the black earth, moss slipping between her toes. A cold hand pressed against her back, pushing her further forward, closer to Mr. Larsen's convulsing body. His eyes rolled loosely in his head, bloodshot and filled with spiderwebbing veins. Foam dripped from in between his tightly clenching teeth.

"Careful."

Elba turned back to see Hanna standing with her eyes closed, hands clasped from either side by the ring of her sisters that had formed around her. She, too, had begun to shake. Her thin lips were parted slightly, rapidly moving as though she were chanting an incantation. Elba admitted to herself that she didn't understand the first thing about witchcraft—she only knew that it frightened her, that she had fallen unwittingly into something deeper than she knew, and that she desperately wanted to know more.

In the passing of her former self, she had commandeered dominion over her destiny. An outcast all her life, a girl on the fringe of society. Suddenly, she was a part of something greater, a sister to several others who undoubtedly longed for the same. She had never been different from the others, not really—just alone. These women belonged to each other, found purpose in each other. Maybe that was all she needed.

But every inch of her skin was crawling and she felt compulsion turning in her stomach. As she stepped into the very center of the clearing, the ground dropped out from underneath her and she was falling, hurtling without control. She had entered into a world that she didn't understand to obtain a power she thirsted for in her bones.

Control over her own unyielding days and nights that passed without resolve had thrown her headlong into this moment. Promises of freedom and the end of futility, of purpose and of someplace all her own and the achievement of everything she ever wanted. But the dusted pages of a story she had read over and over in her mind lay split down the spine in front of her. It seemed as though in the concourse of her life she had meandered in a circle, leapt from the height of a towering city, and fell into the clouds.

"*Careful.*"

Sweat gathered on Elba's brow as she stared intently at Mr. Larsen, struggling inside a body that, at this moment, was not his own. His skin glistened like plasticine, his own sweat pooling in the pit of his stomach and collecting in the concave valley of his chest, spilling over the edge and falling to the ground like hot summer rain. His fingers curled in clenching fists, clutching handfuls of thick black moss that stained his fingernails and left the ground beneath him a mess of claw marks and mud.

"Our Mother lives within us," announced the woman in white to her daughters around the clearing. "She subsists in our every breath, and it is by Her gracious will that we may breathe life. To thank our Mother for the many gifts that She has bestowed upon us, we have gathered here today to render homage."

The anticipation of the women encircled around the great black moss buzzed like static in Elba's mind, filling her head with a persistent ringing that drove her teeth together. An electric current that burned like fire in her blood. Mother turned to face her directly and beckoned with open arms. Grinding bone against weathered bone, Elba dug her fingernails into her palms and took another pace forward. Cautiously, more hesitant than before. With every wayward stride, she felt more and more like she was stepping into a trap.

The guarded, troubled look on Elba's face said to the woman in white that she didn't understand her purpose in whatever was to unfold. Mother recognized this, and so she took a more direct and unencumbered approach.

"Our Mother has chosen you to bear Her sacrifice."

It was too late to turn and run. Elba felt the energy coursing through the air, static sparking all around. Mr. Larsen's body went limp and his eyes turned dark as Elba understood what Mother demanded. The clearing filled with labored moans as her sisters writhed on their feet, reveling in the ecstasy of her pain.

"Will you submit to the All-Mother's will?"

Elba surveyed the women circled around her, all of them joined together by their hands. Outwardly, it was a symbol of communion, a gesture of sisterhood—but Elba understood it as a threat. They had her in a cage, surrounded on all sides, and there was nothing she could do to escape. These were their unconditional terms of surrender—in truth, she had no choice.

"Yes."

A bolt of lightning passed through Elba in an instant, consumed her body, and entered into her mind. Like maggots and mealworms burrowing their way into the center of a corpse, Elba felt something else inside. An alien presence, invasive like a weed. It began to push her out. With useless fingers grasping at the edge of a cliff, she tried to maintain her grip. But it pushed harder and her fingers slipped and she fell down the back of her throat.

[VIII]

The house on Salem Avenue stood tall against the midday sun, beating down onto the rotted wood and glinting off the faded stone. Years of sorrow and neglect had caused the roof to collapse and allowed its inhabitants to fester underneath the surface like a wound. A den of rats, diseased and decaying bodies discarded in their graves, secluded from the cleaner parts of town. The house was a trap, laced with sweet nectar to lure the rodents in, only to keep them there to suffer and to die. It hadn't always been that way, but Officer Boscoe was happy to let the ancient ruins of the city do their part to keep the haunted vagabonds off the streets.

But murder was a more serious matter. He had no regard for the slumbering vagrants who wasted away on aerosol and fumes. Confined to a prison of their own making, there was little need for further quarantine. But the girl called Johanna Parker—she required something more. Interrogation at the least, a brief interview off the record. He wouldn't even need to enter the house. He would be more than happy to question her on the dilapidated front porch, where he paused in shock and disgust. The steps were soft from maggots and termites chewing through the wood. He climbed them carefully, refusing to balance himself on the railing, which had succumbed to corrosion and rust. Sharp bits of twisted, orange metal spiraled like fireworks out of control. The sparks had landed on brittle bones and set the rest aflame.

Officer Boscoe approached the door to the broken house and knocked on the splintering wood. It echoed through an empty house, devoid of furnishings and comforts of any kind. He would have rung the doorbell, but it had been destroyed either by vandals on the street or the inhabitants of the house themselves. Officer Boscoe waited for a reply, for someone to open the door, but no such response came.

He hesitated, peering through the frosted panes of glass in the door, weighing whether he should break the law and enter the house or turn away and abandon his most promising lead. Without a warrant, he would enter uninsured, but he wondered whether there was anyone inside to protest. He didn't wonder for very long before punching out the glass and reaching his arm through the door, fumbling for a moment until he found the lock. Gently, he swung open the front door of the forgotten house and stepped inside. The smell nearly forced him back out, filling his head like sour liquor. He gagged but continued deeper in, searching for Johanna Parker.

"This is HFPD. My name is Officer Boscoe. I'm looking for a girl—"

He nearly tripped over a lump lying across the floor. The electricity had been shut off and the rooms were cast in darkness from the overgrowth crawling up the sides of the house. Bodies lay scattered like landmines, buried just below the surface. The smell was of a battlefield, steaming with shit and blood. But none of these men were dead—they were still breathing, lost in another world. Sleeping off a high that they would return to chase when they awoke. He could have them all arrested, hauled away someplace his taxes would pay for. He chose instead to let them rot for free. Let them sink into the dirt of their own accord. He could wait.

The lonely rooms of the house offered no help as to the whereabouts of its other inhabitants, no hints as to the location of Johanna Parker. Perhaps they had fled in anticipation of his arrival, abandoned their only home rather than risk investigation. But the girl knew more than he had learned and he would do what he needed to discover what that might be. What she had been keeping and who she had been protecting. She had to have been either a witness or an accomplice—the Larsen girl's account suggested that much, supported by her association with Bishop Ford supplied by Elba Reed. This girl knew something that she wanted desperately to hide.

He climbed a rotted staircase to the second floor of the house and, finding nothing at all of value, he proceeded higher still. At the very peak of the house he found an attic space fashioned into a bedroom. The roof had, for the most part, collapsed and the rotted beams had been removed, leaving behind a room exposed to the sky. The walls still stood and, at the far end of the room, a shattered window let in streaking rays of sunlight. They refracted through a little vase, which held a withered, white rose, dying of thirst. A mattress in the center of the room reeked of vomit and sweat, as though it had been salvaged from a dumpster heap or from the sick ward of a foreclosing hospital. The walls were adorned with playful scrawling, some of it in crayon, some of it in paint. This had been the room of a child. He felt pity at the thought but did what he could to ignore it. A man had been killed, and all the clues had led him here.

He began to search what little of the room there was, opening cabinet drawers and pulling back bedsheets, looking for anything that might be available as proof. There wasn't much in the room at all. He found dead mice and rusted nails, nothing much in the way of evidence. He discovered old drawings signed "Hanna" at the bottom. He could state with certainty, at least, that this was her room.

Then, out of the corner of his eye, he spotted a loose plank in the farthest wall. It was leaned unlike the others against the far end of the room, vertically, as though it were meant to be inconspicuous. A spare piece of roofing, left behind for some other purpose. He approached and peeled it back to find that it was nothing more than a makeshift closet, clothes hanging from protruding nails. T-shirts and flannels, jackets and skirts. And he saw it, barely hanging on by a thread—a grey, tattered sweater. The sleeves were in shredded ribbons, the cuffs were frayed to bits. It smelled of sour mud soaking in dishwater and burnt grease. Salvaged from someplace downtown or donated by the family of someone who had died. It was undoubtedly the mark of poverty, an article needed above all else to survive the winter, or else to leave the wearer shivering naked against the cold.

A phantom twinge like a useless limb that had fallen asleep and was suddenly jolted awake ate at him from the outside. It gnawed away at his stubborn brain, eating his professional apathy until it could taste his less impartial thoughts. But he dismissed those wandering sympathies and insisted instead on dispassionate work. He tore the sweater from its hook and fled from the room.

As he descended the stairs from the upper room and hurried toward the front door, anxious to be gone from the place, some distant sound made him stay a moment longer. A deep groan from below, a callous sound that resonated throughout the house, the sort of sound that old houses make. But not this house—Officer Boscoe didn't trust his senses here, not when the air was laced with poison. The deadly fumes of a sunken tar pit, sulfur and ash clouds that wrapped their gaseous tendrils around the throats of their victims. Suffocation like the throes of sleep that drag men away to endless slumber. In this house, the dying drifted away without hesitation, happily breathing in the vapors without resistance. But Officer Boscoe refused the offer and listened more closely to the pitiful moan. Full of sadness, full of fear. This was not the sound of a haunted house. This sound was coming from something very much alive.

His muscles tensed underneath his skin, which was cold and tense to the touch. The sound came again, echoing throughout the empty house as he listened for the source. He thought that it must be coming from below and searched the place for the entrance to a basement or cellar of some sort. Tucked underneath the staircase, a small wooden door stood expectantly, waiting for his hand.

The handle shown in dim light, a cracking glass knob casting daggers that refracted across his face. He obliged and turned it slowly, careful not to cut his hand, and swung the door inward with a wooden scream. It was a dead thing, a ghost that had been nailed to the wall. He descended this last flight of stairs with a decisive apprehension. Whatever lay below, caution was the best course of action. He held his flashlight in one hand and his standard-issue Glock in the other, pointing them both toward the darkness.

With each step downward, his breath shortened in his lungs and his arms shook a little more. The beam of light from his flashlight shot from one side of the staircase to the other, darting away into the unseen recesses of the cellar below. The sound grew louder, groaning in the dark as he imagined what he might find.

At the bottom of the staircase he found a door painted black with broad, uneven strokes that shone like inverted stained glass—it consumed all light that crossed it. Just on the other side, the sound of something dying came more deeply and distressed than he had heard before. Whatever it was sounded unbearably sad, wounded beyond its body, bleeding in its soul. Holstering his Glock, he reached his arm out toward the handle. His fingers grasped it slowly, pulled the great thing outward, and he fell inside.

The room was dark and smelled of sour rust, corrosion eating through the floor. Officer Boscoe shone his flashlight into the endless void, terrified of what he might discover. He listened silently, breathlessly for the sound to come again, but it had stopped altogether. Sweeping the empty room, his beam of light passed suddenly over something wet and shining on the floor. A dark trail glistening like a snake winding its way through the dark. He prayed that it was just a puddle of water collecting from a broken pipe, but he knew this prayer would go unanswered. He brought the light back and saw that the trail was red.

He traced its path across the floor, around a sunken pool depressed into the stone, leading him to a small door flush with the wall, seamless like a hidden passageway, secured by a padlock and chain. Whatever lay behind it, these people that lived like rats in this house did not want it to escape. From underneath the doorway ran the little stream, tears of blood running down a silent face. It was fresh, steadily trickling toward a gutter that led from the empty pool out through the foundation of the cellar. He stepped carefully, footsteps falling against cold flagstone with an empty echo in the dark. As he came closer to the door in the wall, a quiet groan sounded from the other side. Less desperate and more pitiful, as though it had resigned itself to die. Heavy sobs followed by a wounded sigh.

He thought quickly how best to breach the door. He had no backup, no battering ram or crowbar on his person, and he had no time to wait. Aiming his flashlight at the padlock, he pressed himself against the wall, drew his Glock, and fired. The groaning grew loader as the lock shattered and the chain fell free to the floor. Without another moment's hesitation, Officer Boscoe threw open the door.

Crumpled in the corner of the closet lay the brutalized remains of what had once been a young woman, stripped of her clothes and bound by her feet. Her ankles were swollen and bruised, as though they had been broken. Her stomach had been ripped apart, meat torn from the bone by crude instruments—teeth or hacksaws. Blood poured from her abdomen as she cradled herself in her arms. The smell was of something decayed and left for the dirt, abandoned by the world above and given instead to the worms. Wet and warm, lifeblood spilling from a mangled corpse. Her breath was shallow, grasping at thin air. These were not people who lived in this house—these were animals.

Officer Boscoe lifted the young woman in his arms and carried her from the cellar, through the twisted corridors, and out of the rotted house. In the unflinching honesty of the daylight, her face shone through the bruises and strands of knotted hair. He saw in her deep, blue eyes a familiar sadness. The same look he had seen before in the photograph pinned to his wall. And suddenly he knew her, recognized the hopeless façade she wore on her face. He held the broken body of Riley Mason, the missing girl.

After months of fruitless searching, in the final moments of her life, she had fallen helplessly into his care. With a rattling shudder and a final gasp, her eyes widened as she looked into the face of her savior and she fell limp. His arms shook from a sudden weight as he set her gently on the ground. Blood comingled with his tears and the mud dried purple beneath his fingernails. Here, in this house of the damned, the undead held the living hostage. They posted an impossible ransom and committed murder without notice. Anger burned deeper than the pit of Hell inside him, hot in the bowels of his gut, shifting continental plates and disturbing fault lines as it threatened to erupt. Magma bubbled in a violent, steaming brew just below the surface of his skin, about to burst through and burn the city down.

And the cracks began to show, veins crawling like spiderwebs along his forearms, snaking up across his chest in fracturing formations. His blood ran hot and filled his body with explosive energy, flammable like gasoline. Fumes gathered like a storm cloud in his mind, crackling with an electric fever that spread across the exhausted expanse of his mind. The years had worn him down and left his heavy heart brittle in the heat of a blaze. The smallest spark would set him aflame. Then, as if the house on Salem Avenue were tempting him to act, the front door of the rotted place swung open in the breeze. The mesmerizing void inside that haunting house defied him to enter again, taunted him from a distance as if it dared him to turn his back and leave. But this city had tested him too far—the fire was lit inside him and, in an instant, he was consumed.

In a singular motion, and with a swift and steady stride, Officer Boscoe drew his weapon and—

One.

He was in the house, moving like a tiger through the dark, finding his prey as if by instinct. Another lump on the floor –

Two.

Another body on the streets—

Three.

Passing through every vacant, darkened room, he canvassed and surveyed, sweeping through the house like a plague. Indiscriminate, without consideration or thought for who they were. His victims had no mind, no presence in this world—they had been living as though they were already dead. But their blood ran warm across the slanted floor, soaking through the dark and sinking into the soft and rotted wood to leave a gory stain. The lost souls of Hager's Fancy would be found today.

Four.

The gunshots rang out in the dark like thunder, striking the ground where their empty bodies lay.

Five. Six.

One after another, without hesitation, not bothering to take aim—

Seven.

His arm became an extension of his mind, moving of its own volition, sightless but drawn by every blind intention to the roaches on the floor. In the dark, he couldn't see their heads bursting and their brains spattering like puss against the walls.

Eight.

He had murdered insects and rodents before, conducted exterminations of the city's swarming pests. He had lain traps around their nests, lured them from their secret places out into the light. But this time was different—he had never stepped into the dark, trespassed beyond the borders between their hive and home. These vermin had dug in deep, infested the city with filth and rot before embedding their nest in its spine.

Nine.

The broken house had been turned on its head. Once a haven for rotting souls, the house on Salem Avenue was burning at the stake. A sacrifice, an example. But Barry Boscoe didn't care. He only saw its twisted bones and its fractured, crumbling face. He had struck it in its blackened heart and happily caused it to bleed. Wounded by the fatal blow, it stumbled where it stood. Black blood poured in open streams, weeping rivers that converged in an ocean of bitter tears. Dripping from its jugular, flowing from its throat.

Ten.

These crippled animals that he put out of their misery were not victims at their core—these were players in a dangerous game. Gamblers without a chance in Hell, the losing hand of a swindling house. But they had placed their bets and their faith in the promises of something that wasn't true. The unforsaken life of another world, the illusory dream in which they slumbered, stolen away like liquor in their brains, bleeding out for the duration of their days.

But there was more to this place than he ever understood, some darker element to uncover still. In the very foundation that supported the framing of the house, evil had found a way inside. Officer Boscoe wondered how long it had been there, just how tainted had his city been since its founding. Hager's Fancy was sour in its roots, softened at the core, and decomposing from inside. There was a greater corrosion eating away at the rusted spokes of the city, some more deadly disease spreading among its inhabitants than that infecting the nameless vagabonds lying useless and wasted on the floor. Depravity unlike any he had seen in all his tired years, a force at work in the underbelly of the mountains that was beginning to work its twisted way into the head of the beast. He had witnessed the horrors that it committed with his own eyes, carried the broken body of its work from this afflicted place in his arms.

Eleven.

A soft groan escaped from a withered old man who struggled to bring himself to his feet—

Twelve.

The man collapsed again, face-first against the floor. His arms stretched out before him, reaching hopelessly at nothing in front of him for any means of escape, clawing at the empty air. Useless legs kicked out in spasms, futile gestures against his slaughter. There was nothing he could do, nowhere he could go to stop it from happening. He was already dead, beaten and bloodied beyond repair. Bits of him were missing from his chest, blown away and scattered across the floor. Thick blood spilled from his body like a bursting dam, his skin ripped away from his gaunt and shrunken muscles and his bones were broken by the fury of a bullet. He couldn't breathe, couldn't think. But the world would not let him go.

Through the blistering fever of his mercurial high, he saw an enormous man in uniform holding a loaded gun pointed toward his face, stalking without relief, a predator prowling through the haunted night. His eyes were piercing high beams, daggers of electric light. He could not see any semblance of his face—his identity had fallen away behind a wall of rage. It had become him, assumed control of the blood in his veins. This was no longer a man. Unthinking, unfeeling, moved only by the hunger that a vociferous beast felt in its gut. This one lusted for blood, not to feed but to feel, to spill in an ancient sacrifice to a lonely god of war. But there was no god, no sacrifice, only the impetus of pain and the often-hollow promise of something more.

With an act of violence more suited to the maws of a mythic monster, the forceful arms of the manticore that had been a man grabbed him by the loose rags he wore wrapped around his torso and pulled him to his feet. He looked into its opaque eyes, empty but for the hollow, poison glow of white fluorescents staring back. He was truly gazing into a soulless void concealed beneath a mask of meat. Or perhaps his former self had simply fallen away in the crucible of his task and left behind something less feeling, something necessarily less human. He felt the smoking barrel of the gun slide against his skin, still burning hot as it forced its way into his mouth, burning his tongue as he tasted lead—

Thirteen.

[IX]

The clearing had emptied before Elba awoke. Her head throbbed and her throat was sore, as though she hadn't drunk water in days. Cautiously, she picked herself up off the ground and looked to the trees around her. There wasn't a sign of anyone in sight, only dense forest beyond the outstretched fingers of the black moss covering the ground. Spores that shot like thorns from the earth, threatening to expand their reach. Elba took a hesitant step forward before pausing and turning in circles around the spot where she stood, unsure from which direction she had come.

Panic began to take root, teeth sinking into her skin, and she ran. She stumbled as she planted her foot in the center of the clearing, deep into the monstrous sea, catching on the tangle of black moss. But something else was caught where she fell—there, under her feet, concealed beneath the overgrowth, lay Mr. Larsen's body. Pale and beginning to bloat, blue in his fingertips with a deep, red gash cut straight across his throat. Elba was unsure whether he had been purposely disposed beneath the moss or whether the earth had begun to reclaim him to his grave.

Taking to her feet, standing deserted in the woods, a sudden fear gripped her unlike any she had felt before. Her skin felt tight against her bones as it demanded to be torn away. Sobbing between involuntary gasps for air, struggling to find her breath stuck somewhere in her shriveled lungs, she wanted to run from the place, run away and never return to the cursed and sunken city that she had always known since her stolen childhood days. She wanted to run away and never stop running, not even when this day was a far-off, forgotten nightmare lost in the recesses of her mind.

But she was frozen, fixed immobile in place, rooted to the ground like the horrible moss reaching between her toes, grasping for her throat. She couldn't breathe, clawing at her neck while the black ocean swallowed her alive and filled her lungs with rot. She fell to her knees and ripped it from the earth, crying out in silent desperation as her fingers found its cruel heart buried beneath the mud. For every artery she severed, countless others connected in a tangled web to the center of it all, feeding the source of the poison thing with fail-safes sufficient for the most paranoid of minds. The fruitless effort wore her sharp resolve to a blunt and useless instrument beating against the earth. She collapsed to the ground in a useless heap, exhausted and spent from the trials of the day, defeated by that coven of false sisterhood that had used her for their own devices. Overcome by thoughts of betrayal and revenge, she buried her face in the dirt.

PART THREE

[I]

The ground beneath Salem Avenue was awash with smoke, as if the earth had been set on fire. In the blood-stained sacristy beneath the blasphemous house, Johanna Parker breathed in deeply and let it fill her lungs. Hell was burning down below, and Hanna felt high on the fumes.

A small flame flickered at the center of a freshly drawn circle on the floor, set in the empty pool sunken into the stone. Hanna fed it dutifully from her store of brittle kindling and eagerly watched it grow. A wrought iron tripod stood like an altar above the flames, suspending an ancient, arduous cauldron from its neck. The fire licked hungrily at its base, a thousand devil's tongues tasting the blackened char. Hanna tossed bits of shriveled moss into the flames, pieces of shimmering silver, which had been dehydrated and shelved in glass jars for several months. It shattered like glass in the heat and birthed bright sparks, tumbling in somersaults through the air. She smiled at the sight, warm and inviting, deceptive as all fires dancing in their gilded cages. A moment's cruel distraction, a single absent thought, and the clever, hungry beast would leap violently from its lair. *Tiger, tiger, burning bright—*[12]

"Careful."

Mother's voice sounded soft yet stern across the room, a steady note carried by a seasoned soprano. The Queen of the Night.

"I'm sorry, Mother."

And she was sorry. Hanna hated to disappoint Mother, in that moment more than ever. Hanna was engaged in a lesson in witchcraft, a trial that she wanted desperately to pass. She had lived all the memories of her life in Mother's encompassing shadow, a broad, sweeping sail towering above her that guided her ship through tempest-tossed seas. Still, she sometimes stood at the helm and wondered what lay in another direction.

From the other side of the room Mother stood dutifully before the small closet that held all manner of secrets. Hanna had never seen inside—she had only ever heard strange noises, haunting moans that she had feared since she was a child. But Mother was never afraid, not of anything in this house nor of anyone in this city. Not even the massacre of the mindless mob spilling out across the floor upstairs had swayed her from the narrow path she trod. Though they had been called away from the ritual in the woods, alarmed at the fading voices crying out inside their heads, Mother was intent to resolve the dissonance ringing in her ears. There was purpose in her days that drove her onward more fervently than any threat she received could ever sway her charted course.

---

12   William Blake, "The Tyger," *The Poetry Foundation, The Poetry Foundation, 2020.*

Though the world outside the wailing walls of that hollow house condemned her like a disease, an incurable virus embedded in their blood, Mother knew better than to listen. Here, in the dark and hidden depths of the earth below, she commanded power beyond the understanding of those who lived in the tired town of Hager's Fancy. Hanna had seen what she could do, touched the smallest fraction of it, embraced even that tiny piece so fully that it ripped through solid fragments of her skull and tore open a hole in her mind.

Mother plucked some squealing creature from atop the highest shelf of the closet and threw it into the bubbling brew boiling in the cauldron at the center of the room. The muffled cries of some wriggling animal turned to panicked screams in the unbearable heat before ceasing altogether. Mother tossed in a few more sprigs and fallen leaves, things that smelled of fresh mud and fallen rain. Once living sprites that had burst into the world with the showers of spring but had shriveled and died with the bitter winds of fall.

Steam rolled like a billowing cloud across the room before dissipating under cover of smoke. Droplets of sweat had collected on Hanna's skin and fell in rolling streams down the center of her back. Mother stirred the steaming potion, thick and heavy as a midwinter broth. Hanna peered over the brim of the cauldron to see tiny pink hands and feet floating among thick strands of auburn hair and dark liquid like blood. Mangled organs torn open and green fluids leaking out from inside, sunken eyes staring back from beneath a half-formed face.

Mother's voice filled her head with a familiar urgency, an energy that demanded to be heard. No matter how Hanna tried, she couldn't quiet her mind.

"*Mother is pleased with our sacrifice.*"

Hanna watched as the fire burned brighter, as the flames climbed higher and the room grew hotter. Her throat closed up against the smoke but her lungs cried out for more. The taste of it warmed her body, touched her blood with the soft breath of a sleeping babe. And she was apart from all else, existing somewhere between worlds as a passenger on a speeding train racing through an endless tunnel. But Mother took her by the hand and brought her back to Earth.

So Hanna sank beneath the cellar, slipping away to another place where she drifted through the heavy smoke, suspended in the air. Parting like a crimson, velvet curtain, the smoke revealed Mother's face, fallen from disappointment or some other, more severe failure. In the distance, Hanna heard defeated groans—no, the sorrowful sounds of sobbing wails. Guttural cries of pain like an animal that had seen the death of her young. Echoing across the vast expanse of the sky, the mourning song of a wounded beast resounded among the clouds. And there stood Mother, framed purposely by the moon, holding in her outstretched, bloody palm the skull of a slaughtered child. She crushed it in her hand as a thick, white liquid streamed from its severed head.

Hanna collided with the floor in horror, speechless from shock and disgust at the sickening sight. Concern spread like cancer across Mother's sullen face as she strode through the air, thick columns of smoke curling around her ankles like snakes prepared to strike.

"What's wrong, love?"

Hanna couldn't find the words to say, but Mother already knew. There were no secrets in this house, nothing kept from Mother's watchful eyes. The invasive prodding of a surgeon's knife felt around inside her head, digging through flesh and fear to find what lay hidden inside. Within moments, Mother had found out the truth. Catching a glimpse of Mother's intentions freely flowing in her mind had sent Hanna falling from the skies in fear. Neither one had ever seen the other like this, so opposed in all dimensions as to seem, in any regard, unknown.

"*What greater sacrifice than a mother's child?*"

Mother gestured toward the rancid brew, boiling over its brim, spattering the stone below. Hanna choked on the black bile in the air as the stench forced itself inside, prying its way into her nostrils and clawing down the length of her throat.

"*Our Mother's children have abandoned Her, poisoned Her, defiled Her sacred body, and bled Her dry.*"

The order of her days collapsed in a mangled mess before Hanna's eyes and congealed like coagulate blood inside her mind. The purpose of everything she had done in Mother's name, every gruesome task and grisly test. Befriending the loneliest girl in school only to lure her into a trap. She had seen the ceremony performed time and time again, watched her youngest sisters stolen away by the night, but she had never participated in this stage of the ritual—she had never been able to fully grasp at the truth.

"*The rite is unfinished and your sister has left us. But we both know where to find her.*"

Though she knew that it was not her place to question the unfathomable will of Mother, Hanna had never understood her role in the recruitment of Elba Reed. Though they had been called away before, intent to return before Elba awoke, the ritual could still be completed. Hanna had believed in those promises made, the power over her own life that lay just beyond her reach. In the sudden recognition of every-thing she had done, she regretted ever stepping foot down the wayward streets of Hager's Fancy. Hanna could still hear Elba's screams.

"To practice Häxan is to honor the glory of our Mother and atone for our sins against the Earth."

There was nothing Hanna could do to stop the vomit spilling freely from her mouth and out onto the floor. It was acid rain, burning whatever it touched, eating away at her jaw until there was nothing left but a gaping wound. Her tongue fell loose and numb down her throat as her teeth corroded to dust. Or perhaps the noxious fumes from the fire caused her to hallucinate. Dancing in shades of purple and green, the flames lashed out to kill.

Weakened and afraid, Hanna stumbled to her feet and ran toward the cellar door before it slammed shut in her face. She turned slowly to see Mother standing gaunt behind her, blood falling in tears from her eyes, staining ruby droplets dripping down her cheeks. She wept for her daughter, who had turned to run away.

"Stay with me."

Hanna stopped frightfully in her tracks as she felt herself slipping, falling backward into the void that existed someplace her mind could not go, the limits of thought at the precipice of oblivion. She cried out with what voice she could muster, begging to be here, but the familiar impetus of a foreign soul pushed her over the edge and the emptiness swallowed her whole.

[II]

The headquarters of Hager's Fancy Police Department had stood downtown for a century, guarding against those who would tear the city down. Its ramparts proved peerless in the past, watching from above as hardened men ran headlong into the storm. But the building had crumbled and the men had died, long ago succumbing to the tyranny and chaos of the streets, giving way to the anarchy that roamed free without reproach. The Gilded Age was over and the rust had begun to eat through.

Barry Boscoe sat at his desk, poring over the years. Case after unsolved case stared back at him under the harsh fluorescent lights of the office. He knew each face, remembered each offense that had stolen them away. When he had first joined the force, he was filled to the brim with optimism and a schoolboy's understanding of justice. The city seemed new in all its glistening glory, if only through the eyes of a child. But something had changed in Hager's Fancy, whether it was the wearing of the years or his own sense of dread that darkened every avenue, every alleyway he passed suspiciously by. A shadow had been cast like a curse overhead, throwing the city into endless night.

"Officer Boscoe."

He looked up from his desk to see Lieutenant Davis walking briskly by, headed with purpose toward her office door. Her uniform was newly pressed, her shoes clicking loudly against the tile floor. She gestured with a flourish over her shoulder.

"I'd like a brief word."

His skin crawled along his bones in a shivering panic, fearing that he had been found out. The blood he had spilled on Salem Avenue had lost him nights of sleep. Pearly eyes sunk deep in darkened skulls saw through to his burning heart. The screaming echoes of gunshots and lightning scattered like cracks in his mind. He knew his innocence couldn't last.

Already the waves were crashing across his face, sweat collecting in the folds of his brow. Lieutenant Davis reserved her reprimands for serious infractions only, severe violations of department protocol. His slaughter on Salem Avenue would certainly qualify. Stepping into the lieutenant's office, his heart battered against his breast like a hurricane, gripped by chaotic winds that beat inside his chest. It pounded in his brain, breaking against the back of his skull—the rolling thunder of a summer storm.

"Have a seat," Lieutenant Davis said sternly, holding out her open hand toward a lonesome chair on the opposite side of her desk. Barry Boscoe sat as the chair creaked loudly under his weight, its crusted, leather padding giving way.

"I'm sure by now you've been briefed on what happened down on Salem."

She knew. There was anger in her voice, supplemented by sadness that betrayed her stoic façade. She didn't want to tell him—she must have been afraid of what he might do. But he remained calm, feigning ignorance of homicide, of riotous revenge that left the city soaked in blood.

It had always been department protocol to forego investigation of the house on Salem Avenue. Not to ignore its illicit affairs, but to maintain a deferential distance. The helpless and the homeless had a place on Salem, a place apart from society's streets. It had been a prison of their own making, a cell of their own design. So long as they remained hidden away and harmless but to themselves, the authorities of Hager's Fancy had been willing to let them be. But Barry Boscoe had made that arrangement no longer necessary.

"No, ma'am," he lied through the skin of his teeth.

"It's a matter that concerns you directly." Lieutenant Davis made sure to look him in the eye, to challenge his account of events and dare him to refute her founded claims.

"Ma'am?"

"You remember that young woman from South High who disappeared, Riley Mason? Her case had been of great interest to you."

And Barry Boscoe was back in that house, sunken in the stone cellar as he held the missing girl in his arms. Her lifeless eyes like iridescent pearls staring up at him from sunken sockets, swollen underneath her face. The weight of her body, frozen and stiff, tearing at his veins. Her blood running thick over his hands.

"Of course. It still is."

"Her remains were found discarded in the woods beside the interstate."

He knew this, of course. He had been the one to do it. But he maintained a troubled expression, making sure to convey a manner of surprise.

"Discarded, ma'am?"

"Well, it was strange," she said. "Not so much discarded as displayed. Almost as if she had been posed. Arms folded, eyes shut. And there was a dead bouquet of wildflowers placed between her hands."

"That is strange."

He couldn't leave her, abandoned by the city, broken on the street. But he couldn't call her in. The mangled mess of bodies strewn across the floor inside the rotted house had prevented him from reporting her death. The suspicion would be focused squarely on him, the circumstances insurmountable and the evidence clear.

But all parties involved were deceased, and they no longer cared for justice or the truth. They wouldn't mind if he remained innocent and free, unwilling to report the incident and turn himself in. Better to forego that responsibility and wait for them to be discovered in due course. And he had no sympathies left for them, not after everything they had done to the stolen girl. Her life had led her to a similar fate as theirs, but there were mourners to grieve her death. In dedication to her brief but treasured life, he had treated her with a father's respect, arranged her body as though she were resting at peace and bid farewell as she crossed over to another place. He had neither reservations nor regrets.

"Take the rest of the day," Lieutenant Davis said. Her voice was honest and full of sympathy but unyielding in her regard for the truth. "This can't be easy to hear."

"I think I'll be alright, ma'am."

"I wasn't asking."

She did know. A look in her eyes, a pulsing vein in her temple. There, beneath her calm expression, she was telling him to run.

"Take as long as you need."

This was an order of desertion, an advocate's warning that the scene would most certainly lead back to him. Perhaps it was an understanding of his actions, or at least a sentimental reluctance to lock him inside a cage. Suspicion would be staved off for a time, but forensics told a story in blood. Whatever her intentions, she could not forestall the pursuit of justice. The least she could do was alert him to the chase.

He stood slowly from his seat, extending his arm for a handshake, which Lieutenant Davis curtly refused. She did not want to see him chained in iron, but she disapproved of the things he'd done. Collecting his courage and taking stock of his shame, he stepped out from the oppressive walls of the Lieutenant's office and stepped out into the expansive world beyond his corrugated cubicle.

The chilling winds of autumn swept through the empty streets as Barry Boscoe's blood beat against his chest. He felt as though he were floating outside of his body, surveying the city from above. The darkened spokes of asphalt streets stretched out for unending miles, dizzying spaces that brought him back down to the earth. But he could still smell it in the clouds, a boundless, invigorating scent unlike anything he'd ever smelled before. Intoxication sweet as sin, he breathed in freedom pure as bliss. But there was a looming danger in the air that thrilled his swift escape.

Climbing into his father's old '67 Cadillac, Barry Boscoe sped away from that downtown precinct and toward someplace unknown. Excitement staved off the panic as he wondered where he would go. Someplace further than he'd ever been, big enough where he could disappear. Kissed by the sun and swaddled by the sea. Jacksonville, or Miami. He would need to start over, excise this part of his life and hide it away forever. Murders and massacre, hopeless faces staring back at him from the bulletin board. Years of fruitless worry wearing on his mind, the consequences of missteps and mistakes that refused to die. In his professional line of work, the ghosts of failures past haunted well into the night.

But it would be difficult to forget what he was leaving behind. The city of his childhood, the governing seat of his memory. He had always seen his youth through rose-colored recollection, painting the past like Norman Rockwell. In truth, he feared that Hager's Fancy had never really changed, that he had only grown to realize the city had never been emerald green. He switched on the radio in search of something to drown his thoughts.

As he drove beyond the sunken valley in which Hager's Fancy sat, the world stretched out before him. Endless, rolling mountains aflame with the fires of fall as the leaves shed their shameful summer shade. The vast expanse of autumn's Appalachia swelled like an ocean breaking against the bulwark of his ship. In the distorted reflection of his rearview mirror, he watched the city sink beneath the waves.

[III]

The small house on the south side of town grew dark as the evening sun disappeared beneath the lip of the valley. A chill wind stole away the heat of the afternoon as Elba Reed sat on the edge of her sofa, staring at the other end of the room. A dark stain had soaked into the carpeting where her father had stood, where she had scrubbed for days on end after burying his remains in the backyard. Nothing had been able to remove the black spot from the floor.

Her mind, too, had been stained. Poisoned wine seeping underneath her skin, turning her blood sour and cold. She hadn't slept through the night since she awoke alone in the woods, too terrified to close her eyes. Voices clamored inside her head, screaming among themselves, fighting against the frightening memories replaying in her mind. She didn't understand the language they spoke, but the passion in their voices was clear. All of them spoke words of violence—all of them wanted her dead.

The days had grown long in the absence of sleep, folding one into the next as she remembered what those women had done. Elba recalled the clearing in the woods, the sight of

Mr. Larsen struggling against himself as they held him in invisible binds. Hanna's smiling face, giddy with glee at her pain, happy to have been included. Participation in power, a seat at the Last Supper. Persuasion to partake in all manner of misdeeds. Elba had wanted nothing more than the world when she spent the night on Salem Avenue. But now, living in the aftermath, she wanted nothing to do with witchcraft at all. No false friendships, no magic tricks. She could feel her own power pulsating inside her, and it was real.

Burning brightly like some galaxy far away, existing in between space on an untenable plane. There were no spells or potions to summon this sort of power from somewhere in the dark. This incredible, electric energy had filled her mind, called out to her from the black, empty corners of the universe, and received her response in kind. She had been to invisible places where no one else could go, slipped through shadows to a realm of undiscovered strength. It was parallax and paradox, madness and mystery. She had only just begun to unravel its secrets.

Although the journey to the other side exhausted her, she couldn't resist exploring that foreign world. The perilous uncertainty of it frightened her almost as much as the thought of self-sovereignty thrilled her aching bones. Fear and freedom together drove her to indulge herself once more. Her eyes closed to the coming night and found darkness on their own. She relaxed her mind, falling backward into herself, and soared across the clouds. Lightning flared in fiery bursts sending jagged splinters across the sky, fracturing the atmosphere like a stained-glass sunset. She breathed in the air, tasted the spark-singed smoke.

And far beneath her, in the distance of an unremembered time, the untouched valley that would become Hager's Fancy sat nestled in the crook of the mountains. Elba surveyed the endless tide of auburn trees and autumn leaves falling from their place in the sky to the frozen ground below. And through the thinning branches of the forests, she saw the terrible black spot stretching out across the weeds, suffocating the countryside and sinking its gnarled roots into the dirt. Securing its stranglehold on the city that would one day succumb to its grip.

When she opened her eyes again, she lived someplace aside, a refracted mirage of what she knew. Distortion electrified in the prism of thought, her mind a frenzied, tumultuous place. But in that dizzying chaos, in the absolute static of anarchy, she focused her sights on the world. With a half-finished notion of a thought, she ripped herself from the curses of the past and prepared to wage war with the present time. Summoning the strength of an endless energy that coursed through the threadbare fabric of her universe, she tore the front door from her house and reduced its frame to splinters, which she held suspended in the air. A snap of her neck and she sent them soaring like daggers into the wall.

Her power didn't lie in secret rites or ridiculous words. After all, she had liquefied her father with a thought. This was deeper, more primitive than anyone on Salem Avenue understood. She had eaten of their Mother, tasted Her fungal flesh, but their faith was misplaced in the fruits of the earth. They worshipped a worldly god, but Elba belonged to the stars. And she saw them, standing in a circle around her, hands held tightly together, eyes closed as they stole away her mind. Each of them complicit, all of them culpable for the crime. She would see to it that they were paid back in kind.

Combustion lingered like a dare on the tip of her tongue—she knew no sweeter taste. The image amused her, the forest in flames. An immolation of witches. A thin smile stretched across her cracking lips, pleased by the vibrato in their screams. They sang her a beautiful chorus as the flesh fell in smoldering strips from their bones. It almost stirred some pity in her stomach, but she enjoyed the sound too much.

Johanna Parker's voice was the sweetest of them all, crying out above the rest, begging for it all to end. It would, but not before Elba saw her blood steam through her pores and her boiling skin melt away. Witchcraft dealt in desires—deep, dark, and deadly. Elba desired that they all be strung up for their sins. Her own intentions betrayed their reckless tutelage, but she had already thought to tear herself away. She drew her power from instinct, molding it to herself, allowing it to shape her and control her every breath. Energy coursed through the marrow in her bones, tingling in her fingertips like the spark at the end of a fuse. She thought she might just let it blow.

What they had done to her demanded more than retribution—Elba would make them suffer. The sort of naked humiliation that she had endured at their hands. A public execution befitting the crime of witchcraft. She thought of the time and place, the perfect venue, the manner of carrying out the sentence. The woods would be poetic but practically impossible to spring a trap there on her own. Perhaps at school, on the steps of St. Matthias, the very place of the vigil for Bishop Ford. But none of these could be accomplished without a great deal of effort on the part of Fortune playing into her hands.

Then, out of the corner of her eye, lying discarded on a corner table, Elba spotted a flyer that she had received through the mail. It had been sent to her from St. Matthias.

A plain piece of white paper, branded at the top in macabre, stylized letters:

The Bishop Ford Memorial Performance
of William Shakespeare's
Macbeth

She saw it all igniting in her mind, burning bright as iron weld in flames. A horrible, gruesome spectacle that brought a twisted smile to her face. Elba hadn't set foot in St. Matthias in however many days since she absconded from the forest and hid secluded in her house. She had intended entirely to abandon the play, to muddle through the rest of her years, drifting aimlessly between this world and another, more present place. But this would be too delicious to miss.

She foresaw the old Pembroke Theater, heavy with age and weak from neglect, engulfed in a blinding blaze. The audience, stunned silent, forced to watch the grisly show. Johanna Parker, the evening star, would sing for them all. Elba had not yet conjured fire, but she would try.

The night air bristled with erratic energy on the eve of a swelling storm. The skies above Hager's Fancy were thrown into chaos, colliding on an atomic scale. Lightning flashed before her eyes as she reached out into the void. To her discomfort and unease, it reached back. Somewhere in the dark, some vessel of dynamic energy responded to her own. And she saw it, blinking in the night. From the depths of the black ocean of shadows, a pair of bulbous, emerald eyes gazed endlessly through to her soul. Despite its alien, hypnotic glow, she understood the imp for what it was—a familiar sight, a stray cat sitting on the windowsill.

Its dark hair, black as the night that enveloped its shape, stood on stilted end. Elba wondered at the visitation, a curious sight that caused her discomfort. The lonely thing, vagabond in its own right, beggar on the street. It had a knowing intelligence, a glinting grin that twisted its otherwise innocuous face. Underneath its matted, unkempt fur the whirring of a mind at work, dark machinations turning over like clockwork, intricate and fragile as the same. Elba thought to disrupt the mechanisms inside.

With an intuition like drifting away to sleep, she slipped from her own body and sunk into the sea. Falling forward through the spaces between, across the dividing plane. As Elba descended into another life, she forced the spirit of it from its place.

And suddenly she saw through his eyes, piercing into the night as his lean and slender body shivered against the midnight chill. He pressed against the cold glass of the windowpane, raising his back in an arch to brush beside, to test if it would give way. She moved within him, as though her own back bowed in unison with his. She was within him, dictating his every step, overcoming his sovereign sense. She possessed him entirely.

Her feline face formed a twisted smile in satisfaction at the feat as she anticipated her greatest performance yet to come. She would play the part of the Porter, and she would play it well. At last she understood her role—she would welcome her sisters to Hell. With the grace of an autumn leaf falling to the frosted ground below, she leapt from her perch on the windowsill and dashed away into the night.

[IV]

Time had struck the city like paralysis, and Elba could feel it
in her bones. Reverberations from the past bled through like
watercolor on canvas. She had been to the other side, seen
her bitter world transposed, and come to know the horrors
therein. The sins of another time that were buried beneath
the blacktop but breaking through the cracks.

And those sins lingered like hallucinations in her mind,
poison under the pavement that seeped into the soil and
soured the city streets. Elba had wandered out of space and
found herself frozen in fear, gripped by an alien force. A cold
sweat, a shuddering chill that drilled into her teeth. Grinding to the roots, ripping the stone fruits from fertile ground,
and casting them like litter aside. The endurance of evil
withstood the ages, practiced by the coven of witches in the
woods, nurtured like a mother and her precious, newborn
babe. Their curses persisted in the citizens of Hager's Fancy,
who sat expectantly in the dark, sinking into their polyester
seats as Elba stood petrified on stage.

She gazed out across a rippling sea, blank faces staring
back through soulless eyes. The lights were low, dim enough

to hide their snickering smiles. But the floodlight had found her, blinded her to all else. Daggers to the eyes, she felt it pierce her, driving all attention to her.

Alone at the center of the stage, the only woman in the world. She felt the gravity of her performance impress upon her, dragging her down below, deep into the earth. Suffocation began to set in, collapsing her lungs beneath the impossible weight of enormous pressure. Her fingers dug into the dirt, clawing her way back to the surface, but she only fell further in. A loud knocking came from offstage. She lifted her eyes and breathed in the hot, industrial air.

"Here's a knocking, indeed!" she began, finding her voice in the back of her throat. "If a man were porter of Hell-gate, he should have old turning the key."[13]

The costume sat heavy on her shoulders, an oversized set of rags and a lopsided beret. Her face had been painted like a clown, exaggerated features forcing a frown as a single tear ran down her cheek. The trapdoor at the center of the stage groaned as she shifted her weight, threatening to collapse as it had before and fall out from under her. She reached into her pocket to produce a large, rusted key. Another knocking came from offstage.

"Knock, knock, knock! Who's there, in the name of Beelzebub?"[14]

Elba pranced about the stage, fully committed to the act. She reveled in the odd charade, delighting in the souls she would condemn. In gleeful anticipation of her final act, she mimed maître d' to Hell.

---

13 William Shakespeare, *Macbeth, The Folger Shakespeare, Folger Shakespeare Library*, 2020, 2.3.1-3.

14 Ibid., 2.3.3-4.

"Here's a farmer that hanged himself on the expectation of plenty. Come in time, have napkins enough about you. Here, you'll sweat for it."[15]

Scuttling to the other side of the stage, she made way for the souls of the damned to fill her hall. The trapdoor creaked beneath her feet as she bounded across. The heat from the spotlight beaming down from above had caused her to sweat. With a ridiculous flourish, she pulled a white handkerchief from her pocket and waved it about her face. She touched it gently to her forehead, smearing the paint as the colors ran together. Knocking again, louder this time.

"Knock, knock! Who's there, in the other devil's name?"[16]

She danced back across, stuffing the handkerchief into her collar like a judge's cravat. With the oversized key in her hand, she gestured wildly as if she were holding a gavel, calling order to the demons in her domain.

"Faith, here's an equivocator that could swear in both the scales against either scale, who committed treason enough for God's sake, yet could not equivocate to Heaven. O, come in, equivocator."[17]

Knocking, desperate now.

"Knock, knock! Never at quiet. What are you?"[18]

She feigned speculation before shivering from an invisible chill, wrapping her rags around her.

---

15   Ibid., 2.3.4-6.

16   Ibid., 2.3.7-8.

17   Ibid., 2.3.8-12.

18   Ibid., 2.3.15-16.

"But this place is too cold for Hell. I'll devil-porter it no further. I had thought to have let in some of all professions that go the primrose way to the everlasting bonfire."[19]

A final knocking came, the loudest of them all. Elba turned to look offstage and saw a group of her peers, prepared to enter the scene.

"Anon, anon! I pray you, remember the porter."[20]

She darted offstage with the practiced poise of a lumbering fool. Once out of sight, the act disappeared and Elba assumed an alternate air. One of sincerity and purpose as the darkness beyond the stage consumed her. Her brow furrowed and her plans came together, gears and cogs fitting one into the next as the machine droned with clandestine activity. She strode directly to the dressing room, where she found herself a seat. There she would wait, listening for her cue. The play would unfold according to the script, murder after murder, scene after scene, until Johanna Parker returned to the stage. Then, Elba would play her part.

Act III rolled slowly across the stage like a mid-summer storm cloud sounding its thunderous alarm. Men were killed and kings betrayed as Elba focused her mind. Blood spilled freely from the throats of thanes and spattered across castle walls. The banquet scene at last arrived, calling forth the bloody ghost. Elba rose up from her mouldering grave and floated from the dressing room toward the stage.

She waited in the wings, beside a weapons prop table, listening to the soft reverberations of her classmates' voices, murmurs through the walls. The story passed with painfully slow progression. The audience remained silent, save for the

19   Ibid., 2.3.16-19.

20   Ibid., 2.3.20-21.

occasional coughing fit induced by the swirling dust in the air. Elba could feel the age of the building in every groaning creak and moan, the stage grinding like the hull of an ancient ship sailing toward the sirens' shores. Only there was no mythic allure to drag them all to the bottom of the sea. Their demise would fall to her own hands.

Her fingers cracked with electric bursts that she drew from some other place, that invigorating energy that she had tasted only a few times before. She knew that it was dangerous and she knew that it could kill. The air around her hissed with intemperate heat as she reached out toward someplace beyond the theater, through the thinning atmosphere, inviting interference from across the temporal plane. She needed only snap her fingers and break her sister's neck.

But that would be too clean, too painless a fate for her, and for the rest who had stolen her away. Elba plucked an old, rusted dagger from the prop table and admired it in her hand. Its cold, corroded steel came abruptly to a point, which she pressed against the tip of her finger. She drew just a drop of blood before she slipped the dagger into the pocket of her rags, concealed in the folds of her costume. All she would have to do was wait.

The play concluded its first act and the audience prepared for intermission. The scene ended as the lights came down and the theater was plunged into darkness. Haunting music played through the house as members of the stage crew bustled about, carrying away pieces of the rudimentary set, returning with a large, black cauldron. Elba's heart shuddered with excitement. The stage was set and the players stood ready, robed and wrinkled like hags. Hanna Parker stood among them, staring at Elba's painted face. Her makeup remained smeared in a distorted grimace, a frown that said more than Elba could. The two had not spoken since the woods.

"Hello, Elba."

The remark was matter-of-fact, no warmth or pleasure in the greeting. Elba thought nothing of it, as she bore none in return. But she would bare all in time, naked in power for the entire town to see. Her own fingers trembled with the energy of another world, ready to leap across the universe and tear this girl apart. Facing Hanna here, Elba shivered at the thought. But she did not want to play her hand too early.

"How have you been?"

Something in Hanna's voice sounded different, more mature. More assertive than before, as if her voice were not her own. As if Elba questioned whether she exercised control. And she was suddenly in the woods again, fallen prey into their trap. But this time, Elba had lain one of her own, a spider in her web, mandibles salivating in expectation of a meal. The bloodlust raced underneath her creeping skin, building like a symphony or a wave about to crest.

The crescendo neared a fever pitch as the stage crew set the cauldron in place. The audience filtered back into their seats and the music began to fade out. Before Elba could speak another word, Hanna and the other witches stepped out from behind the curtain and took their places on the stage.

The lights rose on a gruesome scene, sickly greens and gory reds shining down on a Halloween sight. Three witches in rags hunched over a bubbling brew, belching billowing smoke from the gaping mouth of the black cauldron. Pale fog rolled like rattling waves across the blustering heath, the final breath exhaled from a dead man's mouth, completing the spectacle of the moors.

"Round about the cauldron go—in the poisoned entrails throw. Toad, that under cold stone, days and nights has thirty-one sweltered venom, sleeping got. Boil thou first in the charmed pot."[21]

One of the witches tossed a rubber frog into the cauldron as they all circled about in a mesmerizing dance, echoing a chant that seemed itself to turn in dizzying somersaults on itself. Elba resisted joining in the spell herself as she watched from her place in the wings.

"Double, double, toil and trouble—fire burn and cauldron bubble."[22]

They each cast in turn, adding ingredients more ghastly and gruesome than the last, tossing plastic props into the great and horrible thing. Swollen clouds of white smoke rose on the stale air of the theater and dissipated into the angry beam of light above.

"For a charm of powerful trouble, like a hell-broth boil and bubble."[23]

Pyrotechnic lighting flashed across their faces as thunder rattled the room. Elba was uncertain whether it sounded from the speakers or the sky above.

"Double, double, toil and trouble—fire burn and cauldron bubble."[24]

Faster now, the chant escaped them against any intentions, spilling from their lips like wine overflowing from chalices made of gold. Intoxicating liquor, hypnotic to the tongue. The witches themselves stumbled drunk into the

---

21   Ibid., 4.1.4-9.

22   Ibid., 4.1.10-11.

23   Ibid., 4.1.18-19.

24   Ibid., 4.1.20-21.

spell, conjuring in rapid succession. With each new rhyming couplet, their spastic motions jerked more erratically, uncontrollable movements that belonged to someone else.

"Scale of dragon."

"Tooth of wolf."

"Witch's mummy."

"Maw and gulf of the ravined salt-sea shark."

"Root of hemlock digged in the dark."[25]

Elba stared transfixed from the shadows as she thought they might really be casting some spell. The false fire burning at the base of the cauldron cast their faces in the garish fashion of a taxidermist, excelsior shavings stuffed underneath sallow, leather skin. But Elba knew magic, and it was much more visceral than this.

"Finger of birth-strangled babe, ditch-delivered by a drab."

"Make the gruel thick and slab."

"Add thereto a tiger's chawdron, for the ingredients of our cauldron."[26]

A final dance around the fire, the chant a steady rhythm of primal nature, the words losing their worth in the pounding beat of feet against the floor and voices rising to the clamoring clouds.

"Double, double, toil and trouble—fire burn and cauldron bubble."[27]

With a steady breath and determined stride, Elba stepped forward from her hidden place offstage, pushing back the heavy curtain and marching onto the proscenium. The harsh light burned against her skin as she stared out into the crowd.

---

25   Ibid., 4.1.22-25.

26   Ibid., 4.1.30-34.

27   Ibid., 4.1.35-36.

This time, she saw their faces, their eyes like ancient jewels set loosely in the coronet of their hollow heads. Vapid, unencumbered by concern. But their piercing gaze in a single beam bore into Elba's brain. Her stores of energy were suddenly stripped away as her face fell in discomfort to match her painted frown. The witches ceased their undulations and turned to see her, uninvited, acting against the dictates of the script. And there stood Hanna among them, alarmed at Elba's appearance.

"What are you—?"

The moment had arrived—she had been there in her mind. The theater engulfed, windows shattering and patrons screaming. Hanna burning for her sins. She had felt the heat of the flames. But she would not conjure fire from her hands, nor could she feel the familiar pricking of energy like needles in her skin. The inertia that had threatened to burst from her fingertips before had vanished from the theater. Instead, she stood terrified in front of the entire school and its benefactors, all of whom had attended in support of the memory of a man they had despised.

"Get off the stage," urged one of the other witches, oblivious to Elba's intentions. But Hanna seemed as if she knew. Her eyes widened, concerned and filled once more with the life of her, that apathetic air draining entirely as though she had regained control. She let out a panicked, pleading cry as her voice cracked with sudden sobs.

"Elba, please—"

"No."

She drew the dagger from her rags and trained it on Hanna's chest. The other witches ran hurriedly offstage, abandoning the ancient ritual and letting the show come to a screeching halt. The audience remained silent, save for a few selective murmurs. Most of them hadn't the slightest idea how *Macbeth* was supposed to unfold. Still, some were beginning to suspect that something had gone wrong.

"Elba—"

There was something Hanna wanted desperately to say, but Elba had no desire to hear it. The trapdoor creaked underneath her feet, which she planted firmly center stage. The cauldron continued to bubble, spewing smoke overhead as the lights flickered from the thunder raging in her mind. She struggled to breathe in the punishing heat of the spotlights, sweat spilling in heavy droplets down the sides of her face. Her makeup ran in staining streaks, which hid the tears gathering in her eyes.

Hanna reached out her hand toward Elba, who held the dagger outstretched and aimed directly at Hanna's heart. But Elba held firm, strengthening her arm and maintaining her grip on the handle. Every moment filled her mind to the bursting point, the witches and the woods and the house on Salem Avenue. She pressed the point of the dagger against Hanna's chest, forcing her to stop where she stood. The entire theater trembled as the audience at last understood that something was terribly wrong.

Fury fumed in Elba's fists as fire sparked the smoke rising in her lungs. It would be easy to take a single step forward, to push the cold steel deep into Hanna's heart, to spill every ounce of her blood out onto the stage. To send her life flowing freely from her chest as the whole of Hager's Fancy looked on in useless horror. Or it should have been, if not for her own misgivings. Something subtle inside pulled at the sinews in her muscles, marionette strings drawing the dagger back.

Reflections of another world, mirrored in reverse, echoes across dimensions. Images of what might have been. She sensed true sorrow in Hanna's sobbing, memories that ripped out her heart. Regret and rejection of everything that Mother had done, of everything that Hanna had endured. The hatred that burned brightly before suddenly collapsed into a smothering heap of embers and ash.

The cinders steamed as tears fell from above and forgiveness overwhelmed her weary heart. Elba's arm dropped to her side, the dagger heavy in her hand, as Hanna took one final step forward. And there came between them an understanding, the truth transmitted in thought. Hanna held Elba in a close embrace for the briefest moment, but the trapdoor buckled and the floor splintered underneath.

They both dropped like stones in water, falling forever down to Wonderland below. The stage rose up into the sky as the world around them froze in midair. Elba saw it all in excruciating detail, the sharpened splinters of shattered wood tumbling in endless somersaults, the cauldron and its electric contents spilling out across the stage, wires and sockets exposed to the broken planks.

In immobile moments, they plummeted through to the trap room far below. A cold and empty place, darkness consuming the concrete floor and cobweb ceiling underneath. A room of shadows that hadn't been surveyed in years. As they twisted in the dark, Elba saw a circle drawn in white—

She heard her legs snap before she felt them break. Her head hit the concrete as Hanna's body collapsed on top of hers, heavy and limp. Unable to breathe, gasping hopelessly for air, Elba let out a silent scream. The pain was dizzying, white hot in her head. It blurred her vision, promising to take it all away. She thought for a moment to give in and let herself sink away, but she felt something wet and warm flowing between her hands.

She lifted Hanna off her broken body, setting her gently onto her back, only to see the dagger plunged deep into her breast, the handle pointing toward the sky. Blood poured, vulgar and intimate, from Hanna's lifeless form. The dagger had found its way directly into her heart.

A maddening cry came from the dark, shrieking at the bloody, violent mess. Mother, laced in white, ran screaming into the circle on the floor.

"*What did you do?*"

"Nothing, I didn't—"

As Mother cradled her daughter's stiffening corpse, other women, like spiders, crawled out from the dark and held Elba's arms in place. They pressed their weight against her, crushing her wrists and forcing her hands splayed open. All of them were robed in red, simple vestments that signified a deeper purpose. More of them moved to her legs, which were twisted and bent, bleeding and split open to the bone. Wails of grief turned to screams of rage as Mother seized her broken legs and forced them far apart. The women stripped Elba of her oversized costume and pressed their dirty fingers to her stomach, jagged fingernails dragging along her abdomen.

"Don't fucking touch me!"

Another of them drew a long, silver instrument from her robes—a slender sickle that glinted in the stray stage light. Mother seized it in her hand before holding it against Elba's skin.

"Why are you doing this?"

Elba was pleading for her life, but she feared that her breath was wasted on the mercies of witches. She could see that they were, all of them, lost to the worship of the world.

"Please—"

"*It is too late to stop it,*" Mother cried inside of Elba's mind. "*Häxan cannot be denied—the ritual must be complete. If you struggle, our cuts will not be clean.*"

A commotion had risen in the theater, members of the audience and students in the cast rushing toward the front of the house to see what had happened, their thunderous footsteps echoing from the other side of the world. But the stage had caught fire and the curtain was burning up above. In the freeing desperation of fear, Elba gathered what strength she had and reached out to the universe from someplace within. A moment of silent uncertainty passed before it reached back and grasped her by the hand, filling her to the brim of her brow with a bristling, perilous energy. She screamed as her mind split open, tearing through her skull with the heat of a dying star.

Mother pressed the point of the sickle to Elba's stomach and ripped her body open wide. Glistening streams of blood and gory bits of meat spilled from her abdomen. In an unthinking instant, Elba snapped the necks of each of her sisters in the room—she saved Mother for herself. Their lifeless bodies collapsed like crumpling paper as the fire above raged out of control. Elba heard Mother's screams in her mind but she saw only blinding light. Whether she had become fully imbued with absolute fury or some higher, less earthly sense, she attained existence beyond thought.

Elba rose up on broken legs, standing on her shattered feet as her muscles and organs fell out onto the floor. Throwing herself forward, she gripped Mother by the throat. Her fingers were fire that branded and burned, eating through flesh like acid to the touch. Mother shrieked in pain as her skin boiled from her bones, muscles bursting from the heat and nerves blackening underneath. But Elba kept her heart beating, preserved the sensations in her brain. Her own skin began to blister and boil, her body trembling from the impossible power she possessed.

The pressure mounted like a bullet in a gun, a powder keg catching fire and exploding outward in a burst of kinetic light. She held it back for as long as she could, but she was a conductor, calling lightning to her body as though she could conjure it down from the sky. She made sure Mother felt it all before crushing her heart and grinding her bones to dust. And in the death of Mother, she was complete, the captain of her destiny at last. In all the tragedies she endured, Elba had found the peace of days. But there was nothing she could do to stop the fire from consuming her entirely as her body vanished into the flames.

In the shockwave that ensued, the earth beneath the burning theater collapsed inward on itself. The old Pembroke jostled in the air before splitting down the middle, an enormous crack in the foundation darting upward to the very peak of the roof. A radiant gleam pierced the dark, the brilliant full-phased moon shining vividly through the fissure. At once, the walls were ripped apart and the theater crumbled to pieces. Brick and stone tumbled down onto the audience below as a crater opened like a grave and the rotted dirt swallowed them all.

***

Night fell soft over Hager's Fancy in the deafening aftermath of the day. The city grew silent and the trees stood bare as the purple sky unveiled diamonds overhead. Far away points dancing in the clouds, distant and cold galaxies of undiscovered horrors waiting to be told. Those stars glistened with a remote indifference, watching from above as the Eye of Providence, callously guiding the course of the universe.

NECROPOLIS

FALLING DOWN

Beneath the blossoming sunrise over San Lorenzo, where the blacktop ran thick and slow, Michael Foster woke with an unexpected start. He had been falling down, faster than the force of gravity, helpless to the horrible fantasy in his head. Hurtling toward the desert sands, past the jagged mountain peaks, he plummeted at a pace far greater than any he had known. In the alarming velocity of the descent, his eyes refused to shut as he surveyed the landscape below. A valley of dry bones, besieged by a rattling sound that echoed through the clouds. Flesh and blood grew out of the ground and pulled the bones together, tendons and sinews sewing separate bodies together. Skin grafted onto their muscles and meat as they rose up from the dead, breaking free from their graves and crying out that their hope had gone. But there was no breath in them.

The mattress shifted under the weight of his impact as he felt the rusted springs press into his body. His memory had suddenly fled and he could not remember anything other than pure sensation, no details of the dream that had a moment before gripped him by the throat. He rarely could, unable to explain the horrors in his head. Those were unaccounted hours, darkened places in his memory that were hidden away from view. He often wondered where those moments disappeared, whether they had truly existed at all. Whether some piece of him had been taken, stolen away by the secrecy of the night.

Angry at no one but himself, he rolled onto his back with an indignant huff and groaned at the golden sunlight streaking into his room. His alarm clock glared at him from his nightstand, burning brightly in the dark—never had 5:30 a.m. looked so menacing as displayed in piercing, electric red. It began to scream, an ugly, terrible pitch puncturing his eardrums and drilling into his brain. He threw his arm over to the nightstand and slammed his fist down with a reckless disregard. Moloch demanded he make a sacrifice, and so his body would burn on the pyre of industry. The call to worship drew him like venom from his bed and brought him back to life.

Reanimation required little more than a shock to the system and the threat of living on the streets. He had considered for a moment remaining in bed, calling in sick and staying at home to nurse the fever that had been burning inside his head for the better part of a week. But his supervisor would have his head if he missed a day of work without giving advance notice. Across the city, where the glass façade of Pacific Union Towers refracted daggers of light into his eyes, his desk stood surrounded on all sides by the thin, carpeted walls of a cubicle.

Michael tore himself from the comfort of his bed and threw his curtains wide, revealing the skyline of the city below. Far above the desert sands, towering over the jagged mountain peaks, the magnificent summit of Los Huesos glistened downtown with the radiance and gleam of a thousand golden flames catching fire in the sky. An oasis in Arabia, the mirage of a madman wavering in the insufferable heat. Beckoning to the innocent passersby, unaware that the glittering towers holding up the sky stood hollow overhead, deceptive self-importance that promised impossible things.

At the center of it all, Pacific Union Towers cast shadows over the great expanse of the suburban sprawl and the desert beyond. Tucked away on the southern side of the 37th floor, Casualty Insurance Co. waited patiently, almost indifferently for his arrival. A hostile place uninviting in the cruel fluorescent glow of the overhead lights, though this failed to eclipse the afternoon aggressions of his supervisor. Whether the man maintained an agreeable disposition solely for his ten o'clock meetings or his morning mixture of medium roast and prescription painkillers had worn off by lunch, he adopted a decidedly more menacing demeanor as the day wore on. A predator on the prowl, stalking his prey among the thicket and the thorns.

Among the grasslands of the desert plains, where the discontent grew out of control like weeds across the earth, he found the inattentive employee and pounced with bloody claws. A jungle to be sure, a vicious tangle of thicket and invasive species spawning in the underbrush before tearing the canopy apart. In the oblivious world between, Michael managed to assemble the distorted mirage of a career. There he would spend his days, dutiful and mindless of the crumbling world outside. But he had already begun to doubt the fortitude of an institution so fragile as to fall at the encroaching appetite of a weevil in the dirt.

He stared deep into his tired eyes in the mirror as his face fell long and wrinkled in the unforgiving light of the bathroom. A harsh, relentless glow that brought every imperfection to the surface, pulling open every pore and draining the color from his skin. He wanted to tear it all away, to rip the flesh from his bones and leave the blood and the puss underneath exposed. But appearances had to be kept, and the people on the streets would consider him accordingly.

Though he felt weighted by the throbbing headaches and bitter sweats that seized him throughout the day, he had no time or occasion to heed their warning calls. Rather than resting for the day in bed sedated by a handful of generic pain relievers, he moved from the temperate steam of the bathroom to the less comfortable climate of his condominium thinking of how he would dress.

His closet was a cramped and dusty corner of the room, filled with an unassuming assortment of collared shirts and wrinkled ties patterned with the most appropriate of checkers and stripes. He selected a short-sleeved, off-white oxford button down and a similarly nondescript navy-blue necktie. Throwing them on like a disguise, he assembled the visage of a gentleman, a mild-mannered cosmopolitan urbanite. Horn-rimmed glasses, cap-toe shoes, and his hair held down with pomade. He slung his leather Vitali messenger bag around his shoulder and walked briskly out the door.

The streets of Los Huesos teemed with activity in the early morning hours. Already the desert heat had drawn the citizens of the sand forward from their mangled hovels and out onto the busy sidewalks. Broken people praying to the gods of the wasteland, waiting for the sweet reprieve of their own salvation.

San Lorenzo was a poor neighborhood on the lower east side, overflowing with the more indigent inhabitants of the city. Those steep, inclining hills far from the salt spray of the sea, rising along the shattered ridge of the snow-capped San Gabriel peaks, held hostage the helpless and oppressed. Angelic as it seemed, the cruelty of the concrete lurked just beneath the surface.

Michael moved among the destitute, dispossessed of their identities and left naked in the heat. Those who had homes had yet to sell them to the incoming classes of professionals, people with money to spare and time to lose. Whether out of some misguided sense of pride or else in spite of their better judgements he couldn't be sure, but he wished they would get on with it. Michael had placed a down payment on his own condominium on the expectation of enormous profit, only to find that San Lorenzo was slow to gentrify.

Still, the neighborhood maintained a quiet dignity, a subdued and stubborn charm in the face of crushing poverty and crime. History storied by a people who had been there long before, who had refused to surrender themselves to the collapse of an inescapable past. Michael could see something noble in the pursuit of a pure and simple life, striving for success in spite of the violence in the streets. To carve out a corner of the universe to call your own—he had tried to do this himself. But the crumbling infrastructure underneath struggled to support the city as the cracks in the concrete threatened to rip the people apart from their roots. They had grown loyal and deep, faithful to a fault, but those faceless bureaucrats seated in the skies above did little to preserve what semblances of civility remained.

Distressingly aware of the time, Michael passed between puddles of vomit and urine that baked in the insufferable heat and dried in a crust on the concrete. The smell of the city sat thick above the sidewalk like smoke that burned his eyes, drawing tears from inside his head. But the vacant corpses lying indifferent on the ground breathed it in deep, unaffected by the rancid fumes that clung to their skin and their clothes. Their senses had been dulled beyond all use by the black venom that coursed through their veins.

As the minutes slipped persistently away, a distorted flash of tailored suits and blazers trim at the waist rushed by, nearly tripping over shoes too new and too expensive to become the dignified modesty of an office ensemble. Michael moved among them, careful not to attract the attention of any particular vagrant, averting his eyes and discreetly holding his breath. But one of them caught his attention, a lonely man sitting cross-legged on the ground in front of a rusted, metal overhead door tagged in graffiti. His clothes were stained with gutter filth and his beard had streaks of grey. His trembling hands held between them a torn and tattered cardboard sign. As Michael passed him by, he read the message scrawled in faded ink:

EAT THE RICH.

The stench of the street filled his head like the hammering of construction crews in the early morning hours. Entire neighborhoods had succumbed to the smell, the grime and the grease that boiled in the sun and baked into the pavement. The primitive den of a pitiful horde, burrowed in so far that their removal posed an impossible task. The effort on the part of the city to amputate them from the body, or else to apply a snake-oil salve to the gangrene, served only to incite combustible concerns. Tensions had increased in the tinderbox to a fever pitch. Any wayward spark would set the city ablaze.

Like a bitter lacquer layered on thick, the odor of San Lorenzo hung still and dense in the air. Michael Foster pushed through it as he stepped in line with the crowd, joining the hurried masses in their familiar morning hustle. It was sometimes difficult to distinguish between the homeless and the inhabitants of the shimmering mausoleums and concrete complexes in the sky. There, secluded in a solace of their own design, detached from the otherwise inseparable arteries that ran the length of the underground, they assumed the role of the other. Solitude, the occasion of their sin, excised them like cancer from society. In that self-inflicted status of isolation, pestilence set in. The people were as diseased as the city, sick in their heads with all manner of rot.

Deep beneath the incontinent weeds, where the earth trembled and the lamplights shook, the metrorail roared to life alongside the fury of the flocking millions. Michael turned the corner to San Lorenzo Station and descended the grinding escalator to the cold and lonely tunnels down below. The crowds jostled about as they stood impatiently in line, jumbling against one another as the rickety, rusted out machine creaked and moaned under their weight. Rather than proceeding step by step, the passengers aboard stood resting on their heels as though they had no other place to be.

Michael stood restlessly in place, trapped behind an enormous woman with a handbag the size of a suitcase, leaning haphazardly on the handrail. He was unable to move past her, caught in a vise that had begun to squeeze his temples and fracture the sides of his skull. He called out politely, asking if she might let him pass by, but his voice fell on oblivious ears.

Resigned either to endure the dreadful descent in languishing silence or shove the insensible woman and send her stumbling end over useless end, collapsing onto the concrete floor and splattering what wasted brains she had, Michael chose to submit to the inescapable and stand in muted protest. His jagged fingernails dug into the palms of his hands as he fell increasingly behind schedule. The escalator descended at a dawdling pace as the minutes escaped his grasp, slipping away with every wasted moment. He glanced half-hesitantly at the watch wound tight around his wrist and saw the second hand tick persistently past twelve time and time again. One minute, two minutes, three minutes, four....

With a sudden jolt of the escalator and a leap from his place on the stair, he darted past the lumbering form in front of him and ran toward the gate. He whipped out his faded, plastic metro card and waited in line as the tired procession of commuters scanned their own, pressing forward through the metal turnstiles and continuing to the platform beyond. He tapped his card impatiently against his fingers like a conductor's baton as he moved at gradual but consistent intervals, closer and closer with every step. A pall bearer for the casket of his days, a clumsy, altogether useless effort to lay himself to rest as he marched incessantly on. Just as he reached his turn at the gate, a young man dressed all in black, hood pulled over his head, shoved him aside and jumped over the gate.

Michael felt affronted at the act, insulted as though he had just been robbed. He had witnessed this behavior before, but the shameless disregard for law and order brought a sudden fire in his gut to light. He looked to the station manager's booth, which was occupied by a broad-shouldered man with an uninterested, weary look across his face. Michael pleaded with his eyes, hoping from a distance that the manager might see and, at the very least, enforce the posted fine. He thought to himself that, had he followed suit and leapt over the barriers, he would be apprehended at once and the extent of the law would be imposed.

The injustice scalded his stomach, burned a blackened hole through his heart. He wanted to call out to the young man, to hold him accountable to the rules that would undoubtedly apply to him. But he failed to find the tenor of his voice, and the young man slipped away. The crowd behind him knocked about with a volatile, unstable fervor that compelled him to move ahead. Defeated by the echo of his involuntary silence, he scanned his card across the sensor and pushed his way through the gate.

The train careened through the concrete tunnels underground as its passengers held tightly to their seats. Michael stood on unsteady legs, gripping a rusted metal pole impaled through the belly of his compartment, tossed recklessly around as it rocked unevenly on its tracks.

He glanced at the faces of the passengers beside him, each of them more crestfallen than the last. The car had been stuffed full with commuters well on their way to work, nearly bursting through the doors. The daily slog across the city took its toll on those burdened with the journey, backs bent and shoulders slumped as they trudged through the thickening smog. The smell corroded his nostrils, stinging his insides like an insidious swarm. He wondered at its source, eyes wandering between overcoats and undershirts protruding through muted oxford button-downs and blushing floral blouses. Perhaps it was the smell of the people themselves, their bodies sweating through their clothes and their breath hanging heavy in the air. Their voices joined together in a barrage of senseless conversations, ringing in his ears like the cacophony of an untrained choir crying Handel's "Hallelujah."

"This is... Porfirio Plaza. Doors opening on the left."

The floodgates broke open and the waters burst forth as the car emptied of half its passengers, only to be filled again with the same sort of figures dressed in slacks, hair drawn back tight against the scalp. A pair of slender women, talking excitedly to one another, boarded with their heads hung low and their voices hushed. Just behind them, dressed in an oversized winter jacket and denim jeans stained with dirt, a tall man entered the car and stood conspicuously beside them. Their eyes filled with disquiet apprehension, shifting among the other passengers surrounding them on all sides.

Michael observed their unease from a distance as the doors shut and the train lurched forward, speeding along its rusted, groaning tracks. Metal screeched against grinding metal, tearing through the foundation of the city with the thundering roar of a hurricane, ripping roofs from houses and knocking buildings to the ground. The man staggered on his feet, tripping over himself and holding tightly to the pole where Michael stood. The two women held onto a pair of overhead handles and took a sudden interest in the floor.

The man slurred a string of stolen words together as Michael watched the women pull away, doing what they could to avoid meeting his bloodshot eyes. But he insisted on their attention, pressing further toward them and refusing to give up the game. Michael didn't know if the man was drunk or high or simply out of his mind. No one else seemed to notice anything particularly out of place, staring down at their laps or getting lost in a weather-worn, paperback book.

Electric tunnel lights screamed by like white flashes of lightning in spring, cracking through the broken sky and splitting open Michael's mind. He saw them all reflected, shattered shards of stained glass falling from above, raining over the summer city with the surprise of a sudden storm.

Though they were all of them enjoined for the moment through the unavoidable communion of public transportation, their individual lives were divided across infinite experiences, refracted by the disparate days and uneven hours that tore the city apart. Uninvited association with members of another class brought the building pressure within the hurtling metro car to an unbearable, agonizing swell. A boil budding beneath the skin, liquid puss and hardened tissue rising to the surface and threatening to burst in a bloody, bruising pulp.

"*This is… 7th Street Metro Center. Doors opening on the left.*"

Michael stole one last look at the two women cowering in the corner, caught by the man accosting them, glancing fearfully about the crowd at anyone who might stand between them. He thought for a moment to help them, to seize the man by his arm and force him off the train, but his own sense of self-preservation forbade him from interfering. He had seen this scenario unfold before—foolish bystanders finding a flash of steel, stabbed in the stomach or shot in the chest for standing firm in the face of fear.

The doors would not remain open for long, and this station was his stop. He had already fallen significantly behind his morning schedule and could not afford to waste further time. Had he sustained a stronger constitution, regarded himself with greater fortitude, he might have made an effort nonetheless. With an uncertain resolution and a swift, uneven stride, he stepped from the car and onto the concrete platform where he fell once again into the crowd.

Downtown Los Huesos swarmed with activity as the morning sun beat down onto the blacktop. The people below swarmed in an excited parade, the procession of insects scurrying across a vulnerable wasteland in an effort to please their sovereign queen. The financial district towered above 7th Street, dizzying skyscrapers dominating the skyline overhead, the Wall Street of the West. Pacific Union Towers soared among the tallest, a pair of impressive monuments to industry, imposing upon the coastal silhouettes that stood in their shadows.

Michael rose above the sparkling sea and the urban sprawl, packed into an elevator ascending Pacific Union South, steadily climbing to the thirty-seventh floor. Pressed between the cheap texture of polyester shoulder pads and the invasive aroma of concentrated hairspray, he tried not to breathe in the poison cloud of perfume and cologne that had polluted the air.

Every other woman seemed to be wearing the latest line of Elizabeth Valencia business wear, imported fabrics and expensive stitching that served only to augment their otherwise inflated egos. Every other man had adopted the shallow visage of a gentleman, Michael among them. Hair trimmed short and parted on the side, held in place by a fragrant pomade, patterned neckties pulled tight, clipped securely to the placket of their crisp, freshly-pressed Oxford shirts. These adornments like a mask made sure that his polished exterior kept hidden his crude condition underneath.

Respectability, that elusive sense of social affect held him above the stinking streets with an elitist air that smelled of stale cigarettes and warm liquor. But they all smelled the same, each of them similarly cynics buried just below the surface of an artificial sheen, rotting from the inside out.

Each new manufactured frame that found its way into the already overstuffed elevator only added to the discomfort— painted faces on parade.

There, in that shuddering box suspended in the air, packed together like so many matches dried in the arid heat, the occupants of the elevator trembled as the cables above creaked and threatened to snap. But the machine droned on until it reached the thirty-seventh floor with a clear, electric chime. Michael stepped promptly between the grinding doors and into a long, unending hallway. Hung at the entrance, in letters blazing red, a large sign declared, "Casualty Insurance Co." Adjusting his messenger bag as it hung haphazardly from his shoulder, he strode with an assumption of confidence toward the office door.

Sitting behind his little metal desk, cramped into the corners of his carpeted cubicle, Michael stared blankly at the hostile, glaring screen of his desktop computer. Humming loudly and giving off an anxious glow, it was a relic from another year, past its prime but lingering on with a stubborn refusal to fall into place at the bottom of yesterday's garbage heap. But the analog clock told time with just as much vigor and faith as any other—until the hands grew weak and its mechanical bones slowed their measured march. Tripping out of step, the minutes would be lost without their calculated counterparts, ticking steadily away.

"...violence on the Red Line this morning. Two women were stabbed multiple times in the stomach by a man in an oversized jacket between 7th Street and San Pedro. They were both taken to Good Samaritan and are last reported to be in critical condition. Witnesses to the attack have stated that the suspect fled on foot. In other news, the sweeping epidemic plaguing the homeless population of Los Huesos worsens by the hour. Without a single report from the *Times*, the *World*, or the *Maine*..."

Michael tried to ignore the buzzing static of the radio, the familiar, grating wail of the most arresting of tragedies. The businesses broadcasting news reports by trade trafficked in calamity. The man in the cubicle beside him absorbed it daily, listened to the litany of languishing men and women fallen victim to the despots of the streets. Dictators of the blacktop, their subjects suffering in the sludge, maintained their miserable rule over the residents of Skid Row. The city had lost control over the expanding empire of poverty and blood oppressed by untouchable tyrants.

Whatever solutions had been devised, each new attempt to curtail the contagion, they were dismantled in an instant with as little effort as could be obtained. The symptoms were acute and the diagnosis was swift, proscribing the patients to the outskirts of society, banishing them to the peripheries of the mind. In all the dramatic renditions of the day's misfortunes and misdeeds, Michael still determined it would be difficult to assign fault where none could be found. But where blame could be assigned in spades, he felt little sympathy.

The computer screen turned black while Michael sat staring at nothing, lost in the half-formed meanderings of his mind. He pressed the space key with a careless shift and brought his spreadsheet back to life. Names of clients crossed by columns accounting for policies and wealth, net worth that far exceeded his own expectations for success. Assets and actuaries, assessments of the future that failed to inspire any doubt. He worked in the fraud investigations division of Casualty Insurance Co., managing the life settlement portfolios of institutional investors. It was a morbid business to gamble on the lives of perfect strangers, but exceptionally lucrative to play a winning hand.

The morning passed in a maddening charade of compliments and niceties, calling the various insureds under the extensive collection of policies to record any changes in health. He was really only meant to discover if any of them had died and to report to the policy owner if they had, but this seemed to him more tactful. And he would get his answer nonetheless, if at the expense of a few fruitless minutes of conversation.

Still, in all the senile sentiments expressed over static-laced telephone lines, he found comfort in their soft, uncertain voices. Elderly women left alone in their fading twilight, men made to grieve for the futility of their work, grateful for a moment's cold reception. But his supervisor disapproved, preferring instead that he work with a detached sense of isolation, ignorant of the living thing on the other side. This was the order of the day—to maintain a disconnected distance from any shade of involvement, to obtain his vital answer and move dispassionately on.

"Yes, ma'am. I understand, but we really aren't concerned with your present financial situation. You sold your policy almost two years ago."

The man whining on with a dreary, indelicate tone in the cubicle beside him had introduced himself as Rinaldo Torres nearly three years ago. Michael had not spoken to him since, and their working relationship seemed not to have suffered in the slightest. He had no doubts that, had he on occasion invited Rinaldo to engage him in small talk and false pleasantries, he might have done something he would regret.

"We just need to know that you haven't died."

With every rude aside, at every snide remark, Michael imagined something terrible. Rinaldo sat oblivious by the window, overlooking the expanse of the ocean, soaking in the sunlight and the sea. He never noticed Michael's tired temperament, the way in which he tolerated the tone of his voice. At once, Michael thought to rise from his seat, to cast aside his stolen sentiments, and crush his calloused heart. To strike Rinaldo across the face and send him reeling from his chair. The neurons firing in his brain would malfunction, fail to inhibit his most animal aggressions. Consumed by compulsions other than his own, he would seize the man around his waist and throw him through the glass, condemn him with an all-encompassed effort to the fate of fallen things— to splatter in a damning display on the pavement far below. Blood and broken bones mangled in a marmalade mess, jellied flesh and custard limbs, liquefied in the force of the impact. The thrill of the murder made his head rush with all sorts of preposterous possibilities. He would never act on his inclinations—but what if he did? God, he could imagine.

"Mr. Foster. Please return to your desk."

In a moment, Michael was back on the thirty-seventh floor. He hadn't noticed that he had stood from his chair and approached the cubicle beside him, that he was peering around the corner at the man he reviled so much. His unencumbered mind had taken over his dispassionate limbs and made him act on impulse. He didn't even know the man, not really, but his every intonation inspired an aggravation, an irreconcilable division torn between the two. Something perverse, an impish instinct contrary to his ordinary intentions.

Suddenly, his supervisor stood behind him, his hair trimmed short but for a ridiculous pompadour, polished patent leather shoes and pinstripes standing tall in the place of a sensible man. Michael turned away and resumed his tedious work.

In the absence of a more momentous morning, the afternoon arrived with the tremendous collision of a violent temper. His supervisor had thrown something very loud and breakable inside his office, shattering into a thousand pieces and scattering across the floor. He heard the familiar crash of a telephone receiver and the indistinct ramblings of a man enraged. Michael paid as little mind as he could, focusing for what his paycheck was worth on the pale, pathetic luster of his computer screen.

He typed arbitrary numbers into indiscriminate cells while holding his head beneath the cubicle, hoping to avoid any unnecessary confrontations with upper management. As he felt his own face flush with red, the door to his supervisor's office suddenly swung open wide with a crack against the wall, and the man himself marched into the room. Michael held his breath but there wasn't any need—his supervisor strode deliberately past and stood at the cubicle beside him.

"Rinaldo, get your ass in my office right now."

"Yes, Mr. Romero."

It was the sort of embarrassment at a father's scolding in front of friends, a reprimand to serve as a reminder of powerless youth, that turned his tongue to ash and caused his heart to sink into his stomach. There, in the wash of acid and bile burning through, the last of his sympathies were dissolved and his blood boiled over in their place. A man without many more reservations, hesitant only at the loss of his own security. But Mr. Romero's bold outbursts were wearing away at the final barriers boarding up his bombarded brain. As Rinaldo followed Mr. Romero obediently through his office door, which he abruptly slammed shut behind them, Michael jumped from his seat and headed toward the hall.

While the men behind the frosted glass were consumed by each other's failures and forgiveness, Michael managed to make himself scarce. Rushing down the hallway and across the southern side of the thirty-seventh floor, he fell headfirst into the bathroom and locked himself in a stall. Hiding away from the wrath of his supervisor had become a routine occurrence, a practiced art of evasion that had saved his sorry skin from a similar admonishment on more than one account.

Michael sat secluded and secure, concealed behind impassable walls of his own invention. Locked inside the confines of his head, he thought of how much longer to remain, not only in the bathroom stall but employed at Casualty Insurance. He considered the worth of his work and the peace of his days, lost long ago in the chaos of his several occupations, each one tearing at the remnants of his forgotten innocence. The withering husk left crumbling in its place lay cracked and shriveled in the heat, bound to blow away at the whispering of the wind—or else, to hold fast to its stalwart roots and snap in the blustering breeze. As he assumed the pose of *Le Penseur* cast in bronze, the bathroom door swung open and another man walked purposefully inside, the heels of his shoes clacking against the tiled floor. The man sat down in the stall beside him, fumbling loudly with his belt and letting his pants fall just above his ankles. Michael looked to his left and noted the shoes of the man, gleaming as though they had just been dipped in ink. Patent leather, the unsuitable shoes of Mr. Romero.

Michael had always thought that public restrooms were uncomfortably intimate. Men made vulnerable in the squatting shame of their helpless situation. On the thirty-seventh floor of Pacific Union Tower South, he listened as his supervisor groaned and pushed a painfully large shit into the porcelain bowl beneath him. The smell was unbelievable, the most offensive stench made all the more unbearable because of the man who had released it into the sterile, antiseptic air. A man whose position commanded some authority, if not some measly measure of respect sufficient enough to stave off revolution.

Despite the iniquities existent among the more senior managers of the stratosphere, Michael had never truly considered mutiny. It was likely on account of their tenure and rank that he stifled his own insurgent ideas. He had kept his protestations to himself, allowed them all to fester underneath until their bitter bile boiled over and burned into his flesh. Mr. Romero had always stood above him, empowered by his place at the company table. But Michael knew the scent of his shit, the sounds he made when emptying his bowels. The most personal of details, more discreet than the obscenities of sex. There could be no more respect imparted between them.

Eager once again to avoid an altercation, Michael left the stall and quickly washed his hands at the long row of sinks set in a pale, granite countertop. It caught the harsh fluorescent light like quartz glistening through wayward drops of water collecting around the faucet. He caught a glimpse of his face in the mirror, tired and worn out after years of worry and neglect. His eyes were dark and his skin had begun to wrinkle across his brow. Just as he moved to turn away and dry his hands, he heard the other toilet flush and watched in a panic as Mr. Romero stepped toward him.

"Hello, Mr. Foster. I wondered where you'd gone."

The glaring light of the bathroom buzzed in his ears, a grinding discomfort that distracted from the gloating man standing before him. As Mr. Romero washed his hands, careful not to let the soap and water splash onto his diamond-studded watch, Michael held his throbbing forehead. He massaged his palm into his brow, pressing against his pounding temple, attempting to alleviate the pulsing ache in his brain.

"You've worked with Rinaldo for a few years now, haven't you?"

Michael stole a desperate glance toward him, wondering at the purpose of his inquiry. His hands were still dripping with water and soap when he reached for a paper towel, taking several between his fingertips and crumpling them together before tossing them into the garbage can underneath. The humming sound of the fluorescents grew louder, filling Michael's head with the static of a thousand screaming radios, all joining together in a riotous eruption of noise. He did not answer Mr. Romero's question, staring instead at the distracting pattern of his necktie.

"He's a good kid, but God, he's incompetent. Do you know what happens when you notify the wrong policy owner that the insured has died?"

The water continued to flow, streaming from the faucet that Mr. Romero had unintentionally left running. He seemed not to notice, focusing his attention on Michael and the injured expression on his face. Twisted wrinkles around the eyes and a frown pulling at the corners of his mouth. Visibly disturbed, tears welling, on the verge of spilling over and falling down the contours of his cheeks. Something discomforting had seized him by the throat and thrown him headfirst into a world of torment. Perhaps an acute migraine brought on by the glare of the fluorescent lights, or else a more malignant source of distress. Whatever the cause of this outward display, Mr. Romero thought to conclude their conversation and return to the list of numbers and names that sat waiting in his office, eager to be called.

"He lost the Pfitzer account. I fired him."

The still, immobile air turned tense at the revelation, strung too thin and threatening to splinter into a million little slivers at the thought of retribution. But his own intuitions were clouded over in the memory of Rinaldo's reaction to the news, his surprise at learning of his final mistake and the unavoidable consequences. A thin smile spread across Mr. Romero's face as a light suggestion of laughter escaped his lips.

"What a fucking idiot."

Michael seized the man by his pompadour and threw his head against the edge of the counter, cracking his skull open and spilling his brains into the sink. He snapped the man's neck away before smashing his head over and over into the granite countertop, splattering the mirrors with blood and scattering shattered teeth across the tile floor.

Michael Foster had been overcome, broken in the crucible of the city streets and snapped in two under the stress of his work. Mr. Romero had pushed him too far and the fever had burst a vessel in his brain. Michael held him tightly by his hair, greased and knotted strands tangled in his grip, blood flowing from an open fissure in his face as the rest of his body fell limp. He dropped it face-first to the floor with a heavy thud, breaking the nose as it crunched against the tile and collapsed into the skull. Michael's own hands dripped with the man's blood in a steady rhythm, adding to the deep, red pool pouring out onto his shoes.

The lights continued to pierce Michael's burning eyes as his heart began to race beyond his control. His breath felt shallow and his skin crawled with a desperate effort to escape his bones. But his will was just where he wanted to be, standing overhead as the bruising body of his supervisor lay brutalized and bleeding out. Michael reached into the depths of his sickening gut, straining to hold himself together. A schism had ripped violently through him, tearing apart the meat from the mind. The spirit was willing but the flesh was weak. Though he felt the vomit boiling in his stomach and rising to the back of his throat, he also savored the taste. He looked down at what he had done and, in the grinning aftermath, he suddenly understood what it meant. He was free.

Brimming with exuberant delight at the bloody work he had done, Michael tore from the scene with a bold, uneven spring in his step. He was unable to contain his overwhelming excitement and he no longer cared that the decorum of the day mandated he mourn for the man lying dead on the bathroom floor. Returning briefly to his desk at the other end of the thirty-seventh floor, he grabbed his leather messenger bag, tossed it neatly around his shoulder, and left Casualty Insurance Co. behind.

The elevator descended at a purposefully painful pace, holding Michael momentary prisoner within its admittedly captivating walls, accented with an art deco sensibility, while its cables creaked and cried out either for maintenance or relief. He was an impatient passenger, pressed against the backmost corner, craving the open air and rushing noise of the traffic in the streets. His mind raced with all sorts of prescient thoughts, envisioning the remainder of the afternoon. An unraveling of the day in bed, elusive hours surrendered to the salve of sleep. The minutes passed deliberately by until the familiar, electric chime of the elevator sounded and the mechanical doors opened onto the lobby. Shimmering structures of steel and copper coating meant to be perceived as art complemented by a fountain falling from someplace up above, splashing playfully at the center of the room. Michael walked briskly past, a man on a mission, determined to return to the comfort of his bed. Bursting with a concerted effort through the burdensome front doors of Pacific Union Tower South, he breathed in the toxic air of Los Huesos and sighed a cloud of smoke.

RESURRECTION

Sewage and smog rolled in billowing waves across the crumbling landscape of the city, obscuring the broken people hidden underneath the skyscrapers. In the shadows of the steel colossus lived nomads of another kind, migrants made to drift in the weary current of still waters, stagnant bodies bleeding in the aftermath of an outbreak. The concerns of the homeless were not quarantined to their forgotten corners of the underworld—the infections that festered deep in their wounds would mature and spread.

Michael meant to traverse the length of Los Huesos, to board the metrorail and ride across the city to San Lorenzo until he could fall fast and freely into bed. But the chaos of the streets had spilled over onto the sidewalk, crowding every path and walkway with the hungry hands and bloodshot eyes of figures without names, faceless forms huddled together against the wind and the sands sent from the dunes beyond the sea. A savage sickness that had seized them from the other side of the stars.

In the blinding heat of the afternoon, Michael failed to see that the disease had found its way to the surface, clawed its wicked way from the foul gutters stinking with human waste, and eaten through the weakest of the wandering fools. Silence screamed out through the echoing alleyways and into the empty streets, abandoned by all but those who hadn't heard. Recklessly, unthinking in the maddening throng, he strode headfirst toward the metro station at 7th and South Street.

Metro Center, the focus around which downtown revolved, stood resolute below the turrets and the towers, the steeples and the spires that soared above the parapets and high into the clouds. Castles and cathedrals, in all their magnificence, could do little to compare. A concrete rotunda around an assemblage of escalators, descending deep beneath the city streets with a loud and anguished grinding of metal. Gnashing teeth enmeshed together as the shrieking wail of an exhausted motor ran beneath the rusted steps. Michael stepped blithely aboard in no particular rush despite the fever raging in his head, allayed enough for now to savor the taste of his freedom. He planted himself firmly on the escalator as he felt the rumbling of the machine against his feet. Deep into the belly of the beast, sliding down its cavernous throat, he made his careless way into the bowels of the city.

As he approached the tunnel leading to the lower platform of the station, Michael saw a young man ahead of him, hobbling unsteadily toward the gates. The man's clothing hung off his shoulders and fell around his waist, the disheveled appearance of a figure in distress. He walked with an uncertain limp, as though one of his ankles had been badly sprained. He wore a hood over his head that obscured him from behind. Michael watched him stagger over to the gate, stumbling against the barriers, and start to press his way through. He could see no attendant on duty to stop the man from jumping the gate, no figure of authority to curtail the tendencies of those without regard for the law. But his anger had been transformed—his newfound freedom commanded his conscience and he cared little what anyone else might say. The man crawled clumsily over the gate as Michael marched forward, swiping his card and calling out in a loud and careless voice.

"Hey, asshole!"

The faltering figure before him paused, nearly tripping over his own uneven feet. He shuffled around in a tremulous about-face, teetering on the tips of his toes. His hood cast a deep shadow across his face, shrouding his eyes in darkness. He moved as though his body were not his own, as though his limbs had been suspended from strings and were manipulated by an unseen puppeteer. Michael moved closer to him, affronted at his insolence, insulted at the sheer contempt for the social order that held this crumbling city together. The collective bargain that had preserved a shred of peace in which he had carved out his former life. The people of Los Huesos had breached their social contract, and Michael had chosen to withhold his own performance.

"The fuck do you think you're doing?"

In the flickering light of the metro tunnel, Michael felt a rush of damp air from underground accompanied by the thundering roar of a train just arriving at the platform below. The smell of the man hit him like a sucker punch in the gut, warm and expired meat left broiling in the sun. Garbage piled high in hot, black polyethylene bags baking on the curb and leaking dark liquid out onto the street. A chittering sound, as of teeth together, sounded in the empty tunnel and echoed against the concrete. He seized the man by his jacket and ripped the hood from around his head. What he saw stole the breath from his lungs and tore his heartbeat from his chest. His blood drained from underneath his frozen face and the indignation that had burned so brightly before in his head had suddenly gone out. Standing squarely in front of him, legs crooked and shoulders bent, was a corpse come back to life.

The flesh of it had rotted, rising in purple contusions and peeling in places where the bones were piercing through. Its nose had entirely fallen away, exposing the brittle skull and tangled mess of shriveled veins and black tissue underneath, woven together in a macabre masquerade. A red death indeed, drenched in the bloody sign of its murderous deeds, dried and caked on thick in a betrayal of innocent alibis. The Annunciation in perverse, painted by a madman with blasphemous intent. More than anything, the figure seemed unaware of this at all, staring blankly with sightless, yellowed eyes. Its arms hung limp and lifeless at its sides, fingers curled like spider legs when the creature has shriveled and died. Michael stood paralyzed and struck by speechless horror at the sight of the hideous thing.

28

28   Tania Bustamente, *A Corpse Come Back to Life, 2020, acrylic ink on watercolor paper.*

At the moment of Michael's greatest disgust, just before he fell headlong into panic, the doors to the metro train below burst open and a torrent of flailing limbs flooded the platform, tearing through the lingering crowds. Screams and splashes of red filled the tunnel as the vociferous horde tore every last person apart. A singular, indivisible mass ripping flesh from bone and feasting on open throats.

Michael stepped hesitantly back from the figure in front of him, shaking beyond control, unable to break into a run. His legs turned to lead as they fell out from under him and he crashed violently to the ground. The crumbling carcass of a man towered over him, sores festering and wounds bleeding as it stumbled forward, arms reaching out in a desperate, starving attempt to—but Michael didn't know. The thing had lost all semblance of humanity, all rational bases, brainless and subject to the control of some more basic instinct. Its fingers had turned black and the skin clung tightly to the bones. Its fingernails had been shed entirely and left soft, deep depressions in their place.

Michael's own fingers shook as he fumbled around in his pocket, desperate to find his metro card and escape back through the gate. Either his hands had numbed to all sensation and lost their use or else he had dropped it someplace in all the chaos. No matter where he had misplaced it, he knew he had to run. His legs failed to find their footing as the rotted thing tripped over its own uneven legs and toppled headfirst to the floor, cracking open its milk-white skull. Dark, heavy fluid spilled out onto the concrete, too thick to be blood. Putrid, oozing brain matter slowly crawling toward him, reaching out with liquid limbs. A burning sense of urgency surged like gasoline through Michael's veins, igniting his otherwise frozen feet and compelling him to stand. He saw the riotous throng clamoring together toward the place where he stood, a teeming hive of ravenous insects subject to their queen. Locusts gorging on the plentiful harvest. Without a moment's regard for the rule of law, he turned away from the metrorail and leapt with a long-forgotten gracefulness over the gate.

With the overrun swarm snapping their yellowed teeth at his heels, saliva dripping in hot streams from their mandibles, their voices wailing like phantoms from their throats, Michael ran as fast as he could up the escalator, out of the tunnel underground and into the sun. The daylight bathed him in golden droplets blinding as the stars, searing his half-squinted eyes through his glasses as he stared at the world around him. An emptiness unlike any he had felt before, the abandonment of a city by its own inhabitants, vagrants who had once poured out into the streets and made the concrete their home.

The droning sound of the downtown traffic had all but disappeared from the afternoon. Silence crept like amnesia into his head, the winter of a well-worn year that had drunk of the summer's spring. In the absence of all the familiar trappings of the day, the financial district of Los Huesos assumed a different face. Alien, a foreign landscape revolving around some faraway star beyond the light of our solar system. A planet past its prime, the desert of a dying land. The peace of silence fallen over the streets sounded like the end of the world. In all the sands that were carried on the reckless whims of the wind, Michael had never known Los Huesos to be kind.

As if in defiance of the aberrant thought, the insatiable horde rushed out into the city and filled the streets with the bloody sounds of a massacre. Virile, young bodies of professionals who had been on their way to work, tourists who had taken to the metro to see the glittering sights, all of them tearing into the silence like carnivores to the kill. At the howling cries of the pack, Michael ran panicked down 7th Street with the speed of a much younger man, aided by the rush of adrenaline that had shot into his veins. He didn't know what had possessed the people behind him, what murderous appetites had seized them in the darkness underground—he only knew that their intentions were far from human.

Before he could tear away from the pursuit and dash onto South Broadway, the roaring sound of an engine struggling to breathe rounded the corner as an enormous Humvee barreled down the street. Michael leapt out of the way before it raced toward the entrance of the Metro Center tunnel, charging across multiple lanes as though it were hurtling out of control. An unstoppable streak of desert sand ripping through the crowd, crushing their skulls underneath tires the size of four-door sedans. Mangled chunks of meat were pressed into the pavement where people had once stood. Bones were crushed to dust and blown away in the wind. But the Humvee did not stop, careening at full speed into the concrete and metal, crashing in a shower of broken glass and twisted steel before erupting into a fury of flames. A plume of black smoke rose above the heat and signaled the disaster to anyone who might be able to help. Michael wondered whether there was anyone left.

Shivering from his teeth to his fingertips, an unfamiliar fear embedded into the fibrous endings of his nerves as Michael sought somewhere to hide. He didn't look behind him as he ran along South Broadway, breaking into a desperate sprint toward someplace far away. His tie whipped along beside him as his feet slipped uncertainly in his dress shoes, threatening to blister and bleed. Sweat fell in heavy droplets from his face and the ends of his unkempt hair, collecting at the bridge of his nose. His glasses slid precariously from their place, as if they might fall to ground and shatter the lenses in their frame. He was careful to adjust them as he maintained his breathless pace, aware that he would be entirely helpless without them.

He didn't know how far he had run when he stopped, gasping for air and doubled over, holding his hands behind his head. His stomach turned in somersaults as dehydration and hunger burned like bile in his throat, crushing his windpipe with a grip that bruised his skin. He hadn't eaten all day and his legs had grown weak beneath him. His condo may as well have lain on the other side of the world—if he was going to make it back home, he would need to restore his strength. Looking around in the aftermath of a terrible collision, disaster embedded in the center of the city, Michael searched the storefront marquees that lined the empty streets. He found one that read *Le Piège* and fell eagerly inside.

The décor was that of timeless luxury, tastefully spilling over like shimmering fountains of light from crystal coronets and golden trimmings that ran the length of the walls. The floor was carpeted in an elegant floral pattern, the dancing crest of the Dauphin in ivory and blue. But gory splashes of red scarred the room with the alarm of a murder scene. A number of tables had been disturbed, tablecloths torn from their tables and shattered porcelain plates fallen atop shards of glass lay littered across the floor. Michael stepped carefully among them, venturing further in.

The morning had been interrupted by the chaos of the streets, breaking through the front doors with the force of a hurricane and feasting on the rotten spoils of the storm. The floodwaters had left the carpeting stained, deep and red, sinking into the hardwood underneath. But Michael saw no bodies among the debris, no mangled limbs or broken bones to tell whatever gruesome tale they could. In their place were pools of blood, still wet and glistening in the manufactured light of the chandeliers. The soles of Michael's shoes had been painted the same scarlet hue, unable to avoid stepping in the gruesome mess.

In desperate search of food, Michael pressed cautiously onward in spite of every screaming intuition telling him to run. He followed the carpeting and the darkened corridors back toward the kitchen, carefully creeping as though he might trigger a chain reaction of land mines blowing himself half to Hell. A heavy, scorching smell hung in his throat, a dark cloud like gun smoke rolling on the air. Step by bloody footstep, leaving a sticky trail of red behind him, he rounded a corner to the kitchen to find a wall of fire blazing on a row of stovetops, abandoned by whoever had been there before him and left to burn in their absence.

A weak spray of chemical foam had fallen over the flames but had done little to suffocate or extinguish their vicious glow. It was contained enough for now, isolated to the backmost corner of the kitchen. Michael watched it with a wary eye as he proceeded to stalk the room for food. The lights flickered uncertainly as he searched among the freezers and the storage shelves.

Scraps lay in pieces across the stainless-steel countertops, bits of lettuce and onion peels tossed aside with broken eggs and bagels made from scratch. He dug a pair of these from the morning garbage and ate freely, without care for cleanliness or taste. An omelet had been prepared and set along the edge of the counter, which Michael also devoured. He opened the doors to an industrial-sized refrigerator and drank from a container of orange juice, freshly squeezed. It spilled from the corners of his mouth and down the front of his shirt, splattering onto the tiled floor.

As he indulged for a moment in the simple necessity, a crash came from somewhere inside. A shattered glass or a dinner plate, or else a broken window from the front of the restaurant. Michael set the orange juice down beside him and listened for any other sound. He heard a low crunching of glass, a quiet disturbance of the otherwise tranquil fallout. Something else had entered the restaurant. He took a steak knife in hand and stepped lightly from the kitchen, peering around the corner. There, shuffling unsteadily through the dining area, were two figures dressed in torn and tattered clothes. Their faces had fallen and their skin had turned sallow with sweat.

29

29   Justin Rohr, *Victims of the Horde, 2020, pencil on paper.*

Michael was unsure whether they had been victims of the horde or whether they had wandered in the same as he had, exhausted and overcome. In the dimming light of *Le Piège*, he saw that their eyes had gone dark. Glazed over with a clouded film, they hung suspended in the air independent of their proper place. A set of wayward souls lost in the screaming havoc, damned to drift the undead avenues that pierced through the lifeless heart of Los Huesos.

Without another exit in sight, Michael stole his silent way back into the kitchen, turning off the lights and clutching the steak knife in his hands, hoping to conceal himself behind rows of stainless-steel cooking stations. There was no door to close and keep locked, no way to blockade himself inside and safe from the predatory half-lives on the other side of the walls. He held his breath, shaking on the cold kitchen floor, praying that they might turn away and stumble back out into the sun. But his footprints lay bare in disloyal blood, betraying the confidence of his hiding place. Michael heard their stealthy footsteps approaching, their unfeeling faces fixated on the perilous pathway laid out before them. They groaned as if they were in pain, pleading with whatever force had possessed them and played puppeteer with their limbs.

As he cowered in the corner of the room, clutching the knife between his fingers, their shadows fell over the doorway. The fire continued to burn brightly against the wall as their faces fell into view, blinded eyes widening at the brilliant light from the flames. Michael was unsure whether they could sense anything at all, or whether they relied on some instinctual sight to hunt. In the blazing light of the fire, he caught a clearer glimpse of them both.

Not rotted and corrupted by disease like the dead man in the metro tunnel—these men seemed very much alive. Agile and fresh, not so stiffened and fallen to pieces, as though they had only been recently deceased. Like the horde that had spilled out onto the streets, faster than a stumbling corpse but less aware and adept than the living. They existed someplace in-between, diminishing by the minute, decomposing by the hour. Bodies that had succumbed to the bloodletting of a parasitic leech, green skin and black veins hemorrhaging underneath.

The pair of them moved carefully, purposeful but with caution, stalking together toward their helpless prey. Blood dripped from their slack jaws and bits of flesh stuck between their teeth. Their humanity had been all but stripped away, preserving instead the cruel atrocity of their savage state. Prowling like a pair of lions, scouting the Savannah on the trail of a wounded beast. But the backmost corner of the kitchen of *Le Piège* was no African pride land, and Michael had claws of his own.

In between silent, shallow breaths, he brought the knife close to his chest and held his eyes shut for just a moment. Suddenly, he was someplace miles away, San Lorenzo far from the sea. In the darkness of his own volition, he saw himself in bed, safe and secure in the comfort of his condominium. The vision inspired in him riotous sparks akin to anger, hot and fervent fury at the bloodlust of the day and the frustration at the downfall of a city in smoke.

He let his eyes drift open again as his grip tightened around the knife, his knuckles burning white from the building pressure. Fingernails piercing the skin of his palms, digging into the flesh of his hands. All he wanted was to return to his bed, to collapse beneath the weight of the morning and fall deeply into the soothing salve of sleep. With the aggravation and abject terror of his predicament grinding into his bones, Michael turned back toward the kitchen and rose unblinking to his feet.

Beside the blazing fire raging in the corner of the room, Michael brought the knife level with his chest as the two figures stared through their blank, unseeing eyes. Their haunting moans grew louder like a death rattle as they approached, excess saliva spilling from their open mouths. Their teeth were bared beneath peeling lips, pulled back and rapidly degrading in the severity of the heat. The stench of death hung thick and low like sulfur in the air, filling his lungs with a fatal dose and burdening his head with the effects of the fumes. Something affective must have been carried on the noxious haze. Spores of a spectral kind dispersing from these apparitions of the grave.

Michael stood cornered on his feet, his back against the wall, watching as the corpses pressed forward, moving as though in tandem. A scavenging pack of hyenas, grinning wide across their gleaming faces, skin stretched tight and thin. Michael looked about the kitchen for anything else to help him, any other weapons with which to arm and defend himself. Lying unassumingly on a countertop to his left, glinting in the dynamic light of the flames, was a large, metal serving fork. It extended the length of his forearm, a smooth wooden handle holding in place a polished pair of twin, steel tines sharpened to lethal points. He reached his other hand out and seized the fork in his grip, prepared to plunge it deep into the broken bodies before him. But his arms felt heavy at his side.

The moment grew tense and Michael grew weary as the fire burned brighter behind him. After another moment's hesitation and a brief instant to muster some strength, he lunged at the figure nearest to him, sinking the steak knife deep into its stomach. It sank like a sword through soft butter, spilling black blood onto the floor. It lodged itself firmly in place, caught between its ribs and embedded in the bone. With a reckless shove behind him aided by the corpse's stumbling inertia, it fell into the roaring flames. An inhuman shriek cut through the silence as the thing was engulfed, arms flailing and legs crumbling underneath. But it did not die, crashing into shelves and setting the entire kitchen ablaze.

Michael leapt from the ravenous flames licking at his heels and collided with the other corpse, knocking it onto its back. He heard a splintering crack echo against the tile floor as he fell on top of its chest, which collapsed under his weight. Its jagged fingernails scratched at his face as its jaws snapped open and shut like the hungry mandibles of a hideous insect. Its fingers found their mark as they ripped through his skin, tearing bloody gashes in his cheek and knocking his glasses across the room. He lifted the serving fork high above his head, deadly tines glinting in the raging glow of the firelight, and plunged it over and over into its softening skull. The black brains of a putrefied man flowed from its ears and spilled from the gash that Michael had gored into its forehead.

He whipped immediately about, his vision entirely distorted without the aid of his glasses. All he could see was the brilliant blur of the fire all around him, a violent orange haze consuming everything it touched. Midas made of flames, turning the world to ash. Michael's own hands reached uselessly across the floor, grasping at nothing but the hopeless prospect of escape, slipping faster by the minute through his grip. But he crawled blindly across the floor of the burning kitchen, over shards of broken glass and through puddles of blackened blood, until his hands at last found his glasses. They were cracked and bent along the frame, but he thrust them onto his face and threw the corpses aside. Driven by the rapidly encroaching threat of the thronging horde and provoked by the engulfing heat swelling behind him, Michael stumbled unsteadily to his feet.

As though time itself had slowed and the dancing of the flames maintained the rhythm of some undying dirge, Michael sprang from the kitchen in a desperate dash toward the door. The heat of the fire blistered on his back, bubbling up beneath the skin like boiling scalds. The sounds of a thousand voices screaming out in unimaginable pain pierced the air with the poignancy of a practiced physician, puncturing the pit of Michael's ears with clinical precision. Tearing through the dining area and out of the front doors, he burst from the restaurant with unconquerable speed and left *Le Piège* behind.

- - -

The streets of the city raced by in a thundering flash, empty pavements and hollow walls streaking past as Michael fled from the thronging swarm. Dark smoke billowed in a menacing pillar overhead, rising against the pale blue clouds as a squadron of helicopters screamed across the soaring skyline. The sound of gunfire ricocheted off the concrete and pierced his throbbing brain. Dire screams echoed in the dour daylight, casting the afternoon in rust. Tears fell in unencumbered streams down the contours of his cheeks as he staggered through the wreckage of the city, his legs nearly buckling underneath his weight.

In the winds that ripped through the treacherous streets, Michael sped carelessly down darkened avenues and abandoned alleyways, far from the terrors that spilled like insects from underground. As he ran further from the sparkling ocean shore and toward the more mountainous outskirts of the city, his legs trembled beyond his control and air hemorrhaged from his lungs like a gas leak. The heat had constricted around his throat and made it impossible to breathe. As the world collapsed in a cloud of ash behind him, Michael turned toward the slopes of San Lorenzo standing tall across the wasteland.

The desert stretched open before him farther than his straining eyes could see. Faded colors dotted the desert like wildflowers dying in the sand, vulnerable and exposed to the heat and the wind and the unrelenting torment of the sun. A field of tents propped precariously in the dirt, ragged and torn strips of nylon and polyester whipping in the breeze. Rusted and rotted out RVs, Airstreams abandoned and forgotten to the years. Positioned at the edge of the urban sprawl, downtown burning at his back and the barren spoils of a fertile past extending out forever before him, Michael gathered his mind and made himself prepared for the crossing.

There, at the base of the mountains rising high against the clouds, the hills of San Lorenzo overlooked the fallen city like a sentry at his post. Michael moved unseeing through the blazing desert, marching as a wounded man toward his homeland, bested by the brutal blows of war. He had been ravaged by the sadists of a despotic state, a sacrifice in a ruthless game that he had never played. Further still, he had not been aware that such a game had been begun at all. In the gory throes of conquest, he struggled to maintain the dignity of a graceful defeat. This enemy was one without a name, without a face or form to call its own, yet was mighty enough to condemn him to the wastes by decree of banishment. His skin was cut by the sands beyond the suburbs, where the vagabonds and vagrants spent their lonesome days and hot, oppressive nights. He had become an exile, joining the ranks of the living dead of Los Huesos. But the bones had risen up from their graves.

Standing at the edge of the quiet encampment, listening for any sort of sound, for some sign of life, Michael stepped forward with abundant caution. The hollow chittering of a rattlesnake echoed in the distance, warning if it could for him to turn away. But the journey was begun and he would have to see it through.

His eyes had dried from the sun and the strain of stumbling sightless through the streets. In the shifting sands beneath his feet, he staggered as though he were drunk, shifting his weight unsteadily between his legs. Exhausted and overcome by dehydration and the heat, he dropped with a pathetic crash to his knees and heaved into the dirt. Loud, relentless retching that tore at his throat and clung like rot to his teeth. Ripping through his stomach and doubling his weakened body over, the convulsions gripped him firmly by the neck and compelled him at once to prostrate himself against the ground. Tears welled in the corners of his eyes as his stifled cries carried over the dunes and out into the empty, scorching waste.

But a snarling like a pack of wild dogs prowling the Sahara interrupted his violent gagging as he turned to look behind. Crawling out from underneath collapsing tents and from within the shadows of the underbrush, bruised and broken bodies rose half-buried by the dirt. Bones brought back to life. Their skin had turned to leather and was bleached by the sun, or else from the loss of color as the blood had dried in their veins. Jagged, crooked bones protruded like a cancer, warped and twisted features of a skeletal throng, risen up from the deserted depths of a mass, forgotten grave. Dark, unseeing sockets spilled down their petrified faces, jaws hung slack, and scalps pulled tight against their skulls. These were not as fresh as the others, not nearly as preserved. There was something less earthly about them. Less human.

Michael struggled to find some last vestige of strength within him as he forced his body to stand. Burdened by fatigue and the overwhelming weight of weariness bearing down on his shoulders, he readied himself to run. With a snap of his tendons and a flurry of sand, he tore away from the ravaging horde and raced headlong toward the horizon. He had no weapons and no other choice but to outpace the maws of death. The ravenous corpses pursued him against their will, acting as if by instinct, compelled to crave the taste of flesh.

As he sprinted through the sand, he scanned the desert for any sort of shelter, some place to shield him from their murderous minds. Along the edge of the encampment, a row of rusted-out RVs rested as though they had been untouched for years. Desperate and fearful for his life, Michael ran toward a distressed camper colored a pale orange and embellished by a collage of graffiti splashed across the side. Pushing past each mound of canvas, kicking up clouds of dust, he grasped the handle of the old, metal door and threw it open with all his might.

He slammed the door shut behind him as he crashed into a wall of cabinets. Stacks of empty Tupperware containers collapsed from their shelves and coffee mugs coated with dust toppled out and shattered on the floor. In the suffocating darkness, trying to catch his breath, he tasted a staleness in the air. There, inside the unearned intimacy of the camper, Michael found the most offensive smell—human flesh baking in the broiling heat of a convection oven. A metal crucible cooking the corpse of a rotted man. He turned around in the tight, confining space of the camper to see a body molding on the bed. Flies gathered like a storm cloud above its head and maggots spilled out of its stomach. Its shirt had been torn from its torso and deep gashes had been ripped open across its chest. As Michael cautiously approached, eyes straining in the dark, the mob of undead collided with the outside of the camper, rocking it precariously on its wheels. He was thrown violently backward from the bed, tripping over the back of his heels and falling to the floor as the rotted body rose to its feet.

Michael's eyes widened at the sight, blood vessels engorged and bulging in their place, nearly bursting as his breath was stolen away. Deep, black liquid flowed from the corpse, thick and slowly from its gut, splattering the floor with blood and maggots and whatever viscous marinade had begun to emulsify in its veins. It stepped toward him on broken legs, bones exposed through sandpaper skin, reaching out with arms like an insect. Advancing with another's mind, grasping with an appetite unknown. Its face was absent, eye sockets empty and falling inward on themselves, a binary system collapsing into a pair of black holes. Through lips peeled back and shriveled against the skull, its teeth shone yellow like the fangs of a rattlesnake, mandibles oozing with venomous saliva.

The walls of the camper closed in on Michael's head, crushing him with the infinite stress of a pressure cooker, ready to explode. The strain wearing like corrosion against the cliffs was growing too great to bear. The desert sands had succumbed to the fury of the rains and a canyon had been gored into his chest. His throat had closed and his mouth had filled with the sensation of cotton against his tongue. He couldn't breathe, couldn't think beyond the towering, skeletal figure leering over him. Steam was building against the roof as the violence of the day screamed inside his head. Bright splashes of blood against the blacktop and bits of meat still on the bone falling to the floor flashed like bolts of lightning in his eyes.

In rapid succession, shuttering like a Super 8 projector, he saw the horrors of Los Huesos played out again as faithfully as though they were real. The rotting man in the metro tunnel. A horde of corpses racing through the streets. Fire searing the flesh from a man as he screamed with his final breath. And he saw Mr. Romero's head split open like a coddled egg cracked against the concrete, bleeding out onto the bathroom floor. His lifeless eyes rolled back into his broken skull, his jaw hanging loose and his teeth scattered across the tile like dice.

And in that moment of mirrored clarity, Michael understood that he had fallen from a towering peak, turned his back to a middling, comfortable life among the clouds in favor of something more depressed. An epiphany like the comedown from a terrible high, head throbbing to the beat of his stubborn heart, pumping in spite of his obvious peril. He had joined the numbers of the dead in the valley of bones. Where the hopeless and forgotten refuse of the city sat suffering in exile, he had fled out of desperation and reckless abandon of the civilized streets burning in chaos behind him. But he refused to settle at the bottom of a riverbed that had dried up long ago.

As the camper threatened to rock onto its side and the dead outside clawed at the door, the broken corpse buckled under its own crippling decay and fell onto Michael's heaving chest. He cried out in disgust as its limbs flailed about, tearing at whatever they could find, ripping through his shirt. He gripped it by the throat, black saliva falling onto his face, and crushed its brittle windpipe. With a herculean thrust of his knees deep into its gut, he forced it off of him and facedown onto the floor. Climbing onto its back, feeling its spine snap beneath him, he held its head in both his outstretched hands. He found that the skull had softened in its rot, pine-patterned veins snaking along like a century egg pickled and preserved in saline. Without hesitation, he beat its head against the floor, over and over with the unbridled ferocity and violence of an ape cracking cockles against a stone. Primal and enraged, reverting with ease to the instinctive nature of his prehistoric ancestors, he bared his teeth as black brains spilled without reserve from what remained of its head. In a matter of moments, blow after blow, he reduced it to a pathetic pile of pulp and jellied meat.

Sweating profusely in the aftermath, drenched in black blood splattered across his face from the kill, he stood unsteadily and stared out the windshield. Through the layers of dust and dirt caked on thick from the years, Michael made out bodies crawling onto the hood, some sliding back down while others climbed over like swarming locusts to the fields. He swiftly took a seat behind the wheel, found that the keys were already in the ignition, and prayed that there were more than fumes in the tank. With a rough twist of the key, he cranked the engine and threw the gearstick into drive. He floored the gas and held his breath.

The camper roared to life and fired like a shotgun shell into the mass of bodies in his path. Blood and bones were ripped to pieces as the undead fell under the tires spinning in the sand, grinding into an unrecognizable purée. A red cloud of blood and dust rose like a new dawn in the afternoon sky behind him as the camper tore across the valley, away from the mob of the undead, and toward the soaring hills of San Lorenzo.

The valley did not take long to cross in the camper, carrying Michael through the brushwood and crushing the wildflowers growing underneath with all their might in the desert sun, struggling to survive on the side of the interstate. With a considerable jolt of the camper's rusted suspension, he raced along the abandoned backroads toward the hills and began to climb the streets of San Lorenzo.

Every straining thread and bolt of the camper groaned from the stress as he passed the same, recumbent vagrants lying unaware on the sidewalk. He paid them no mind as he thought only of his bed, consumed entirely by the prospect of relief waiting for him like an attendant in his condominium. As the whole world fell to pieces all around him, Michael envisioned the familiar comfort like a mirage, wavering delicately at the tip of his tongue, too elusive yet to taste. He was no longer behind the wheel, imagining himself instead drinking freely from the sweet oasis, ignorant of the fires raging out of all control. Sleeping peacefully beneath sheets of silk—

Metal grinding against metal and the sound of steel twisting in the violence of a collision brought him back to the streets, snapping his neck forward as the windshield shattered and the passenger seat was crushed by the brutal force of the engine. The blinding flash of taillights and glinting shards of glass suspended in the air held Michael captive in a moment of fire and blood, raining down onto his face like hailstones from the burning sky above.

He threw the door open and fell helplessly from the camper with a crash onto the pavement, legs buckling beneath him. His left ankle snapped as blood flowed into his eyes. His vision was red and fever stung him as the fear and the panic of the swarm found him vulnerable at last, piercing through his skin and consuming him alive. But he was still breathing, pushing on in spite of the bloodthirsty daggers bared and snapping at his heels. The venom burned bright and boiled in his veins as his voice escaped him in a guttural scream. Michael was unsure whether he had been filled with adrenaline or poisoned by the lucky strike of a rattler's fangs. He wiped the blood from his eyes and saw that the street was empty, that he had cried out in the street all alone.

With his left foot twisted distressingly to the side, covered in blood and stumbling along as tears streamed down his face, he imagined he must appear like a corpse rising up from the headstones of Los Huesos. He turned to look behind him at the city crumbling down below, black smoke rising higher than the mountaintops. Gunfire ricocheted off the concrete and echoed into the hills. The city was under siege, smoldering in the ruins of prominence, a golden era that had come crashing to its knees. A wayward rocket fired by some reserve military convoy careened into the side of Pacific Union South and exploded in a ball of fire.

The blast showered the pavement with glass and twisted beams, crushing anyone who may have been caught underneath. As helicopters soared overhead and split the clouds open in the sky, the sands were swept away with the fading light of the afternoon. In the growing havoc of gluttonous riots that overshadowed the gridlocked streets, a greater calm eclipsed the chaos, which was consumed by the stillness of the sea. The tide beat tirelessly against the coast, lapping at the shoreline, eager to swallow the city whole.

Michael turned away and staggered unsteadily on his feet, which were bent unnaturally in his shoes, as he struggled to climb the hills toward his home, an old brick compound sitting squat at the end of the street. An unbecoming, washed out grey-brown development that nearly sunk into the backdrop of the dirt. His own unit waited dutifully on the third floor, a watchman overhead.

As he approached the front door of the building, he noticed a small, cowering mass of a man sitting outside on the stairs. His frame was thin as though his body had been subjected to all manner of hardship, hunger and heroin alike. A tattered polyester jacket was draped carelessly across his back, fit to the build of a much younger man. In spite of the overwhelming desert heat, his shoulders and his knees were trembling. Michael was unsure whether he had ever seen this man before, whether he had routinely taken up residence on the stoop or else drifted there on the occasion of the wind. Whatever the incidence of his visit, Michael felt pity in his heart.

"Hello," he said, his voice marked by a worn and weary kindness. The man looked up with eyes that had seen more than their share of years. They carried with them the pain of countless days caught in the snare of the city, endless nights of lying hopeless in the dark, attended like a mongrel in a cage. The deadened lamplights once held for him the glamour of ideals and the promises of progress. He had paid for his faith in the institutions of the day, those lonely, fickle frauds like salesmen at the gates. Purveyors of porterhouse peddling mincemeat.

Against the sounds of rioting and destruction erupting down below, the man responded with a low and gentle voice. Gravel in the throat, but softened by the erosion of years. Heavy with the weight of his own considerations, calloused from the buffets and the blows, his answer rang full of brass.

"Sorry for taking up your stoop."

Michael was unsure of how he meant this, whether the man had been sincere or else was expressing some degree of sarcasm. He settled on the latter, assuming that the day had worn on him too. Michael surveyed the fires raging and the gunshots in the streets, the billowing smoke and the shattered glass that covered the city like snow, shimmering in the afternoon sunlight.

"Do you have anywhere you can go?" Michael already knew the answer, but he wanted to be polite. The man looked down at his bare feet, bloodied and bandaged at the heel. Michael looked around the lonely streets of San Lorenzo, careful not to linger for too long. In the chaos and the carnage of the day, he took comfort in the company of another man.

"Why don't you come upstairs with me?"

The man stared almost in disbelief, a warranted amazement at the offer. A gesture of kindness in the midst of horror, the simplest show of sympathy. Recognition of the human spirit recumbent in a broken shell. Michael extended his hand toward the man, who hesitated just a moment before taking it in his own. The two climbed the steps and entered into the building together, each consoled by the other and the false promise of tomorrow.

Michael's condo unit sat depressively above, overlooking the carnage downtown through a wide, unobstructed window gazing out across the city. Through the glare of the sunlight against the glass, the smoldering ruins consumed the skyline as the smoke rose high into the clouds. The sea salt sprayed a useless froth into the air as the ocean foamed around its fangs, hungry for the horizon to fall into the sands. Michael drew the shades and cast the room into darkness.

As the man pressed further into the place, still hesitant and uncertain of whether he might be safe, Michael gestured toward the kitchen, indicating that he should make himself at home. The man smiled softly, his shoulders falling as he finally relaxed, and made his way into the bathroom. Michael listened to the peaceful sound of water falling from the shower before he turned away and left the man to his own devices.

Retreating into the bedroom, Michael removed his tattered, bloodstained clothes and fell at long last into bed. An overwhelming sense of relief cleansed him of the horrors of the day. Mr. Romero, the metrorail, the undead wanderers in the wastelands—none of it remained. In their place drifted far-off memories of sleep and dreams of summer days long dead. In that remote and distant still, he drifted away to somewhere invisible and out of reach. But a dark spot had begun to form beneath his skin, spreading like an unattended stain as it spilled over the edge and soaked through to the marrow in his bones.

FORBIDDEN
THINGS

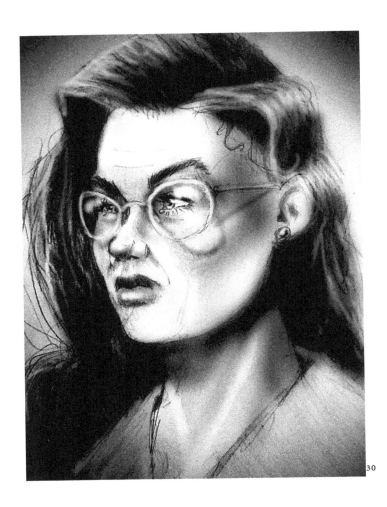

30

30 Justin Rohr, *Clare Montgomery, 2020, pencil on paper.*

Wayward strands of auburn hair fell across Dr. Montgomery's face as the hypertrain roared into Union Station. She took a tentative step back from the edge of the platform, holding fast to her briefcase. Yellow lights flickered like lightning overhead, an electrical storm in the darkness to signal the thundering approach of something unstoppable and real. The wind whipped the front of her jacket and threatened to tear the briefcase from her hands. She tightened her grip, as though she might be blown away without it, and pulled the collar of her jacket close around her neck. Metal screeched against grinding metal, shaking the concrete underfoot.

As the train slowed to a stop in front of her, Dr. Montgomery adjusted her glasses and swept away the hair that had fallen into her eyes. The voice of a disembodied woman told her to stand clear of the train as its doors opened and its passengers filed out. She obeyed, stepping aside and observing each pitiful figure, each pathetic face that stared vacantly ahead. Unreadable expressions of apathy in the early morning hours. She imagined her own must have been much the same—she had practiced. Heavy thoughts weighed down her head and forced her shoulders to shrug.

The train cleared and she stepped aboard, unzipping her jacket and folding it in her arms. She wouldn't need it on the other side, but winters in Washington were cold. Her job required a considerable degree of professional decorum—record snowfall had ensured she dressed the part. Otherwise, she would be tempted to travel in something less constrictive. But the concrete underground did little to shield against the frozen winds that rushed in from the streets.

The train embraced her in its warmth, holding her close to its metal heart. It hummed powerful and deep, the engine pulsating in an organic rhythm as the passengers trembled inside. She turned to see the faces of those around her, ordinary people pursuing ordinary lives. In the anticipation of their departure, they showed no signs of distress. Theirs was the mistaken comfort of a mother's lullaby, sung soft and low to soothe their uneasy senses. Her own could not be calmed. Taking a seat beside the door, she set the briefcase in her lap and laid her jacket tidily on top. The doors closed at the sound of a synthetic chime and she took a final, anxious breath.

With the devastating thrust of a propulsion rocket, the hypertrain soared from the station at a seamless speed, hurtling through the tunnel underneath the city. Dr. Montgomery closed her eyes and folded her hands as if in prayer. She entrusted her life to the unerring precision of the mainframe conductor, calculating their trajectory far faster than she could comprehend. There had never been a single derailment or accident of any kind, something that could not be said of the Washington metrorail. Still, the inertia of the hypertrain unsettled something in her stomach as it raced toward the gate.

In the darkness of the tunnel, a blinding light shone from somewhere up ahead. The colossal power of an immense machine, the gate to the other side. A massive ring revolving around an invisible axis, rotating at a terrifying speed. Energy spewed from the center, radiating outward like spokes on a runaway wheel. Dr. Montgomery clenched her teeth and turned her knuckles white as her heart beat faster and faster against her chest. The whirring of the gate filled her head as the light flashed before her eyes, shrieking from the shadows like a strobing siren's wail. Her entire body shuddered in its seat as the roar of the engines overtook her breath and crushed the air from her lungs. The hypertrain screamed and the world fell away as it all slipped suddenly through the gate.

- - -

The desert sun beat down on the railway tracks that ran the length of the station. Beneath the bleeding sunrise and the dizzying mountain peaks, the outskirts of Los Huesos baked in the scorching heat. Crowds had begun to gather on the platform just as the 6:30 from Washington was scheduled to arrive. With the cracking sound of thunder splitting open the sky, the hypertrain tore through the other side of the gate and careened along the tracks.

As the train approached the far end of the station, Dr. Montgomery braced herself in her seat. She held tightly to the railing beside her with one hand and clung to her briefcase with the other. The sunlight broke through the cover of shattered clouds and refracted through the tinted windows of the train. She took a pair of dark Valencia sunglasses out from her pocket and placed them over her eyes. The doors to the hypertrain slid open with the same synthetic chime as she rose from her seat and stepped lithely from the car.

The city of Los Huesos shimmered in the distance, sky-scrapers soaring over downtown tenements and drifting like a mirage on the waves. The skyline trembled in the blistering heat as Dr. Montgomery swept toward the city, briefcase in hand and the mission on her mind. She hailed a cab that carried her away from the station and toward the center of the city's spokes. There, deep underground, trapped like a titan in Tartarus, lay Talos Industries.

Concrete encased the city like a chrome-encrusted coffin, lowered by pallbearers down into the dirt—but the city had refused to die. The splintered pieces had risen up from the ashes of a broken world and been rebuilt as something better. Marching into the very heart of the city, beating more vigorously than ever, Dr. Montgomery arrived at the front doors of Talos Tower.

A glittering steel colossus, the beaming beacon of an ancient world that loomed like storm clouds over the coast, a bonfire burning to ward away wayward ships from the shore. From the pavement far below, Dr. Montgomery stole a squinted glance at the spires high above, the soaring peak of the tallest structure in the world. Talos was an accomplishment to be sure, but Dr. Montgomery was not there to sing its praises. She had work to do.

She passed through security with ease, submitting herself and her briefcase to the metal detectors just inside before filing alongside technicians and other employees to the elevator lobby. A vast space adorned with the finest décor, fountains and sculptures reaching like monuments to unremembered men, pointed toward the sky. Looking up into the atrium, she paused and stood in silent wonder at the astonishing heights. An endless column that touched the clouds, shimmering in the light of the morning sun. There had always been skyscrapers in Los Huesos, but nothing quite like this. At the ringing sound of a small, metallic bell, the elevators opened their doors and invited passengers aboard. She managed to secure one on the end alone and pressed (-06). When prompted by the elevator panel, she entered the passcode and descended deep below the city.

The sharp glare of the lights along the walls reflected all around, multiplying in magnitude and intensity in the mirrors that hung behind. Dr. Montgomery turned to see herself, only there stood a woman burdened by years. She was lost for a moment in the eyes of the strange figure staring back at her through the other side of the looking glass. Changed in the aftermath of something real, the devastating consequences of understanding, of knowing the man who pulled the strings behind the curtain.

The doors opened to the sixth sub-surface floor as Dr. Montgomery stepped out of the elevator and into a hallway flooded with light. Cruel fluorescents burned above her head, buzzing with anticipation at her arrival. She strode purposefully down the hall, checking the time on her wrist, until she reached Room 0621. With an uneasy breath, hands trembling for some reason she didn't understand, she knocked her knuckles against the door. An unfamiliar voice responded from somewhere on the other side, beckoning her to enter. She turned the heavy handle toward the ceiling as she pressed against the door and fell inside.

At the far end of the room, seated behind a large metal desk and typing vigorously away at his station, a middle-aged man quietly slipping into his golden years peered over the rim of his wire-framed glasses. The window behind him projected a view over the city, past the dusty haze of downtown and out into the ocean spray. It flickered in the manufactured sunlight as the stout man acknowledged another presence in the room. He gestured with a meaty hand for Dr. Montgomery to step further into the room, opening his palm toward an empty chair seated on the opposite side of the desk. She surveyed the limited confines of the room, humble but utilitarian décor and industrial exposures running along the walls. The man's desk was littered with little more than the bare essentials of an office space—a desktop monitor and writing instruments, files and folders arranged in particular order. She approached with the poise of a professional woman and offered her own hand in his.

"Dr. Clare Montgomery, Department of Government and Industry Affairs at the Commission on Interstellar Supremacy."

He stood to greet her as an inviting warmth spread across his face.

"Yes, I remember. We spoke over the phone. Dr. Charles Lewis, Chief Administrator of Research and Development here at Talos. Peace to the Director."

"Peace to the Director."

She took a seat across from the man, setting the briefcase on the floor and folding her arms across her lap.

"I'm sure you are familiar with routine inspections from Washington," she said. Though she had never been to this facility, she had been briefed on its status—**NONCOMPLI-ANT**, in bold letters emblazoned across the cover of last month's report.

"Yes, of course," Dr. Lewis replied. "You'll find that we've made some significant adjustments to our preventative safety measures, in lieu of the language issued by the Department. And we do appreciate the candor in your reports."

Dr. Montgomery opened her briefcase and handed a folder filled with official papers to the man seated across from her. His face fell immediately as he held the heavy burden of its contents, considering what weighty matters might be printed across those pages in fateful ink. Revocation of funding, fines levied against the company for violating some obscure environmental statute. Whatever the penalties proscribed therein, Dr. Lewis understood the intentions behind them. Talos had been a target for many years—an unfortunate side-effect of leading the industry for the better part of the past century. Federal oversight almost rivaled the impudence of corporate sabotage.

"To refresh your memory."

A discomfort quieted the room, falling silent aside from the low humming of the electrical conduits droning just inside the walls. Dr. Lewis tossed the folder onto his desk as his lungs let loose a heavy sigh.

"If we're going to get this over with, I'll need a fresh cup of coffee."

They both filed out of the room and marched down the hall, turning toward a glaring, galley kitchen covered in glass. The coffee machines were already brewing when the clock on the wall struck 8:00. A younger woman dressed in white, hair pulled back tight against her scalp, moved diligently at the kitchen counter. She poured a steaming pot of fresh coffee into an insulated tumbler and turned to Dr. Lewis, who leaned his shoulder against the doorframe.

"This is one of our biotech interns down here in R&D. Makes a mean macchiato. Dr. Montgomery, meet Heloise."

The young intern smiled from the other side of the room, maintaining her distance as though she might be embarrassed, or else in awe of the accomplished woman before her. Dr. Montgomery gave a knowing reassurance with a familiar look in her eyes.

Taking his coffee in hand, Dr. Lewis led Dr. Montgomery from the kitchen and further down the hall. As they turned to walk away, Heloise swept a small white packet torn open at the corner into the trash. Tiny grains like sugar had spilled onto the counter, catching the fluorescents and casting glints of light across the room. She was careful to brush every last particle away, to vanish all traces of the substance and bury it deep beneath old coffee grounds and between used filters that had soaked through and stained. When she was sure that no suggestion of the mess remained, she returned to her desk, gathered her things together, and fled from Talos without a single glance behind.

- - -

Deeper into the maze of corridors and cubicles, buried beneath the concrete and the dirt, Dr. Montgomery marveled at what she could only conclude was an elaborate, monstrous greenhouse. Glass walls two stories tall, intense lighting that blinded and stung. Small figures at the far end of the room, dressed head to toe in biohazard safety suits, worked purposely on whatever assignment they had been given. And at the center spindles and thorns winding upward and down in a dizzying gyre, a towering, black colossus lorded over every corner of the room. A dark specter from another world, an agent of untold terror soon to be unleashed upon the world.

"I believe this was the primary concern of the Department's last report. As you can see, we've made significant improvements."

The glass stood strong as steel, unyielding and thick, bolted between rivets and beams that rose high above. A vacuum seal separated the greenhouse from the hallway on the other side of the glass, ensuring that the contaminant inside could be contained. The workers in their uniforms moved among countless rows of individual specimens preserved in jars, buzzing like insects in a hive, bristling with excitement at their task. This was a vault more impenetrable than a fortress keep, a prison cell more secure than the solitary confines of Thornfield Asylum. In the shadow of the leviathan, Dr. Montgomery was dwarfed beside the looming, grotesque mass of black fungus that had overtaken the greenhouse and begun to crawl along the walls. Dr. Lewis gestured beyond the glass.

"Magnificent, isn't she?"

Dr. Montgomery was awestruck, at a loss for words to properly describe the great, black thing before her. She had read the reports, studied the history of bio-innovation at Talos, even taught herself quantum plasmonics, but it all did little to prepare her for the encounter. Magnificent was not a word that came to mind.

"*Mazuku occidendum.*"

"Yes—I've read the patents," she murmured, her voice faint and her heart heavy in her chest. She struggled to steady her breath as the air in her lungs grew thin. There was no room left in the hallway as the world around her expanded, an assault undertaken against her mind. The floor fell away from under her feet and she caught the violent horror in her throat. Gagging on the coarse, sandpaper flesh of her tongue, she could not quiet the irrepressible thoughts bombarding her head. But the still that followed in the wake of her silence spoke clearly enough.

"You haven't read everything," Dr. Lewis continued. His lips loosened around his words as they began to spill freely from his mouth, blood like wine from an open wound. The inhibitions in his brain had been struck by the precision of an adversary's blow. Dr. Montgomery recovered her senses and pressed him further.

"Tell me what else I need to know."

"That's all very proprietary," Dr. Lewis said, a thin smile stretching his lips across his face. He turned away from the greenhouse, drinking the last of his coffee in earnest, and beckoned Dr. Montgomery to follow. She tore herself from the hideous, vulgar sight of the greenhouse and hurried to keep up with the man who had, a moment ago, maintained a bold and confident stance at the sight of his work, who was suddenly stumbling on his feet. Staggering like a drunken man, unsure of his ability to remain upright. He dashed abruptly into a conference room at the far end of the hall, falling onto the other side of a large door obscured by frosted glass. Dr. Montgomery pursued, pushing heavily against the handle, and followed the man inside.

31

31   Tania Bustamente, *Mazuku Occidendum, 2020, acrylic ink on water-color paper.*

The room was dark, no lights at all and no sign of Dr. Lewis. Taking a guarded step, Dr. Montgomery felt for a light switch, fingers fumbling blindly along the wall. Her hand trembled as she found a small panel, pressing inward and flooding the room with harsh, fluorescent light. There, at the center of the room, sat Dr. Lewis at the head of a large conference table, staring intently at the contents of a sterile glass jar. A small, black specimen squirmed inside—a sample of mazuku from the greenhouse. Dr. Montgomery hesitated to approach, unsure of Dr. Lewis' intentions.

"Have a seat, Clare."

She did, choosing a chair on the other side of the table. The uncertainty in the air was thick, a viscous cloud that cast shadows from overhead. Dr. Montgomery studied the man seated across from her, taking note of the heavy beads of sweat that had begun to gather in the folds of his brow. She hesitated to speak, careful not to break the fragile balance they had struck. The smallest show of discomfort could bring this broken parley crashing into dust.

As she settled into her seat, Dr. Lewis raised the glass container level with his eyes and looked in wonder at the black fungus sprouting thorns inside.

"Do you know why this greasy little fucker is so dangerous?"

Dr. Montgomery considered the question and reflected on the subject of the inquest. There were many answers she could give. She thought of the specimen's first discovery in Elba County, its murderous tendencies that tore through the city of Los Huesos before ravaging the rest of the world. It was a parasitic fungus, one that consumed the flesh of its hosts with the fervor of the most effective carnivores. By all natural rights, it shouldn't even exist—a despot over all other species, holding tyrannical control like a fist around their throats. In the absence of competition, the dominant predator atop the hierarchy of all living things. She settled on an answer invoking the history of the city.

"The mass casualties stemming from the outbreak that began in this city almost two hundred years ago illustrate its potential to overwhelm an ecosystem. Which is why we have been so concerned with your somewhat cavalier attitude regarding its exploitation. We've allowed this corporation to continue its experimentation supporting this nation's interstellar efforts, provided that you adhere to the standards defined in our directives."

Dr. Lewis was satisfied, smiling in amusement at the response.

"So clinical," he replied. "Mass casualties. Exploitation." His demeanor shifted from one of entertainment to one of anger. "You never had any idea what you were doing."

The offense taken at that statement incited argument within Dr. Montgomery's mind. A debate inside herself struggling over whether the heart of what he had said might in fact be true. She refused to surrender to the notion so easily.

"The Director understood what was necessary at the time," she said, "to curtail the swelling poverty and crime that had taken root in this city. Subsequent mutations of the mold to such a devastating degree were unforeseeable."

"But not impossible," Dr. Lewis countered. "We've engineered it in a way to prevent that from happening again. Which you could have done had you taken the time to understand—this isn't a fungus."

He placed the sample directly in front of Dr. Montgomery, setting it almost on the edge of the table.

"It's an egg sac."

The revulsion in her stomach reached upward along her esophagus and sat at the back of her throat. She glanced down at the seemingly insignificant thing, the extremities of its tendrils testing the strength of its cell. The fluorescent lights shone back at her in the reflection of its black and glistening gloss, sleek like leather and fluid like ink. She wondered whether it was instinct or intellect driving the creature inside.

"You didn't consider the lives you were throwing away," Dr. Lewis continued. "You unleashed it on this city."

The sample seemed to sharpen its thorns at the sound of the accusation. Pointed and direct, the stinging needle of an unspoken truth—a coordinated operation to eliminate an entire class of people. Dr. Montgomery could do nothing to deny it.

"And see where it's taken us," she argued. "A golden age of unstifled innovation. Poverty cured, global conflicts ended. Our history stands by the Director's decision."

But the pain in her eyes betrayed the confidence of her voice. Some hidden reservation coming to light. Dr. Lewis seized on the moment, pouncing at the delicate wavering of her loyalty.

"They haven't cured anything—they've only altered its meaning. Progress for the sake of progress. They created a power vacuum and installed themselves at the head of a new society. But we're on the verge of something chaotic and out of their control."

This was the primary purpose of her visit. Dr. Montgomery had known of the dangers of mazuku, the precautions that Talos was taking, but her Department had yet to discover the unacknowledged operations that were festering underground. Developments in interstellar technologies beyond their understanding. She pressed further as the beads of sweat fell from Dr. Lewis's brow and gathered in pools on the table.

"What do you mean?" she ventured.

He folded his arms across his chest and considered for a moment whether to divulge something sitting on the tip of his tongue. He placed his elbows on the table and leaned forward, bringing his face very near to Dr. Montgomery. His eyes grew suddenly intense, burning brightly in their sunken sockets. At the command of a strange and alien voice loosening the reservations holding back those secrets in his head, words flowed like cigarette smoke over his lips and out into the world.

"Clare, it feeds on radiant energy from another dimension."

The sparks caught on the tension stretched thin and set fire to the air. She had studied the theories, did what she could to understand. The science was sound, the potential—limitless. She wondered whether she had gone too far, whether she could believe the sincerity of his words, but she only had so much time.

"Our own visible, three-dimensional universe exists within a higher-dimensional space. Some of those dimensions are imperceptible to us—some of them leave traces. We found one that changed our world forever."

The animated expressions that accompanied this explanation did little to ease its understanding. Dr. Montgomery must have shown her disbelief in the careful lines contorting across her face. In the quiet confines of the conference room, between fits of coughing and bouts of hesitation, Dr. Lewis lowered the tenor of his voice and tempered the speed of his lesson.

"There's an infinite plane that runs through the space of our own. Pure, endless waves of energy in between our universe and every other. Invisible in every respect to our own dimension, though we can measure its effects. But this little fucker," he said, gesturing to the inoffensive piece of black mold moving tentatively inside its prison. "It showed us where to look."

A pregnant pause, bloated with a gestating thought of defiance in the face of threatening defeat. Dr. Lewis looked to the table as he struggled to find the proper words to convey the gravity of his developing line of thought. His breath became labored and his shoulders sat heavy underneath the weight of their burden.

"That's the real danger," he continued as his gaze wandered somewhere far-off and distant. His voice grated against the flesh of his throat and his manner grew distractingly vague. "They couldn't give two shits if a billion more people died tomorrow. So long as their cities survived, their subjects secured. They can't let us open a gateway to another world beyond their control."

The man had been reduced to sweat and stinking breath. His skin had turned pale, his eyes had yellowed around the pupils and drifted in opposite directions. A mass of spoiled meat on the verge of convulsing, rotted underneath the hardening rind. But he was compelled still to speak, his voice hoarse as it spilled like vomit across the table.

"Conquest. Colonization. It's in our beating hearts, burning like fire in our blood. After every advancement and show of progress that we've made, we're still just noisy, primal creatures setting fires in the dark."

Dr. Montgomery could taste the honesty like alcohol on his breath, breaking down the inhibitions in his brain. His words were progressively becoming slurred with the passing of every minute. She needed to prompt him to speak more directly.

"What is it that you're planning to do?"

"We're building a new accelerator," he confessed, his hands shaking and his voice strained. "Like the hypertrains, massive gateways to move us between vast distances. Portals to tear the fabric of space apart, powered by an infinite source of radiant energy. Only instead of traveling across the earth, this one will take us to the other side of the stars."

He started to laugh, a grotesque sound choking through the saliva that had gathered in his throat. Dr. Montgomery tried to question him further, to follow-up her inquiry into this new development, but was abruptly interrupted.

"What do you—"

"We tore Terremoto Canyon through the middle of the Mojave Desert. It wasn't an earthquake—it was an accident. We sent the San Gabriel mountains soaring somewhere into outer space."

There was no stopping him now. The laughter had commandeered his lungs and he could not prevent himself from spewing the truth.

"Hypertrains were just the beginning. This project will be the key to unlocking our future, far away from here. A world beyond the Director's reach. A settlement free from the suffocating weight of the Party's oppression. It's already underway—we're going to escape."

He collapsed into an uncontrollable fit of spasms, gasping at the air while clutching his chest in his hands. The guttural sounds echoed against the empty walls as his left eye filled with blood. Concern for the future gripped Dr. Montgomery as she rose from her seat, towering overhead against the glare of the fluorescent lights.

"I can't breathe," the man rattled, his words thin and hollow as they wafted across the room.

"I know," she replied. Cold and unconcerned, her sympathies turned to steel against the panic that had set into the shriveled man seizing on the other side of the table. The Department's worst fears had been confirmed by his confession—she was nearing the end of her mission.

"Sodium thiazodine. Anyone would understand if you mistook it for the sugar in your coffee."

A stream of bloody tears fell along his cheek as his jaw hung slack and wide. Saliva filled his mouth and spilled out over his dried and cracking lips, splattering onto the pools of sweat that had gathered on the table. The smell of something sour and rusted like corrosion seeped out from in between his pores, the rotten stench of indolent gases escaping a bloated corpse.

"It disabled the neurotransmitters in your prefrontal cortex responsible for telling lies. You don't have enough brainpower left to tell me anything but the truth." She moved to the other side of the table, staring into the deadened eyes of the dying man. "Now you're going to tell me where to find every unacknowledged file, every secret project in Talos' system."

The sound of soft laughter bubbled up from the swollen belly of the pitiful man and discharged from the back of his throat. Deep and full of life, one last effort to overthrow the weight of the city crushing him beneath the surface.

"Only Dr. Lewis has been granted special access," he sneered. A terrifying glimmer sparked through the blood congealing in his eyes. Perhaps the dosage had been too high, or else his brain had suffered some unforeseen side-effect. Whatever the reason, he had to be speaking nonsense. She seized him by the throat and stared directly into the jellied sockets where his eyes had been.

"Tell me where to find those files."

The man spoke with unreserved conviction as he gagged on his tongue, choking back vomit and bile.

"I'm not Dr. Lewis."

Her heart sank into her stomach with the force of a controlled demolition, scattering debris and filling her lungs with smoke. Her blood ran thin and her head was filled with helium. Despite the absolute certainty in his voice, she refused to accept the truth—Talos knew what she had come there to do. On the verge of transfixing panic, she stepped away from the convulsing body of the man slumped over in his chair and turned to run for the door. But the world suddenly slid onto its side and Dr. Montgomery fell to the floor.

Her head floated for a moment above the clouds before it collided with the table, cracking open just enough for warm blood to trickle down through her hair and into her eyes. She strained to see through a scarlet haze, glancing toward the ceiling in time to see the glass container holding the sample of mazuku sitting precariously on the edge of the table. It teetered once over the side, then back onto the table-top before it succumbed to the forces of gravity and inertia and plummeted to the floor. The moment was crystalized forever in time as it turned somersaults in the air, immobile levitation preserved by the immobile levitation preserved like an insect in amber. It shattered upon impact and the specimen inside burst apart, erupting in a cloud of black dust and shards of glass.

Dr. Montgomery could do nothing to stop herself from breathing it in, the particles piercing her veins like barbs and stingers, tearing through the soft flesh inside. She screamed out in pain, clawing at her own face as the grains of black sand seared her nostrils before making their way into her brain.

She was no longer in control, entirely consumed by primal, instinctive fear. The ancient voice shouting in her head had only a single command—*run*. She obeyed, crashing into the door as she threw it open and tore down the hall. There were no other thoughts, nothing left aside from her singular objective to survive.

The path toward the elevator was a labyrinth of twisted corridors winding toward the hallway where she had first seen the monstrous, black cancer swelling inside her mind. But her body pushed on, desperate to escape from the sprawling complex underground and ascend to the sunlight of the city. She turned her face away from the massive greenhouse as she passed, her head throbbing against the inside of her skull. The droning workers were too busy to notice her broken body stumbling along the corridor. But she could feel its presence all the same, an unstoppable force of nature feeding on something intangible, invisible but full of power.

At the end of the hallway, she threw herself against the wall and slid down onto the floor. Her fingers fumbled blindly before they found the elevator panel and pressed the button for the lobby. As the doors opened, she collapsed inside, a trail of blood falling from her nose.

The elevator groaned as it carried her six floors to the lobby, chiming as it reached its destination. She spilled out of the elevator and stumbled once again underneath the glittering chandeliers and golden trim. There was no time to gaze dumbfounded before she hurtled headfirst into a group of Talos employees rushing someplace undoubtedly important. She could not see their faces, her own glazed over with a thin film of blood that had already begun to dry.

As she burst through the front doors of Talos Tower, she was blinded by the brilliance of the sun. Daggers of light refracted off the infinite glass of the skyscrapers and pinned her powerlessly in place. She turned about in the middle of the road, disoriented and out of breath, unsure of which direction to run. The city was no longer a place that she recognized as she found herself suddenly somewhere unfamiliar. The thundering noise of the traffic speeding by was deafening to her ears and the concrete all around her looked the same. She lost her balance in the chaos of the streets and crumbled like paper in rain. Her knees folded underneath the weight of her body before her feet sank into the blacktop. She surrendered herself to the oppressive heat and the aftermath of what she had done.

In the early morning hours beneath the blistering desert sun, Dr. Clare Montgomery collapsed in a useless heap onto the pavement, overcome by the traumas in her head. The city remained an indifferent observer as the sands slipped through the hourglass and gathered in the wastelands beyond the gates. As the silence of the years echoed out into the darkness, Talos stood guard above the skyline, a vigilant sentinel before the stars.

ACKNOWLEDGMENTS

———

Thank you so much to everyone who has had a hand in making this book possible, especially all of you who have helped me fund the costs of printing and publishing through your preorders and contributions. It has been a life-long dream of mine to publish a book and pursue my passion as a writer. I couldn't have achieved this goal without each and every one of you, and I am so grateful for your generosity and support.

Aaron Arnwine
Adam Smith
Adam Taylor
Alexander Wakuluk
Alexis Rojas
Alexis Sabrina Barone
Alfredo Pineda
Amy Bielecki
Andrew Barnhill
Andy Markel
Andy Vargo
Anil Sookdeo
Ben Peterson

Beth Carpegna
Bobby Thigpen
Brant Miller
Brent Gilbert
Brian Day
Brian Vogelgesang
Brian Winterfeldt
Cassy Sottile
Celestino Zapata
Christina Theis
Christopher Russell
Connor Burne
Courtney Dorsey

Damian Chayse
Dani Beau
Darlene Bennett
Denise Wells
Derek Beet
Edgar Colliflower
Edmund Colliflower
Elizabeth Brennan
Emily Ward
Emma Patterson
Eric Koester
Eric Rosenthal
Frank Russo
Frank Russo
Gaby Cusato
Gail Marthrel
Hannah Geesaman
Harrison Ferachi
Heather Stritch-Nees
Ian Carroll
J. M. Boothe
J. W. Edgar
Jack Dudley
Jared Dockswell
Jessica Swarner
John Fossum
John Naylor
John O'Connor
Jonathan Antista
Joshua Poole
Judy Dudich
Katie Egan

Kelly Weiss
Kendra Jordan
Kevin Lerner
Kyle Jamolin
Kyle Murdoch
Lark Herron
Laura Au
Laura Geben
Liam Martin
Margaret Negas
Maria Conner
Maria Sofia
Mary Katherine Theis
Matthew Bosserman
Matthew Mallard
Meghan Parker
Melissa Markey
Melissa Sorto-Zepeda
Michael Bramson
Michael Capuano
Michael DiMercurio
Moira Frederickson
Molly Kennedy
Monica Theis Huber
Morgan Serra
Natalie Theis
Nathaniel Guest
Nche Nobert Beyelle
Nicolas Navarro
Paul St. Clair
Po Kuan Wu
R. R. Dolan, Jr.

Richard Fairley
Robert W. Miller, Jr.
Rusty Wissman
Sharon Winalski
Tania Bustamente
Teresa Moats
Thomas Fazzini
Tim Guest
Timothy Davidson
Tom Jennings
Tristan Longnecker
Xavier McQuiston

APPENDIX

INTRODUCTION

Baum, L. Frank. *The Wonderful Wizard of Oz*. New York: George M. Hill Co., 1900. http://www.read.gov/books/oz.html.

THE BLACK SPOT

Bustamente, Tania. *The Black Spot*. 2020. Acrylic ink on watercolor paper.

Bustamente, Tania. *Mazuku Parricidium*. 2020. Acrylic ink on watercolor paper.

Rohr, Justin. *A Beggar in the Street*. 2020. Pencil on paper.

SALEM AVENUE

Blake, William. "The Tyger." *The Poetry Foundation*. The Poetry Foundation, 2020. https://www.poetryfoundation.org/poems/43687/the-tyger.

Bustamente, Tania. *The Broken House on Salem*. 2020. Acrylic ink on watercolor paper.

Bustamente, Tania. *Elsabeth*. 2020. Acrylic ink on watercolor paper.

Bustamente, Tania. *Häxan*. 2020. Acrylic ink on watercolor paper.

Bustamente, Tania. *The Work of Days*. 2020. Acrylic ink on watercolor paper.

Rohr, Justin. *Elba Reed*. 2020. Pencil on paper.

Shakespeare, William. *Macbeth*. *The Folger Shakespeare*. Folger Shakespeare Library, 2020. https://shakespeare.folger.edu/shakespeares-works/macbeth/.

NECROPOLIS

Bustamente, Tania. *A Corpse Come Back to Life*. 2020. Acrylic ink on watercolor paper.

Rohr, Justin. *Victims of the Horde*. 2020. Pencil on paper.

FORBIDDEN THINGS

Bustamente, Tania. *Mazuku Occidendum*. 2020. Acrylic ink on watercolor paper.

Rohr, Justin. *Clare Montgomery*. 2020. Pencil on paper.

CPSIA information can be obtained
at www.ICGtesting.com
Printed in the USA
FSHW021945211220
76895FS

9 781636 765792